(1) is a major change going to be —

"Whig" (progressive) → reinterpretation of "attorney ship"
               concept of representation   (1) "instructions"

"mercantilist" (conservative) → representatives as enlightened,
                          disinterested arbitrators

(2) Can we trace the spread of the concept that
"those with a stake in society can vote, etc" rhetorically ??
That is, we see how rhetorical practice expands the
public sphere by noting how "stake in society" is spread
out to include more people.

DEPUTYES & LIBERTYES

DEPUTYES
&
LIBERTYES

The Origins of
Representative Government
in Colonial America

---

by

MICHAEL KAMMEN

ALFRED·A·KNOPF

New York

Library of Congress Cataloging in Publication Data

Kammen, Michael G
  Deputyes & libertyes; the origins of representative
government in colonial America.

  Bibliography: p.
  1. Representative government and representation—
U. S.—Sources. 2. U. S.—Politics and government—
Colonial period. I. Title.
JK81.K3   321.8'0973   78-88751
ISBN 0-394-31701-7

THIS IS A BORZOI BOOK
PUBLISHED BY ALFRED A. KNOPF, INC.

First Paperback Edition, 1972

The "Prolegomenon: An Interpretive Inquiry" appears
in a slightly different form in *Liber Memorialis Georges
de Lagarde. Studies Presented to the International Commission for the History of Representative and Parliamentary Institutions, London, 1968*, XXXVIII (Louvain-
Paris: Editions Nauwelaerts et Béatrice Nauwelaerts;
1969), pp. 133–200.

Acknowledgment is made to North Carolina State Department of Archives and History for excerpts from
North Carolina Charters and Constitutions, 1578–1698

Manufactured in the United States of America

For my sons
DANIEL MERSON
and
DOUGLAS ANTON

① this is, I think, a good example of demonstrating how historical issues can speak to contemporary problems.

questions

✑ Preface ✑

Representative government stands high on the list of institutions traditionally cherished in the Anglo-American world. The Declaration of Independence remarked upon "the right of representation in the legislature" as a right inestimable to the people "and formidable to tyrants only." One of the most serious charges raised against George III was that he had "dissolved representative houses repeatedly for opposing with manly firmness his invasions of the rights of the people." For Frederick Jackson Turner, "the rise of representative government" came first in a brief catalogue of important evolutionary developments in early America. Today, the historical problem of how constitutional structures of government originate and develop is especially fascinating because the practical issue of whether such structures can survive and expand is poised so delicately in the modern world.[1]

①   *⚡*

Students of American history have available several excellent studies of the *growth* of representative institutions in the eighteenth century.[2] Yet there is no systematic description and analysis of the seventeenth-century *origins* of representative government in British North America. The lack of such a study suggests a serious deficiency in our knowledge of American constitutional, political, and institutional development, and presents an exciting challenge for research and inquiry. I have attempted in

[1] Turner, *The Frontier in American History* (N.Y., 1920), 2; see Brian Tierney, "Medieval Canon Law and Western Constitutionalism," *The Catholic Historical Review*, LII (1966), 3.

[2] See Jack P. Greene, *The Quest for Power: The Lower Houses of Assembly in the Southern Royal Colonies, 1689–1776* (Chapel Hill, N.C., 1963); and Mary P. Clarke, *Parliamentary Privilege in the American Colonies* (New Haven, Conn., 1943).

my introductory essay to provide the prolegomenon to such an inquiry. My discussion falls naturally into three sections: the historiographical and European background; actual origins in the seventeenth-century colonies, treated chronologically; and finally, a summary examination of patterns, trends, motives, and impulses.

The documentary materials which follow the first part make up a primer in Anglo-colonial constitutional history. In selecting these sources I sought to strike a balance between formal frames of government, such as charters and ordinances, and political realities revealed by assembly journals, personal narratives, letters, and broadsides. Indeed, I have consciously tried to contrast the structural and procedural dimensions of government—static plans and forms against the dynamic forces pressing for change—and thereby to reveal the underlying tensions between them.

It is 350 years exactly since the first representative body met in the English colonies. Now we are more deeply concerned than ever before with the relationship between government and citizen, between "deputyes and libertyes." It is my hope that this book will prove useful to students of history and political science; but also, perhaps, to those persons—legislators and laymen concerned about the future of democracy—who are therefore interested in the origins of representative institutions in America.

An epitome of my "Prolegomenon: An Interpretive Inquiry" was first presented before the International Commission for the History of Representative and Parliamentary Institutions (London: July 19, 1968), and subsequently in a revised form before the Organization of American Historians (Philadelphia: April 19, 1969). I am most grateful to C. C. Weston, David S. Lovejoy, and Gary B. Nash for their helpful observations on those occasions. Wesley Frank Craven, David Brion Davis, Richard S. Dunn, E. Lousse, and J. R. Pole were kind enough to read the "Inquiry" at different stages; I very much appreciate their wise and penetrating suggestions. I owe a particular debt to H. G. Koenigsberger, Secretary to the International Commission, who first aroused my interest in the history of representative government, and whose knowledge of such institutions in early modern Europe is unparalleled. The congenial staffs of the Milton S. Eisenhower Library, the Humanities Center, and especially Jack P. Greene of the History Department at Johns Hopkins University, helped in many ways. I am obliged to Mattie E. E. Parker for generous advice concerning various versions of the Fundamental Constitutions of Carolina, to Mary Menke for clerical assistance, to my wife for "advice and assent," and to Jane N. Garrett, friend and editor, for seeing the manuscript efficiently through to publication.

Ithaca, New York   M.K.
June 1969

ᥰ Contents ᥯

⤧ Part One ⤧

PROLEGOMENON:
An Interpretive Inquiry

From these accumulated considerations it is evident that the only government which can fully satisfy all the exigencies of the social state is one in which the whole people participate; that any participation, even in the smallest public function, is useful; that the participation should everywhere be as great as the general degree of improvement of the community will allow; and, that nothing less can be ultimately desirable than the admission of all to a share in the sovereign power of the state. But since all cannot, in a community exceeding a single small town, participate personally in any but some very minor portions of the public business, it follows that the ideal type of a perfect government must be representative.

JOHN STUART MILL
Representative Government

Introduction—
Historiographical and European Background

DESPITE the considerable number of monographs—many written half a century ago and more—about early American political institutions, and despite the intense, sustained interest of political scientists and historians in representative government, we have no comprehensive and cohesive analysis of the origins of representative government in British North America. A generation ago, when Charles A. Beard felt that representative institutions were everywhere under attack, he devoted two essays to a re-examination of the Teutonic origins theory made famous late in the nineteenth century by Herbert Baxter Adams. Beard studied the problem in antiquity, the Middle Ages, early modern Europe, Stuart England, and modern times—but completely ignored the American colonies, though he would have been well advised and qualified to include them. Beard's contemporary, Henry J. Ford, professor of politics at Princeton, devoted half his volume on *Representative Government* to historical origins, yet he also managed to skip the colonial experience.[1]

Institutional studies of particular colonies have too often tempted the historian to reach conclusions quickly by examining structure without much attention to development. The multivolume general works by Herbert L. Osgood and Charles M. Andrews treated individual colonies authoritatively and sepa-

---

[1] Beard, "The Teutonic Origins of Representative Government," and "Representative Government in Evolution," *American Political Science Review*, XXVI (1932), 28–44, 223–40; Ford, *Representative Government* (N.Y., 1924), part 1.

rately; but they do not offer an integrated presentation or response to the problem. The authors stressed constitutional, imperial, and legal aspects rather than the social and political context of public affairs.[2] Two others, Andrew C. McLaughlin and Alfred de Grazia, attempted to discern a pattern in the emergence of representative institutions in America. Although both men have made thoughtful contributions, their interpretive essays are tentative, unsubstantial, dated, and without very much concern for chronological development. Consequently they are more valuable for their suggestions than for their conclusions.[3]

Perhaps colonial scholars have been intimidated by the imposing and complex historiography which has luxuriated around the elusive origins of representative government in medieval England. As Brian Tierney has observed, "we now have a fantastically elaborate bibliography of hundreds of books and articles devoted to this one question and all the fascinating subsidiary issues that arise out of it—whether the English Parliament was already some kind of representative legislature in 1297 or whether . . . this felicitous state of affairs did not begin to come about until, say, 1327." [4]

If, however, the English origins have been over-scrutinized, surely colonial beginnings have been unduly neglected. Superficially it would seem that the passage of centuries and destruction of documents would make the origins of representative gov-

[2] Osgood, *The American Colonies in the Seventeenth Century* (3 vols., N.Y., 1904); Andrews, *The Colonial Period of American History. The Settlements* (3 vols., New Haven, Conn., 1934-7); and for a capsule summary, Andrews, *The Colonial Background of the American Revolution* (New Haven, Conn., 1924), 31-6.

[3] Andrew C. McLaughlin, *The Foundations of American Constitutionalism* (N.Y., 1932), ch. 2; Alfred de Grazia, *Public and Republic. Political Representation in America* (N.Y., 1951), ch. 3. De Grazia is primarily concerned with theories of representation rather than actual origins. See also Frederick Madden's suggestive essay, "Some Origins and Purposes in the Formation of British Colonial Government," in *Essays Presented to Margery Perham* (Oxford, 1963), 1-22.

[4] Tierney, "Medieval Canon Law," 6-7. See also Peter Spufford, *Origins of the English Parliament* (London, 1967); Edward Miller, *The Origins of Parliament* (London, 1960); D. Pasquet, *An Essay on the Origins of the House of Commons* (Cambridge, 1925).

ernment in England much more mysterious, vague, and subject to variant interpretations than in America. Here only a few generations and the fallibility of men's memories separated seventeenth-century origins from the eighteenth-century celebrations of those origins and their perpetuation. Nonetheless, many of the constitutional battles which occurred and recurred in the eighteenth-century colonies hinged upon bitterly contested, divergent views of the origin and nature of provincial assemblies. Whether the governor or the legislature, for example, ought properly to have authorized the summoning of delegates from new communities depended heavily upon whether representative institutions existed by virtue of the royal prerogative or by natural right.[5] By the 1760's, American Whigs were already making claims for their assemblies almost as extravagant as those made by the Elizabethan Society of Antiquaries for the pre-Norman existence of the House of Commons.[6] The ink spilled and type set by American revolutionary writers have subsequently obscured our proper understanding of the problem.

Bernard Bailyn has recently offered brief but brilliantly incisive observations on the partial re-creation in early America "of a kind of representation that had flourished in medieval England but that had faded and been superseded by another during the fifteenth and sixteenth centuries." Parliament had originally enabled "local men, locally minded, whose business began and ended with the interests of the constituency," as attorneys for their electors, to seek aid from the royal court of Parliament. In return, they could commit their constituents to financial support for the Treasury. Commoners were not usually anxious to serve as Members of Parliament; and the constituencies commonly bound their representatives to local interests in every way possible: by requiring local residency or the ownership of local property as a qualification; by closely controlling the payment

[5] Leonard W. Labaree, *Royal Government in America* (New Haven, Conn., 1930), 174, 177–9.

[6] See H. Trevor Colbourn, *The Lamp of Experience. Whig History and the Intellectual Origins of the American Revolution* (Chapel Hill, N.C., 1965), 7.

of wages; by instructing representatives explicitly; and by making them fully accountable.[7]

By the time governmental institutions took form in the seventeenth-century colonies, however, the English Parliament had greatly changed. "The restrictions that had been placed upon representatives of the commons to make them attorneys of their constituencies fell away; members came to sit 'not merely as parochial representatives, but as delegates of all the commons of the land.'" The primitive conditions of early provincial life, however, resembled in many ways the medieval circumstances conducive to the concept of attorneyship in representation. The colonial towns and counties were in various ways autonomous, "and they stood to lose more than they were likely to gain from a loose acquiescence in the action of central government." It became generally the custom to require representatives to be residents of and property owners within their constituencies, to instruct the deputies, and subsequently to check upon their actions as delegates.[8]

Thus the kinds of questions traditionally raised by English medievalists are critically relevant to an understanding of the origins of representative government in British North America.[9] If the convening of a fourteenth-century parliament was important because at that moment all the operations of government came into sharp focus, the gathering of a seventeenth-century provincial assembly was at least equally vital, given the rudimentary nature then of other government apparatus. We should

[7] Bernard Bailyn, *The Ideological Origins of the American Revolution* (Cambridge, Mass., 1967), 162–3; Carl Stephenson, "The Beginnings of Representative Government in England," *Medieval Institutions. Selected Essays* (Ithaca, N.Y., 1954), 138.

[8] Bailyn, *Ideological Origins*, 164–5. See also Bailyn, *The Origins of American Politics* (N.Y., 1968), 60–1.

[9] See H. G. Richardson and G. O. Sayles, *Parliaments and Great Councils in Medieval England* (London, 1961); J. G. Edwards, *Historians and the Medieval English Parliament* (Glasgow, 1960); H. M. Cam, "The Theory and Practice of Representation in Medieval England," *History*, XXXVIII (1953), 11–26; H. L. Gray, *The Influence of the Commons on Early Legislation* (Cambridge, Mass., 1932); and May McKisack, *The Parliamentary Representation of the English Boroughs During the Middle Ages* (London, 1932).

like to know how early the colonial counties came to be regarded as fiscal and political units; just when the colonial constituencies began instructing their representatives; whether the principle of majority rule was operative from the outset; whether the judicial functions of early American legislatures were as essential to them as to medieval parliaments; whether an indefinite fusion of functions—legislative, judicial, and executive—was as characteristic in seventeenth-century America as in fourteenth-century England; and finally, whether seventeenth-century colonial representatives were passive servants and petitioners of the prerogative to the same extent as their forebears in fourteenth- and fifteenth-century England.[1]

Several of these comparisons, and certainly the last, will undoubtedly be answered in the negative. Because the thirteen colonies developed initially along different lines, the proper way for historians to pose these questions will vary. In some cases, it is appropriate to ask when the assembly ceased to be a high court of appeal. When was this function separated and given to a provincial supreme court? Elsewhere—for example, Maryland —it will be more instructive to ask when the assembly first *sought recognition* as the highest court of judicature.[2] We must also inquire whether controversies ever arose over *plena potestas* in the colonies. Did governors in certain circumstances insist that delegates to the lower houses be fully empowered to make agreements binding upon the community? Did the delegates themselves? Did the constituencies in their turn resist such demands? Few instructions or writs have survived. Consequently many of these questions will be quite difficult if not impossible to resolve.[3]

[1] See George L. Haskins, *The Growth of English Representative Government* (N.Y., 1960), 31–2, 77–8, 93–4, 98, 110; Sir Goronwy Edwards, "The Emergence of Majority Rule in English Parliamentary Elections," and "The Emergence of Majority Rule in the Procedure of the House of Commons," *Transactions of the Royal Historical Society*, ser. 5, XIV–XV (London, 1964–5), 175–96 and 165–87.

[2] See C. H. McIlwain, *The High Court of Parliament and Its Supremacy* (New Haven, Conn., 1911).

[3] Cf. H. G. Koenigsberger, "The Powers of Deputies in Sixteenth Century Assemblies," *Album Helen Maud Cam. Studies Presented to the Inter-*

Because the Elizabethan House of Commons underwent so
many significant alterations, one wonders how these changes
would affect the embryonic colonial legislatures a few decades
later. The Elizabethan era, for example, was conspicuous for the
formalization of procedure, a process denoting maturity in a
legislative body. The first two modern treatises on parliamentary
practice appeared then, as the House of Commons hammered
out its "orders" and recorded them in its Journals.[4] Moreover,
the relationship between Lords and Commons was profoundly
changing. Under Edward VI and Mary, the Commons was a
rather loose and easygoing assembly. The House of Lords was
the more responsible body, and most bills began there. By the
latter part of Elizabeth's reign, however, the roles of the two
houses were reversed. Most bills were now first introduced in the
Commons. The pace of activity was rather reduced in the upper
house, and much increased in the lower.[5]

The medieval concept of attorneyship was still alive in the
sixteenth century, and even made the representation of boroughs
by alien gentry less objectionable than one might expect. There
was apparently no incongruity in employing a stranger as attorney. Paradoxically, as Sir John Neale has shown, the practice
of "carpet-bagging" in the sixteenth century made the House of
Commons a more able and a more national—rather than local-
minded—body. "For how else could the House of Commons
have greatly surpassed the average ability of the community; how
else have provided room for the nation's best available skill and
leadership?"[6] Given these new developments, therefore, one
wonders whether the use of direct representation through residential requirements in the seventeenth-century colonies might
in any sense have *retarded* the development and maturation of
provincial assemblies. Or was colonial society structured and dis-

*national Commission for the History of Representative and Parliamentary
Institutions,* XXIV (Louvain and Paris, 1961), 211–43.
[4] J. E. Neale, *The Elizabethan House of Commons* (London, 1949),
355–6, 363, 384–5, 389.
[5] *Ibid.,* 351, 359, 412.
[6] *Ibid.,* 150–1, 153–4, 14.

tributed so differently as to obviate comparison on this question?[7]

Despite all sorts of illegalities and anachronisms—indeed, because of them—the Elizabethan House of Commons was a mature, effective, and spirited body.[8] Somehow, the miniature legislatures that sprang up a generation later in America would eliminate most of the illegalities and anachronisms; yet the effectiveness and spirit of assertiveness would be quickly transplanted and kept. While that transplantation was in process, of course, a revolutionary party in England would achieve its Long Parliament and lead the country into civil war. As part of the intellectual ferment that precipitated, accompanied, and followed the turmoil, Puritans had hoped to remodel the Church of England into a representative system, and militant theorists would seek to establish a representative framework for the New Model Army. The religious and political stresses of the whole period evoked and reinforced the ideas of representation which were already becoming part of American fundamental law.[9]

In one sense, however, and quixotically, without the "successful" Puritan Revolution representative institutions might have matured even more rapidly in the colonies, for there would have been a steady influx of exiled and harassed parliamentarians seeking refuge in America. As it happened, the English attitude to the growth of colonial assemblies remained ambivalent for much of the seventeenth century. Not until the decade 1676–86 did a policy emerge whereby the creation of an assembly was

[7] Although it provides little assistance in answering such queries, a useful compilation is Hubert Phillips, *The Development of a Residential Qualification for Representatives in Colonial Legislatures* (Cincinnati, Ohio, 1921).

[8] Neale, *Elizabethan House of Commons*, 306–7; Wallace Notestein, "The Winning of the Initiative by the House of Commons," *Proceedings of the British Academy*, XI (1924), 125–75.

[9] Williams M. Mitchell, *The Rise of the Revolutionary Party in the English House of Commons, 1603–1629* (N.Y., 1957); Louise F. Brown, "Ideas of Representation from Elizabeth to Charles II," *Journal of Modern History*, XI (1939), 29, 32, 35, 40; Vernon F. Snow, "Parliamentary Reapportionment Proposals in the Puritan Revolution," *English Historical Review*, LXXIV (1959), 409–42.

formally deemed an act of royal grace. Thereafter, British officials
would oppose the tendency of colonial legislatures to exercise
freedom of action equal to that of Parliament. But by then it
was already too late. The colonists may have acquired the *legal*
right to representative forms of government from the Crown;
but in actual practice they had discovered those forms anew
for themselves.[1]

Although representative government in British North America may have been inevitable, there was nothing inevitable about
the particular ways in which it evolved, or the surprising institutional uniformity that emerged from diverse constitutional origins,
or the rapid growth to maturity. The colonies being primitive,
provincial, and relatively homogeneous, for example, the early
legislatures might very well have remained unicameral and met
infrequently, every second or third year.

A great many of the queries that spring to mind can be
answered, at least tentatively, at this stage; and I shall attempt
to answer them in Sections II and III below. Numerous other
problems will require fresh research into the fragmentary evidence. Nonetheless, they are worth noting as part of this inquiry:
What were the effects of topography and demographic change
upon the early growth of representative government? In what
ways did colonial factionalism shape the evolution of colonial
legislatures? Did it make an appreciable constitutional difference
which came first, the assembly or royal government, and whether
the assembly could confront a royal governor with established
precedents (as in Virginia and the Carolinas)? How was the
lower house affected when the council began to be appointed
rather than elected?[2] How was the lower house affected when
the judicial role of the legislature changed? And finally, just
what did representative government mean to the different ele-

[1] Labaree, *Royal Government in America*, 173–5; J. R. Pole, *Political
Representation in England and the Origins of the American Republic* (London, 1966), 513–14.

[2] See H. Hale Bellot, "Council and Cabinet in the Mainland Colonies,"
Transactions of the Royal Historical Society, ser. 5, V (1955), 161–76;
Martin Wight, *The Development of the Legislative Council, 1606–1945*
(London, 1946), ch. 1.

ments in colonial society? Surely its value varied from group to
group, at any given time, and indeed changed for particular
groups during the course of the seventeenth century.

Three basic considerations may usefully stand as determinative elements hereafter. First, that the origins of representative government are to be found in the earliest experiences of
colonization, particularly in the political organization and administrative functions of the commercial corporation in the
colonization process. Second, that about twenty years were required at the outset for representative institutions to materialize,
stabilize, and take permanent form in each colony. And third,
that their origins must be precisely pinpointed along a chronological calculus of change: Virginia and Bermuda in 1619–20;
Massachusetts Bay, Maryland, Plymouth, Connecticut, and New
Haven between 1634 and 1639; Barbados, Rhode Island, the Leeward Islands, and Jamaica between 1639 and 1664; the Carolina
and Jersey proprietaries between 1665 and 1681; and the trouble
spots of the early 1680's—Pennsylvania, New Hampshire, and
New York. Between 1704 and 1758, assemblies would emerge in
Delaware, the Bahamas (1729), Georgia (1755), and Nova Scotia;
but their story, however interesting, is anticlimactic.

The Origins of Representative Government in British
North America: *Seventeenth-Century Chronology*

Colony	English settlement first established	First assembly	No. of deputies	Became bi-cameral
Virginia	1607	July 30, 1619	22	pre-1660
Bermuda	1612	Aug. 1, 1620	16	unicameral
Mass. Bay	1628	May 14, 1634	24	1644
Maryland	1634	[1635?]		
		Jan. 25, 1638	24	1650
Connecticut	1636	May 1, 1637	12	1698
Plymouth	1620	March 5, 1639	17	unicameral
New Haven	1638	June 1639	4	unicameral
Barbados	1627	1639	22	1639
St. Kitts	1624	c. 1642	24	c. 1672
Antigua	1632	c. 1644		c. 1682
Rhode Island	1637	May 19, 1647	24	1696
Montserrat	1632	post-1654		1696
Nevis	1628	c. 1658		post-1672
Jamaica	1655	Jan. 20, 1664	20	1664
N. Carolina	1663	1665	12	1691
S. Carolina	1670	July 1671	20	1691
E. Jersey	1664	May 26, 1668	10	1672
W. Jersey	1675	Nov. 21, 1681	34	1696
N. Hampshire	1633	Mar. 16, 1680	11	1692
Pennsylvania	1682	Dec. 4, 1682	42	unicameral
New York	1664	Oct. 17, 1683	18	1691

❧ II ☙

The
Seventeenth-Century
Colonies

❧ I ☙

Virginia and Bermuda

On July 30, 1619, in sweltering heat, the little church at James-town, Virginia, was the scene of the first legislative assembly in British North America. Twenty-two deputies elected by eleven constituencies met with Governor George Yeardley and six councillors. One year later the same number of councillors and 16 deputies gathered in the church at St. George, Bermuda (Somers Island); and so a second English colonial assembly was established. Both wobbled hesitantly at first, but they survived and endured.[1] The initiative for both assemblies came from London, from the concerned leadership of the two commercial companies engaged in these overseas ventures. Because Virginia was less profitable than had been expected, and Bermuda more politically chaotic than was desirable, representative assemblies were envisaged as stabilizing institutions designed to alleviate the listing and rough-sailing characteristic of early colonization. In Virginia, the assembly was primarily an economic expedient; in Bermuda, more of a political one.

[1] The charter of the ill-fated Council for New England, sealed in 1620, included provisions for a legislative assembly. The scheme resembled the later Carolina proprietary arrangements in some respects, but was still-born. See Richard A. Preston, *Gorges of Plymouth Fort* (Toronto, 1953), 170 ff.; Bernard Bailyn, *The New England Merchants in the Seventeenth Century* (Cambridge, Mass., 1955), 6.

The Virginia Company charter of 1612 had provided for a reorganization of the Company's governmental structure. Powers previously exercised by the council were transferred to a "Court and assembly" of the adventurers. Since 1609 this assembly had helped determine the council's membership and the Company's economic policy. In addition, after 1612 it could also admit new adventurers, control the selection of officers for both Company and colony, and—most important—draft "such laws and Ordinances, for the Good and Welfare of the . . . Plantation, as . . . shall be thought requisite and meet." Thereafter the assembly met regularly as "an ordinary court," and quarterly in a great court at which major questions were examined. In the colony, meanwhile, a council representing the leading planters had been established to advise the governor. Consequently, once the charter of 1612 took effect, only the gathering of a general assembly of the planters in Virginia was needed to complete a government structurally similar to that existing for the adventurers in London.[2]

In the decade before 1619, "the rigours of Martiall Law" and the dispersion of settlement into private plantations had undercut the Company's economic hopes and viability. The new proprietary ventures instituted since 1617 led to a diversity of interests and a dispersion of settlement that threatened the colony's very existence. Because these private plantations involved the investments of important groups of adventurers, there were urgent reasons why their interests should be directly represented in the colony's government. By 1618, both of the Company's warring factions in London recognized the need for changes if the colony was to remain cohesive, develop economically, and provide profits more bountifully.[3] Though convening an assembly of the leading planters has been the most striking innovation in historians' eyes, we must not forget that it was merely one part of a

[2] Wesley Frank Craven, *The Southern Colonies in the Seventeenth Century, 1607–1689* (Baton Rouge, La., 1949), 87 and n.43, 111–14. See also Nora M. Turman, *George Yeardley. Governor of Virginia and Organizer of the General Assembly in 1619* (Richmond, Va., 1959).

[3] Andrews, *The Colonial Period,* I, ch. 9; Craven, *Southern Colonies,* 122, 126–7, 129–36.

broad program for change. We must also bear in mind that while the new governmental structure of the colony reflected that of the Company in London, the powers of the several component parts were not altogether analogous.

The first function of "the generall assemblie" was to consider the important documents and decisions recently passed by the Company in London. The adventurers there were not obliged to act upon suggestions from the Jamestown assembly; but suggested amendments would be considered seriously, especially since Company officials hoped to make Virginia attractive to new colonists. For the next twenty years, economic considerations and social imperatives—the need for profits and planters—would be paramount in the assembly's development. The king's desire to establish a tobacco monopoly led him to authorize the calling of an assembly in 1628, the first one to be held legally under Crown auspices.[4]

That first session in the sticky summer of 1619 was short-lived. Illness and pressing business locally led to a rapid dispersion after five days. But within a few years the planters became zealous of their general assembly, "than which nothinge can more conduce to our satisfaction or the publique utilitie." By 1624, the impetus behind representative government emanated from within the colony rather than from London. Even so, the planters were less concerned with legislation than with achieving effective administration, counsel and consent. The initiative behind the assembly had shifted, but not its felt purpose.[5] Even after 1630 when annual assemblies became regularized, they were rather frail bodies. Membership was not ardently sought nor their deliberations especially respected. During the earliest years there really was no House of Burgesses as such. Representa-

[4] John Pory, speaker of the first assembly, wrote an admirable "Reporte of the Manner of Proceeding in the General Assembly . . . at James City . . . July 30–August 4, 1619," printed in *The Records of the Virginia Company of London,* ed. Susan M. Kingsbury (Washington, D.C., 1906–35), III, 153–77. Craven, *Southern Colonies,* 163.

[5] *Journals of the House of Burgesses of Virginia, 1619–1658/59,* ed. H. R. McIlwaine (Richmond, Va., 1915), 27; Andrews, *Colonial Period,* I, 197–8, 204.

tion from the burghs and hundreds was not regarded as a separate branch of government, but as ancillary to the council. Although there is evidence of separate action by the burgesses as early as 1632, there was little conflict of interest between the elected members and the council until almost mid-century. Shortly thereafter, and certainly before 1663, bicameralism was established.[6] Royal instructions to Governor Wyatt in 1639 and Governor William Berkeley in 1641 had finally provided full Crown consent for the House of Burgesses. And in 1641, the proud but primitive colony built its first state house. Not surprisingly the legislative chamber reproduced rather closely St. Stephen's Chapel, where the House of Commons sat.[7]

In Bermuda a scheme of proprietary subcolonization had also been inaugurated during the 1610's. The consequence, as in Virginia, was a diversity of interests and a dispersal of settlement by 1620. Simultaneously, the Somers Island Company, like its parent Virginia Company, was racked by dissension; and as the struggle worsened, the whole question of the representation of shareholders in influencing managerial policies became increasingly important. The factious leaders were obliged to turn to the shareholders for support, and in so doing the latent political roles of the generality were made manifest.[8] In this case politics—the struggle for power—would serve as the labor pains accompanying institutional birth.

Just prior to 1620, unrest among the colonists in Bermuda had reached proportions far more dangerous than in Virginia,

[6] For the Ordinance and Constitution of 1621, see Kingsbury, *Records of the Virginia Company*, III, 483-4; and see McIlwaine, *Journals of the House of Burgesses, 1619-1658/59*, 57-65; Bernard Bailyn, "Politics and Social Structure in Virginia," *Seventeenth-Century America. Essays in Colonial History* (Chapel Hill, N.C., 1959), 97 and n.24, 102; Craven, *Southern Colonies*, 165n.

[7] Charles M. Andrews, *Our Earliest Colonial Settlements* (N.Y., 1933), 27. See generally J. A. C. Chandler, *Representation in Virginia* (Baltimore, Md., 1896), ch. 1; Elmer I. Miller, *The Legislature of the Province of Virginia* (N.Y., 1907).

[8] William R. Scott, *The Constitution and Finance of English, Scottish and Irish Joint-Stock Companies to 1720* (Cambridge, 1910-12), II, 266. Henry C. Wilkinson, *The Adventurers of Bermuda* (2nd ed., London, 1958), 138-40.

verging twice upon civil war. Unlike the older colony, where executive authority had been too strong, Bermuda had fallen into confusion because of the absence of effective governors— indeed, in 1618 the lack of a governor altogether. In the absence of properly constituted authority, and with the news in 1619 of an unwanted choice for governor, the settlers began to ask why the London adventurers, "sittinge by their warme fires and full flesh potts," should impose upon them "newe and unknowen men to be their Governours?" In October 1619, Nathaniel Butler arrived with instructions to summon an assembly as quickly as possible, because "every man will more willingly obey lawes to which he hath yielded his consent." So far as the adventurers were concerned, the purpose of this assembly was twofold: to raise taxes for badly needed public services in Bermuda, and to quell the political rumblings there. Given the Company's revised plans since 1618, as Professor Craven has observed, "there was good reason for seeking in every way possible the full co-operation of the colonists in the enforcement of many new regulations." So far as the planters were concerned, the assembly offered an opportunity to expand their control of the colony, diminish the London adventurers', and develop a sense of their common interests.[9]

Because Bermuda was more factious than Virginia, the first assembly in the sea-washed colony followed exact rules of parliamentary procedure much more carefully than had been the case at Jamestown. Because the interregnum of 1618 had left Bermuda without recognized leadership, one of the planters' first actions in their new assembly was to define the authority of a governor whose commission lapsed before the arrival of his successor. The powers of the assembly were enlarged and clearly fixed by the proceedings of the second assembly in 1623. The planters' participation in raising taxes helped to facilitate the imposition of levies unspecified in the original plan of settlement. Between

[9] Wesley Frank Craven, "An Introduction to the History of Bermuda," *William and Mary Quarterly*, ser. 2, XVII (1937), 197–8, 201–2; *ibid.*, XVIII (1938), 23–30; *The Historye of the Bermudaes or Summer Islands*, ed. J. Henry Lefroy (London, 1882), 190.

1619 and 1623, then, the government of Bermuda was transformed, and the settlement entered its second decade with the power to tax and the principle of representation irrevocably joined.[1]

The original assemblies in Bermuda and Virginia differed more in function than procedure. The judicial responsibilities handled by the Virginia burgesses were already provided for in Bermuda by 1620, where the dispensation of justice had been less arbitrary anyway. The Virginia assembly became a court as well as a legislature, thereby safeguarding the right of petition. In Bermuda, the delegates needed only to set two fixed days in the year for general assizes. Perhaps because the colony's life was less complicated than Virginia's, or possibly because Governor Butler had accomplished his mission so well, the assembly decided to meet every second year rather than annually as advised in Butler's instructions.[2]

The first American assemblies, then, both initiated under the auspices of commercial companies, and both possibly sponsored by Sir Edwin Sandys, originated in circumstances and ways rather different from the New England legislatures founded in the 1630's. The powers of delegates in the two oldest colonies were more restricted than in Massachusetts Bay because they met less frequently, under the close supervision of the governors, and because their acts were subject to review and disallowance by the companies in England.[3] Bermuda and the Plymouth Colony provide interesting examples of representative governments, structurally similar but functioning with different degrees of effectiveness. Both had unicameral legislatures with limited judicial roles. Both had residential requirements for representatives.

---

[1] Butler's invaluable account of the 1620 assembly appears in *The Historye of the Bermudaes*, 190–203.

[2] Craven, "Introduction to the History of Bermuda," *William and Mary Quarterly*, ser. 2, XVIII (1938), 29–30, 34.

[3] George L. Haskins, "Representative Government in Early New England: The Corporate and the Parliamentary Traditions," in *Liber Memorialis Sir Maurice Powicke. Studies Presented to the International Commission for the History of Representative and Parliamentary Institutions*, XXVII (Louvain and Paris, 1965), 85–6.

But Plymouth's General Court, meeting with much greater frequency, and stronger than the executive, would assume a more vital role in the governance and society of the Pilgrim colony.

◄§ 2 §►

Maryland and New England

Between 1634 and 1639, representative assemblies were established in Maryland and four New England colonies: Massachusetts Bay, Plymouth, Connecticut, and New Haven. There would seem to be some coherence in their closely proximate origins. In contrast to Virginia and Bermuda, the initiative for assemblies came essentially from within the colonies; Maryland stands as a partial exception because Lord Baltimore's charter empowered him to make laws with the "advice, assent and approbation of the Freemen of the . . . Province," assembled by the proprietor "in such sort and form as to him or them shall seem best." [4] Although representative government helped clarify the structure of the emerging polities of these five younger colonies, it was less urgently needed as a stabilizing device than in 1619–20. And while representative institutions obviously were highly desirable, their exact nature was as yet rather unclearly defined. Assemblies appeared in the 1630's as a convenience for both magistrates and the citizenry, and also as tangible symbols of the search for a proper distribution of community power. Unlike Virginia and Bermuda, representative governments in the 1630's were rooted in the early charters of these colonies, or else were quickly implanted therein (Plymouth being the exception). Like the first two company colonies, however, the existence of assemblies in all five would very considerably antedate the direct presence of the Crown.

An assembly of some sort met in Maryland as early as 1635. The earliest of which we have knowledge, however, was a pri-

---

[4] *The Federal and State Constitutions, Colonial Charters, and Other Organic Laws,* ed. Francis Newton Thorpe (Washington, D.C., 1909), III, 1679–81. See also Elihu S. Riley, *A History of the General Assembly of Maryland, 1635–1904* (Baltimore, Md., 1905), 1–30.

mary body convening in January 1638. Thirteen months later a representative assembly gathered; and for the next eleven years Maryland's legislature was never clearly one kind or the other. Some members responded to individual writs, as did the peerage of England. Others came on general writs calling for the attendance of all freemen—either in person, by deputy, or by proxy. Such a mixture moved rapidly and inevitably toward a bicameral organization. Those summoned by special writs tended to identify with the larger propertied interests, and consequently with the governor's council. Delegates of the freemen tended to be linked with particular hundreds, the original unit of representation, and after 1654 with the several counties. Though demands for a discrete lower house occurred as early as 1642, separation did not come until 1650. Thereafter, the Maryland legislature became fully a representative body. The terms "burgess," "delegate," and "deputy" were used interchangeably, though burgess became less common after the first few years, and delegate more so. By 1661 six counties had been established and were represented by 16 men. From 1650 until 1732, there were no cases of nonresident delegates.[5]

In New England the pattern of development was cut somewhat differently, but significantly there *was* a pattern, primarily shaped by the Bay Colony. The Puritans who migrated there in 1630 had the presence of mind to bring—along with personal possessions, livestock, and barrels of beer—their company's charter. They thereby ensured that the General Court of the Massachusetts Bay Company would eventually become the legislative assembly of the colony. Even so, the process by which this transformation occurred was complex, curtained by half-known conflicts, and by no means inevitable in the form and time it took. Since those 10 or 11 freemen of the Company who chose to emigrate were also assistants or officers, the General Court and the Court of Assistants were virtually identical in 1630. It made little practical difference, then, which body managed the Company's

[5] Andrews, *Earliest Colonial Settlements*, 153–4, 157, 165–6; Phillips, *Development of a Residential Qualification*, 169–77, 183; Craven, *Southern Colonies*, 205–8.

affairs in America. When the tiny General Court first met in October 1630, it gave the assistants the power to select the governor and deputy governor (from among themselves), to make laws, and select officers to enforce them. On this occasion, John Winthrop and his peers invited more than a hundred colonists who were not freemen to observe. Somehow the desire for approval and consent without yielding the privilege of participation seems to have prompted the invitation; in fact, this surprising concentration of all governmental power among fewer than a dozen men would continue effectively until 1634. But a steady erosion of that power occurred in the interim.[6]

Even before John Winthrop arrived in 1630, the small band of colonists under John Endecott had been permitted to select two members of the governor's council. In the spring of 1631, Winthrop and his fellow magistrates decided to admit to freemanship a considerable number of men. Thereafter, the General Court and the Court of Assistants ceased to be coincidental. In 1632, a tax requisitioned by the latter group was resisted when the independent-minded minister of Watertown gathered his congregation and warned the members against paying taxes to which they had not consented. When summoned before Winthrop, the protestants deferred to his argument that the colony's government, unlike that of a corporation, was "in the nature of a parliament" wherein the assistants, the freemens' delegates elected at large, had full power both to legislate and levy taxes. Nonetheless, the magistrates made a major concession, and "ordered that there should be two of every plantation appointed to conferre with the Court about raiseing of a publique stocke." The Watertown protest had thereby led to the inauguration of representative government for the limited purpose of taxation.[7]

In 1634 the constitutional transformation was completed.

[6] G. H. Haynes, *Representation and Suffrage in Massachusetts, 1620–1696* (Baltimore, Md., 1894); George Lee Haskins, *Law and Authority in Early Massachusetts* (N.Y., 1960), 26–8.

[7] Edmund S. Morgan, *The Puritan Dilemma. The Story of John Winthrop* (Boston, 1958), chs. 7–8; *Records of the Governor and Company of the Massachusetts Bay in New England,* ed. N. B. Shurtleff (Boston, 1853–4), I, 95–6.

That spring the freemen appointed two deputies from each town to consider crucial questions to be brought before the General Court in May. In the course of their discussions they asked to see the charter, from which they discovered that indeed all laws were properly to be passed by the General Court. Winthrop admitted this was so, but pointed out that there were now so many freemen that "it was not possible for them to make or execute laws, but they must choose others for that purpose." Deputies did in fact attend the May meeting, and proceeded to promulgate resolutions that exceeded Winthrop's wildest expectations: that only the General Court could admit freemen, pass laws, and grant lands. A general representative system was also established. The freemen of each town might choose two or three delegates to prepare business for the General Court and legislate there. As a result, the Court became an elective body consisting of some 20 deputies, plus the governor, his lieutenant, and the assistants. The General Court thereby resumed the powers granted it according to the charter, and fully displaced the Court of Assistants as the fulcrum of the colony's government.[8]

Thereafter, the logic of development seemed to be guided by gyroscope. In 1636, the legislative parity of the two elements in the General Court was acknowledged. Five years later, the Body of Liberties reaffirmed the right of each town to choose deputies, and in 1644 that silly dispute over a stray sow produced a permanent separation and bicameralism. The General Court simply formalized what had for some while been accepted practice.[9]

As, after long experience, we find divers inconveniences in the manner of our proceeding in Courts by magistrates & Deputies sitting together, & accounting it wisdom to follow the laudable practice of other States. . . . It is therefore ordered, first, that the magistrates may sit & act business by themselves, by drawing up

[8] *Winthrop's Journal. History of New England, 1630–1649*, ed. James K. Hosmer (N.Y., 1908), I, 122; Haskins, *Law and Authority*, 29–31.
[9] Phillips, *Development of a Residential Qualification*, 21; Morgan, *Puritan Dilemma*, 171; A. P. Rugg, "A Famous Colonial Litigation," *Proceedings of the American Antiquarian Society*, n.s., XXX (1920), 217–50.

bills & orders which they shall see good in their wisdom, which having agreed upon, they may present them to the Deputies to be considered of, how good & wholesome such orders are for the country, & accordingly to give their assent or dissent; the Deputies in like manner sitting apart . . . may present to the magistrates, who, according to their wisdom, having seriously considered of them, may consent unto them or disallow them; & when such orders have passed the approbation of both magistrates & Deputies, then such orders to be engrossed, & in the last day of the Court to be read deliberately, & full assent to be given; provided, also, that all matters of judicature which this Court shall take cognizance of shall be issued in like manner.[1]

Again, there was nothing inevitable about bicameralism in Massachusetts Bay. Puritan society there was still comparatively homogeneous, especially within the elite leadership of saints in the General Court. When the first deputies were admitted in 1634, they had resisted the assistants' inclination to act as an upper house. After all, the deputies' superior number would serve more effectively in a unicameral body. Moreover, when Lord Say and Sele and other Puritans of high birth proposed from England in 1635 that they emigrate upon establishment of a hereditary House of Lords in Massachusetts Bay, the magistrates reluctantly but firmly refused. Bicameralism, then, was simply the result of a felt need to formalize a balance of power: the deputies were determined to compel the magistrates to give up their "negative voice," while the latter were equally determined not to yield.[2]

This whole tale of complexities transpiring between 1630 and 1644—much oversimplified here—has traditionally been spun around the engaging figure of John Winthrop. Fair enough, except that the central problem has not been brought into sharp focus. The Puritans who settled in Massachusetts had thorough familiarity with local government, and could re-create it easily. But almost to a man they lacked direct experience through in-

[1] Robert C. Winthrop, *Life and Letters of John Winthrop* (Boston, 1864–7), II, 294–5.
[2] Samuel Eliot Morison, *Builders of the Bay Colony* (2nd ed., Boston, 1958), 83–5, 91–3; Andrews, *Colonial Period*, I, 451.

It seems that, at larger levels, this problem is increasing *this problem is played out*

volvement in central governments. Therein lay the difficulty: how to establish, systematize, and develop central authority—patently necessary by 1632—and define its proper relationship to local government. Because of his vision and responsibility, Winthrop found the necessity and nature of provincial governance his special concern. During the 1630's, his problem was not merely how permissive or authoritarian he should be; it was how to accommodate the authority of the state (which then seemed so invidious in England) to the needs of changing and dispersing communities of men.[3]

Massachusetts Bay compressed into the years 1630–4 a process that took almost twenty years to complete in the older but smaller Plymouth Colony. There the settlers all assembled once each year to elect the governor and assistants. Not until the mid-1630's did this very slowly expanding society begin to incorporate subordinate towns. By 1638, the dispersion and difficulties of gathering a primary body together regularly were all too apparent. Therefore, the freemen who had assembled for the March court voted to elect representatives to join the governor and assistants four times annually in passing legislation. From 1638 until 1652, however, *all* freemen were obliged to attend the election court in June. The establishment of a representative system in 1638 clearly reflected the freemen's desire to keep control of the General Court as an instrument of taxation; and indeed, by 1640 it had "become the sole governing authority in the colony." Its powers were extensive, judicial as well as legislative. With good reason the towns watched the General Court carefully and zealously. Because laws proposed at one legislative session were not voted on until the next, the delegates had ample opportunity to consult with their constituents. Plymouth's settled communities had years of experience with local government to draw upon. Not surprisingly, they looked closely at the first assembly which gathered in Plymouth on March 5, 1639, and scrutinized its successors with equal care. The assembly remained unicameral,

---

[3] For a valuable town by town analysis of 528 deputies, see Robert E. Wall, Jr., "The Membership of the Massachusetts General Court, 1634–1686" (unpubl. Ph.D. dissertation, Yale University, 1965).

established a residential qualification from the outset, controlled its own membership, and enjoyed remarkable stability and continuity in membership.[4]

Connecticut's General Court, patterned after Massachusetts Bay's, met for the first time at Hartford on May 1, 1637. It was composed of two magistrates and three deputies from each of the three river towns. Its meeting was required not only by the need to form an independent government, but also to raise men and supplies for the Pequot Indian war. The General Court quickly assumed nearly complete control over the towns; indeed, the relationship was similar to that of their counterparts in Massachusetts. Early in 1639 a convention of all the freemen adopted the Fundamental Orders, which provided for two annual sessions of the General Court, to which each town would send four deputies. Thereafter, very little legislation appeared concerning the organization or powers of the General Court. Nevertheless, its business was extensive. Many extra sessions were held in addition to the two scheduled each year, and its work was legislative, judicial, and administrative in nature. As in Massachusetts, committees were relied upon extensively—a logical outgrowth of the use made of committees by English trading companies in transacting their business. The Royal Charter of 1662 essentially confirmed the institutional arrangements already in existence, and the General Court remained relatively constant until its reorganization and shift to bicameralism in 1698. (After 1644, the deputies had an equal voice with the magistrates; either group might veto legislation.) During the later seventeenth century there was a slight increase in nonresidential representation, but less than in Massachusetts.[5]

In 1639, the body of freemen in New Haven's quiet colony chose 12 men deemed fit to be magistrates; and from them seven were selected by lot actually to serve. In October they resigned,

[4] George D. Langdon, Jr., *Pilgrim Colony. A History of New Plymouth 1620–1691* (New Haven, Conn., 1966), 85–8, 93–8.

[5] Nelson P. Mead, *Connecticut as a Corporate Colony* (Lancaster, Pa., 1906), 7–20; Mary J. A. Jones, *Congregational Commonwealth. Connecticut, 1636–1662* (Wesleyan, Conn., 1968), 31–2, 65–6, 82–6, 90–3; Phillips, *Development of a Residential Qualification*, 86.

whereupon all the freemen elected a magistrate and four deputies to manage public affairs. Thereafter, these officers would be elected annually at a general court. In October 1643, an assembly was convened in New Haven at which for the first time the outlying towns were represented. Milford, Guilford, and Stamford each sent two deputies. The General Court met in two annual sessions, and remained unicameral until its last (and plenary) gathering late in 1664 when Connecticut absorbed her smaller neighbor.[6]

Amongst Maryland and the four New England colonies, then, we find several new developments in the later 1630's and the rough outline of a common pattern. As compared with Virginia and Bermuda, the time lag between initial settlement and the inauguration of representative government had been much reduced. Consequently, in all five there is a certain vacillation at the outset between the assembling of primary and representative bodies. Being small, and (except for Massachusetts Bay) lacking the immediate stock company origins of Virginia and Bermuda, there was even a greater tendency to experiment with primary gatherings. Finally, we find the origins of representative government in Plymouth, Connecticut, and New Haven influenced by developments in Massachusetts Bay, whose surprising reach would eventually extend even to the Caribbean.

◄§ 3 §►

The Caribbean Colonies and Rhode Island

James Hay, second Earl of Carlisle and nominal proprietor of Barbados and the Leeward Islands after 1636, began to struggle with problems of effective government there just when Roger Williams encountered a similar challenge in the wilderness outpost that would become Rhode Island. There must be something politically divisive about an island mentality, for both men faced

[6] Isabel M. Calder, *The New Haven Colony* (New Haven, Conn., 1934), 106–10, 117–22.

fractious, local-minded, and highly independent enclaves spotted here and there in little clusters. In both places a stormy prehistory —characterized by insecure executive authority, particularism, and factionalism—anticipated and precipitated the establishment of representative government. Like Rhode Island's several plantations, the Leeward Islands enjoyed *de facto* local independence for some years before being drawn into a unified framework. Both Barbados and Rhode Island, like Connecticut and New Haven, owed much of their early autonomy to their highly tenuous constitutional status. And in both colonies the settlers acquired a decade's experience with local government before being asked to accept participation in the centralization of authority.[7]

On isolated occasions before 1639 the governor of Barbados had called meetings of all the planters to consider business of great importance. After 1636, an extraordinary rise in population occurred. In 1639, when the Earl of Carlisle tried to wrest proprietary control from the trustees by dismissing Henry Hawley as governor, Hawley appealed for popular support by granting Barbadians the right to elect a representative assembly. A year later, the king and proprietors sent commissioners to Barbados to remove Hawley. Their efforts succeeded, and so did Henry Hunks as interim governor. But the assembly Hawley had called endured. From 1639 until 1641, its functions were essentially counsel and consent: 11 councillors and 22 burgesses stood for eleven parishes in a bicameral body. In 1641, under Governor Philip Bell, they gained the right to initiate legislation. During the 1640's, sessions were frequent (at a tavern in Bridgetown), the two houses cooperated rather closely, their power and autonomy were considerable. In the next decade, the assembly resolved many problems and secured many powers (over finance and public works, for example) despite the presence of Francis Lord Willoughby, whose commission as governor gave him ex-

[7] J. H. Bennett, "The English Caribbees in the Period of the Civil War, 1642–1646," *William and Mary Quarterly*, ser. 3, XXIV (1967), 359, 361 ff., 373; Andrews, *Colonial Period*, II, 6–26, 258–61; Vincent T. Harlow, *A History of Barbados, 1625–1685* (Oxford, 1926), 331–5.

tensive powers. After 1652 an ardent group of parliamentarians,
led by Colonel Thomas Modiford, even sought representation in
the great Parliament at home! During the decade of the 1660's,
however, a decline in white population linked with a rise in
Willoughby's authority as governor led to a gradual decline in
the assembly's governmental role. Its members surrendered power
of the purse in return for land grants, and permitted the thrust for
independence characteristic of the 1650's to die.[8]

The Leeward Islands were effectively opened to settlement
by Barbados, and legally under its governance until 1672. St.
Christopher elected its first assembly of burgesses—24 young
planters—early in 1642; they re-ordered the colony's laws, and
remained unicameral until the 1670's. Antigua, peopled almost
entirely by Barbadians, acquired an assembly in 1644 or 1645. It
rapidly became the most aggressive in the Leeward group, con-
stantly seeking powers at the governor's expense—a tendency
accentuated by the fact that the governor usually lived in Nevis
or St. Kitts. The assembly remained unicameral until the early
1680's. During the 1650's, tiny assemblies of planters appeared
in Nevis and Montserrat, which became bicameral after 1672
and in 1696, respectively.[9] Once the Leeward Islands became a
royal colony in 1672, independent of Barbadian control, Governor William Stapleton called together representatives of the
island councils for consultations. The first occurred in 1674,
though these early meetings were essentially executive councils
rather than legislative bodies. The first general assembly met at
Nevis in November 1682, and another in 1683. This new federal
structure possessed a legislative authority recognized as binding
upon each of the four constituent islands, however their own local
delegates may have voted. From the outset the General Assembly
confronted all the serious problems of the coming generation:

[8] Frederick G. Spurdle, *Early West Indian Government* (Palmerston
North, N.Z., [n.d.]), 12–20; Harlow, *History of Barbados*, 25, 51, 65, 97–
100, 102, 124–7, 134–5, 140.

[9] Bennett, "The English Caribbees," 362–5; Andrews, *Colonial Period*,
II, 258–9; Vere L. Oliver, *The History of the Island of Antigua* (London,
1894), I, xviii–xxviii.

finance, defense, local representation, and proposals for a unified legal code.[1]

Just after St. Christopher and Antigua first achieved assemblies in 1642–5, committees from the tiny Rhode Island towns met in convention; so that, curiously, the first assembly virtually preceded the actual creation of a central government. As early as 1640, provision had been made for two annual sessions of a General Court. A strong sense of localism, however, delayed implementation until May 1647, when a mixed primary and representative body met at Portsmouth. From then until 1663 every town was represented at every assembly. Thereafter, indifference became rather commonplace. The 1647 gathering simply assumed the form and functions of a General Court, without formal proclamation. Until 1663 the body was called "the Representative Committee" or "the General Court of Commissioners." Not until the new charter was obtained did "General Assembly" become the standard term. After 1648 six representatives attended from each town, and the group gathered alternately at the four leading localities. After 1663 both annual sessions met at Newport, there were no restrictions upon the assembly's legislative power, and very little nonresident representation. Agitation for bicameralism, strong in 1665–6, did not succeed until May 1696; and the federal system in Rhode Island bore a surprising similarity to the constitutional structure of the Leeward Islands after the 1670's. Significant and symbolic was the remarkable retention of a local role in the legislative process during the early assemblies. Bills might originate in the towns as well as within the General Court. Indeed, early in the 1650's there was very nearly a complete reversion to exclusively local government.[2]

[1] C. S. S. Higham, "The General Assembly of the Leeward Islands," *English Historical Review*, XLI (1926), 190–209; Higham, *The Development of the Leeward Islands Under the Restoration, 1660–1688* (Cambridge, 1921).

[2] *Records of the Colony of Rhode Island and Providence Plantations*, ed. John R. Bartlett (Providence, 1856), I, 147–55; Osgood, *Colonies in the Seventeenth Century*, I, 332, 345, 355–9, 363–4; Patrick T. Conley, "Rhode Island Constitutional Development, 1636–1775," *Rhode Island History*, XXVII (1968), 55–63.

One final assembly came into being during this quarter century from 1639 until 1664: that of Jamaica. Captured from Spain in 1655, it received from London a civil government in 1661 through an elected council of twelve who would advise and assist the governor. Although he was empowered to summon an assembly of elected freeholders, writs were not finally issued until 1663, when 20 members were chosen from the several settled districts in proportion to population. On January 20, 1664, the first assembly convened, and again in May. It immediately passed money bills and sought control over taxation. In so doing it was following the practice of Barbados and Virginia during the 1650's, rather than English usage (where the House of Commons had not yet begun to appropriate supply and examine the royal accounts).[3] As in Barbados, the assembly was bicameral from the beginning.

Between the outbreak of the Civil War in England, then, and the Restoration of Charles II, representative governments were inaugurated in six Caribbean colonies and Rhode Island. And during these same years, of course, maturation, considerable autonomy, and in several cases bicameralism evolved in the older colonies whose assemblies had been established earlier. Certain generalizations about this period emerge with sharp clarity, while others must remain tentative. For the first time, parliamentary developments in England had a *direct* impact as sources of encouragement, emulation, and appeal. This was especially true in the Caribbean, but it shaped Roger Williams's thoughts on political organization as well.[4] In various ways the gathering of the Long Parliament in 1640 would assist and encourage fledgling parliamentarians in America. In Barbados, news of the Long Parliament made the assembly much more assertive, and in 1643 Charles I was warned that the Barbadians "had all turned to the way of the parliament and were lik to shake off . . . obedi-

---

[3] Agnes M. Whitson, *The Constitutional Development of Jamaica—1660 to 1729* (Manchester, 1929), 20–9.

[4] Alan Simpson, *Puritanism in Old and New England* (Chicago, 1955), 58.

ence to his Majeste." [5] In Virginia, Maryland, Massachusetts Bay, and Plymouth as well, colonial assemblies enjoyed a new self-confidence and even sophistication. In every case the date 1640 marks a very real turning point.

The Restoration and events immediately following would also have a visible impact, especially in the Caribbean. There the existence of executive authority had uniformly preceded the introduction of assemblies. The latter had managed during the 1640's to wrest from governors rights that might easily revert, given some shift in the balance of power. That was precisely what happened in Barbados, St. Christopher, and Antigua during and after the 1660's; and in Jamaica between 1665 and 1671. In each case representative bodies had been launched at a propitious time, had flourished initially, overreached themselves, and fizzled out after the demise of the Protectorate. In Barbados, a decline in white population, emigration of the wealthiest planters to England, and the influence of Francis Willoughby, Lord of Parham, were all responsible. In St. Christopher, the same factors plus Sir Thomas Warner and the French presence proved decisive. And in Antigua, Willoughby alone turned the tide.[6] Since the politics of Roundheads and Cavaliers had been explicitly played out in miniature amongst these early Caribbean assemblies during the 1640's and 1650's, it was not surprising that the altered balance of power in England after 1660 would be re-enacted in the islands as well.[7]

[5] Bennett, "The English Caribbees," 368, 370; Andrews, *Colonial Period,* II, 302, 322.

[6] Harlow, *History of Barbados,* 134–5, 140; Bennett, "The English Caribbees," 365–6; Higham, *Development of the Leeward Islands,* 225; Spurdle, *Early West Indian Government,* 21–4.

[7] N. Darnell Davis, *The Cavaliers & Roundheads of Barbados 1650–1652* (Georgetown, Br. Guiana, 1887) chs. 8–14; James A. Williamson, *The Caribbee Islands Under the Proprietary Patents* (London, 1926), 114 ff.; Harlow, *History of Barbados,* 51 ff.

~§ 4 §~

The Carolinas and Jersies

The beginnings of representative government in Jamaica in 1663–4 were strikingly transitional in nature. Influenced by earlier developments in Virginia, Parliament, and the New Model Army, and resembling Barbados's legislature in important respects, the Jamaica assembly also anticipated some of the new developments originating in those colonial assemblies organized after the Restoration. It profited from the various experiences of other colonial assemblies during the 1650's; emerged from the outset as a surprisingly mature, bicameral body; and offered opportunities for self-government partially designed to attract new settlers.[8]

With colonization of the Carolinas and Jersies after the 1660's, representative frames of government came to be regarded as *stimuli* to settlement rather than *responses* to it, as had been the case between 1619 and the 1640's. During those early years representative institutions had often been a convenience for the rulers, an expedient way of securing political stability and consent to altered economic planning. By the 1670's, such institutions were seen as much more than conveniences and expedients; they would safeguard the rights of settlers, and therefore were essential to the proper foundation of New World societies. Paradoxically, however, representative assemblies were now provided for by proprietary boards of trustees—potentially the most authoritarian kind of governors.[9] Where the Carolinas, Jersies, New Hampshire, Pennsylvania, and New York were concerned, a few farsighted men eventually saw that representative government would stand as almost the *sine qua non* of successful colonization.

[8] Whitson, *Constitutional Development of Jamaica,* chs. 2–3. And see *Journals of the Assembly of Jamaica From January the 20th, 1663–4 . . . to April the 20th, 1709* (Jamaica, 1811), I, 1–47.

[9] Wesley Frank Craven, *The Colonies in Transition, 1660–1713* (N.Y., 1968), 91–2.

Many others lacked their vision, however, and therein lay a source of sustained tension.

In 1663-4, the Carolina proprietors planned that laws in their intended colony would be made by an elected assembly with the consent of governor and council, subject of course to the proprietors' disallowance. The revised "Concessions and Agreement" drawn up in 1665 provided governments for three separate settlements at Albemarle, Cape Fear, and Port Royal. Each would be called a county and given a separate administration (with its own governor, council, and assembly). A central government was provided by the famous Fundamental Constitutions of 1669-70. Altered ever so many times during the remainder of the century, these essentially called for a unicameral and biennial assembly. It would include a governor, the proprietors or their deputies, landgraves, caciques, and elected freeholders from each precinct. The last-named group would no longer be privileged to initiate legislation. And it was understood that the whole complex scheme would only come into being gradually.[1]

In one sense the degree of self-government anticipated by the proprietors contracted between 1663 and 1670. The liberal arrangements of 1663, with two representatives from every tribe or parish, had not been intended as permanent by the proprietors: merely an early inducement to attract colonists. When no permanent settlement devolved under these terms, the proprietors voided them. Under the 1665 plan a fixed number of deputies, twelve, would constitute the representative part of each assembly. After several decades' experience, the proprietors still had not brought governmental theory into full congruence with political reality. In 1691, they intended to have just one governor and one legislative assembly for their whole domain—even though there were by then two discrete and very different settlements. Because such an arrangement proved utterly impracticable, the colonists of North Carolina (née Albemarle) were permanently

---

[1] *The Colonial Records of North Carolina,* ed. William L. Saunders (Raleigh, N.C., 1886), I, 43-7; *North Carolina Charters and Constitutions, 1578-1698,* ed. Mattie E. E. Parker (Raleigh, N.C., 1963), 74-104, 107-240.

given a separate legislative assembly and a deputy governor as chief executive.[2]

So much for the elaborate theories of those unthinking proprietors. In actual fact an assembly sat for Albemarle some time before June 1665; there must have been assemblies in 1665, 1667, and 1669; and they became regular after 1670. Theoretically the delegates met with the council as one body. In practice the governor and proprietors' men deliberated separately until after 1691, when bicameralism was formally established.[3] The so-called parliament that developed between 1670 and 1691 included the governor, his council of six, and 20 elected delegates whose function was restricted to action upon proposals presented by the governor and council.

The southern settlement on the Ashley River had a similar theoretical framework, but developed under significantly different circumstances. In 1663–4, a group of 46 experienced planters from Barbados contemplated making a new colony within the Carolina grant, and asked to have the government of it placed in their own hands. The Barbadian adventurers were pleased by their exploration of the Cape Fear region in 1663; so pleased, in fact, that they drafted a scheme of colonization which included the assurance that all freeholders would participate in the election of deputies to a general assembly. For a time settlement remained sparse below the Albemarle, so this liberal document failed to become operative. The Barbadians were nevertheless persistent. When a colony finally materialized in 1670, the governor failed to summon an assembly because of inadequate population. Thereupon, two unauthorized individuals issued election writs, and the local parliament of 15 thereby elected (plus five councillors) was South Carolina's first. Commonly called Owen's Parliament, it convened in July 1670. A year later, after the authorization of Governor Joseph West, the first legal parliament

[2] Charles Lee Raper, *North Carolina. A Study in English Colonial Government* (N.Y., 1904), 16–21; Phillips, *Development of a Residential Qualification,* 202–4.

[3] *Colonial Records of North Carolina,* I, 101, 167; Raper, *North Carolina,* 24–5.

met.[4] It was racked by factionalism, and dissolved quickly. Thereafter, 20 freeholders would be elected biennially, and meet as
often as plantation affairs required. But for twenty years to come,
in both Albemarle and the southern colony, the councils dominated. Perhaps this was inevitable so long as both colonies remained so small.

In 1682, a revision of the Fundamental Constitutions increased the power of the freemen. The proprietors decided also
to divide the settlement into counties, each with equal representation in the parliament. Grand councillors, noblemen, and representatives of the people would still sit together in one house;
but all laws had to be passed by a majority of each of the three
groups, thereby creating a kind of tricameral assembly. In 1691,
with factionalism rampant in South Carolina, the proprietors
actually suspended the Fundamental Constitutions and altered
the government. The old council, partially elected, was replaced
by an appointed body of proprietary deputies. Thenceforth, the
southern colony had a bicameral assembly in which the Commons House would have the dominant voice. By the close of the
seventeenth century, following a brief controversy in 1696 over
constitutional questions, the assembly emerged as a major political institution under moderate leadership.[5]

Representative bodies matured in the Carolinas more slowly
than in New England, the Chesapeake, or several of the Caribbean islands. Institutional development required a longer gesta-
tion period, and in several respects proceeded hesitantly. A partial explanation rests in the relative absence of local government.
South Carolina had very little to speak of until the eighteenth
century; and in Albemarle the system of courts remained rudimentary. By contrast, local government in New England preceded
or emerged alongside representative assemblies. The experience

[4] E. E. Rich, "The First Earl of Shaftesbury's Colonial Policy," *Transactions of the Royal Historical Society*, ser. 5, VII (1957), 56–7; Andrews,
Colonial Period, III, 194 and n.3, 196; *The Shaftesbury Papers. Collections
of the South Carolina Historical Society* (Charleston, S.C., 1897), V, 203–4,
290–5, 311–32.

[5] M. Eugene Sirmans, *Colonial South Carolina. A Political History,
1663–1763* (Chapel Hill, N.C., 1966), 37, 51, 61–2, 66–70.

and confidence gained locally helped reinforce the rapid rise of legislative power.

Beyond the retarding effect of weak local institutions, two other characteristics are noteworthy in understanding the origins of representative government in the Carolinas: uncertainty and the influence of Barbados. Proprietary government was extraordinarily indefinite and unscrutable. No one could be quite certain about the organization and procedures of the polity, or know just what was meant by the proprietors' "will and pleasure." The Concessions and Agreement of 1665, which would be so important in the life of East New Jersey, proved useless in Carolina when colonization on Cape Fear collapsed in 1667. In understanding why South Carolina's assembly soon outstripped Albemarle's, one must keep in mind not only the uniqueness of Charles Town (and the excess of nonresidential representation that developed in the colony), but also the impact of Barbadian colonization and the hope of attracting New Englanders. The influence of New England and Barbados appeared both in the Declarations and Proposals of 1663 and in the Concessions and Agreement. Shaftesbury's colonization schemes of 1669–70 were aimed especially at attracting Barbadians. Such families as the Yeamans and the Colletons brought the governmental experience of the Caribbean islanders to bear upon public affairs in Carolina; so that several decades after the Ashley River settlement began, the Commons House was still dominated by the Barbados party.[6]

In the colonies of East and West Jersey the development of representative institutions was also contingent upon proprietary bodies and their peculiar relation to the freeholders. Consequently, bitter struggles for power occurred in the 1670's and 1680's. Although government in both the Carolinas and Jersies really began with the same Concessions and Agreement of 1665, assemblies matured much more readily to the north. The presence of self-governing Puritans before 1665 was a major contributing factor.

[6] *Colonial Records of North Carolina*, I, 39–42; Andrews, *Colonial Period*, III, 203, 247–8; Sirmans, *South Carolina*, 44–9.

Proprietors vs. freeholders

New Englanders had established themselves at Middletown, Shrewsbury, and Woodbridge, and brought with them institutional assumptions that had been developing for a quarter century. These people bridled at the absolute authority claimed by the proprietors. They insisted that they were freeholders in their own right, rather than by virtue of some proprietary patent. In 1667, almost a year before the first Jersey assembly formally gathered at Elizabethtown, "The General Assembly of the Patentees and Deputies" met at Shrewsbury, giving prior experience and assertiveness to East Jersey's initial delegates. The three towns of the Monmouth Patent sent representatives to this special body for several years, though it exercised only local functions.[7]

In East New Jersey, according to the Concessions of 1665, the proprietary governor would appoint his council of six to twelve men. The assembly would initially include twelve elected deputies; and the entire body sitting together would have full lawmaking powers. In April 1668 the first elections were held, and late in May the new assembly consisted of seven councillors plus two deputies each from Bergen, Newark, Woodbridge, Elizabethtown, and Middletown.[8] The Monmouth towns would only participate on condition that the self-governing rights they held under grant from New York's Governor Nicolls would not be impaired. Such conditions were unacceptable, and their delegates were not seated. Shortly thereafter, Middletown and Shrewsbury refused to pay a tax voted by the assembly, citing in defense their seven-year exemption under the Nicolls patent, whereupon a complex series of rebellions unsettled East Jersey for several years. Legal assemblies met in November 1668 and 1671. An unauthorized body, denounced by the proprietor, Philip Carteret, came together in May 1672, but its records were suppressed, and a new gathering was not summoned until November 1675. This frustrating impasse, so embittered by differing conceptions

[7] Andrews, *Colonial Period,* III, 141–2, 146–7, 156; Edwin P. Tanner, *The Province of New Jersey, 1664–1738* (N.Y., 1908), ch. 19.

[8] At subsequent assemblies deputies also attended from the Delaware settlements. Cf. John E. Pomfret, *The New Jersey Proprietors and Their Lands, 1664–1776* (Princeton, N.J., 1964), chs. 2, 4.

of the proper nature of government and colonial sovereignty, could only be resolved through appeals to England. The result, of course, was complete victory for the proprietary claims. For more than a decade the East Jersey assembly, stimulated by the Long Islanders' influence, would seek to achieve its proper role in the colony's government.[9]

In West New Jersey, a Quaker proprietary, the extraordinary Concessions and Agreements of 1676–7 were drafted to guarantee popular self-government. All legislative power would be vested in an assembly of 100 elected members. Voting would be annual; and election by secret ballot. A ten-man commission would serve instead of a single executive. Although the Concessions were never actually put into effect, the document's eventual impact was considerable. It emphasized consent—"for we put the power in the people"—and when the first elected assembly convened at Burlington on November 21, 1681, every effort was given to establish its supremacy. Provision was made for its annual election, and all officials were to be selected by and accountable to the legislature. It met with fair regularity thereafter, probably in two sessions each year. Even so, the exigencies of imperial policies and provincial politics made government most uncertain in the 1680's; in 1683 an extraordinary assembly of the freeholders sought to usurp Edward Byllynge's control over the proprietary. In 1691, following a brief period of executive government, the West Jersey legislature began to stabilize. Representation was by divisions called tenths until 1694, when counties were established. In 1692 the council ceased to be elected by the assembly, and was thereafter appointed by the governor. In 1694 a new law apportioned 55 representatives among the four counties. Two years later the two houses began to meet separately.[1]

[9] John E. Pomfret, *The Province of East New Jersey 1609–1702* (Princeton, N.J., 1962), 28–30, 56, 59, 63, 67–9, 83–101, 107; *The Grants, Concessions, and Original Constitutions of the Province of New Jersey. The Acts Passed During the Proprietary Governments* . . . , eds. Aaron Leaming and Jacob Spicer (Philadelphia, Pa., 1881), 14–18.

[1] *Ibid.*, 404–7; John E. Pomfret, *The Province of West New Jersey 1609–1702* (Princeton, N.J., 1956), 96–7, 114, 128, 130, 133, 135–49. See also John E. Pomfret, "The Problem of the West Jersey *Concessions* of 1676/7," *William and Mary Quarterly*, ser. 3, V (1948), 95–105.

There had been very little nonresident representation in West Jersey; and in 1698 a residential qualification was passed by the East Jersey assembly. In 1702, following years of chaotic feuding between proprietors and freemen over government arrangements and land grants, the two provinces were reunited as New Jersey, a Crown colony under the governor of New York. The proprietors kept their property rights but surrendered governmental power. In November 1702 Governor Cornbury was instructed to call an assembly. He did so, and it first met in 1703 amid frantic maneuvering for leverage. Thereafter, the New Jersey assembly—structurally united yet politically divided—resembled those in Her Majesty's other American possessions.[2]

Developments in West Jersey inevitably influenced contemporaneous events in Pennsylvania—especially the proprietor's attempt to construct a viable government. William Penn had helped to draft the Concessions and Agreements of 1677, and would experiment with equally large and unwieldy legislative bodies for his own territory in 1681-2. It is important to note also that the abortive Fundamental Constitutions of 1683 in East New Jersey called for 144 representatives elected by the freemen.[3] Given the opportunity to innovate governmental structures in the later 1670's and 1680's, there was a clear inclination toward institutional gigantism, especially considering the smallness of of the settlements. Various reasons are apparent, strikingly diverse but all equally important. First was the profound influence of James Harrington's *Oceana*, and that utopian author's proclivity for vast legislative bodies. Secondly, one must consider the view then commonly held of human nature as self-interested individually yet more trustworthy in large numbers. The later Stuart mentality had greater faith in society as a whole than in its particular members.[4] Thirdly, and perhaps most important,

---

[2] Phillips, *Development of a Residential Qualification*, 135, 138–41; Andrews, *Colonial Period*, III, 177–80.

[3] *The Grants, Concessions, and Original Constitutions of New Jersey*, 153–66.

[4] See Harrington, *The Commonwealth of Oceana* (London, 1887), 178, 193; H. F. Russell-Smith, *Harrington and His Oceana. A Study of a 17th Century Utopia and Its Influence in America* (Cambridge, 1914), ch. 7;

there was the Quaker experience with social organization through endless well-attended meetings: meetings for worship and sufferings, business and preparative meetings, monthly and quarterly meetings, and even women's meetings.[5] Fourth and finally, the element of seductive colonization contributed. These large, unwieldy bodies did have a strong participatory attraction. Since European emigrants were being sought in considerable numbers, the inducements of full citizenship and the chance to shape one's destiny seemed an irresistible lure.

~§ 5 §~

Pennsylvania

In 1681 William Penn received his proprietary charter from Charles II. A year later, very much influenced by the theories of James Harrington and Algernon Sidney,[6] Penn promulgated his first Charter of Liberties. For years past in England, Penn had demonstrated his concern for effective representatives, residential requirements, and "frequent parliaments, the only true check upon arbitrary ministers." When he actually came to write a frame of government, Penn considered many variations and drafted many versions. Almost all of them called for regular elections, annual parliaments, and the secret ballot, thereby safeguarding "all of the privileges of the English House of Commons." And the proprietor showed consistent concern for regulating the representative's responsibility to his constituents.[7]

Algernon Sidney, *Discourses Concerning Government* (London, 1763), 14, 17, 41–2, 308, 438–9.

[5] Rufus M. Jones, *The Quakers in the American Colonies* (London, 1911), *passim;* Edwin B. Bronner, *William Penn's "Holy Experiment." The Founding of Pennsylvania, 1681–1701* (N.Y., 1962), 91.

[6] In 1679 Penn worked diligently for the candidacy of Sidney, who had sat in the Long Parliament. In 1680–1 Penn consulted the republican Sidney directly about a colonial frame of government. See Joseph E. Illick, *William Penn the Politician. His Relations with the English Government* (Ithaca, N.Y., 1965), 11–12, 42; Russell-Smith, *Harrington and His Oceana,* 165–83.

[7] Mary Maples Dunn, *William Penn. Politics and Conscience* (Princeton, N.J., 1967), 29, 31, 34, 89–92.

Even so, the earliest draft of Penn's 1682 Frame projected a government dominated by a landed aristocracy and less liberal than those functioning in many other colonies. As he made revisions in successive drafts, Penn gave the lower house the right to initiate laws, and some other concessions. But then early in 1682, Penn shifted to a more conservative scheme. An upper house of 72 wise and substantial men would be elected by the freemen. The right to initiate legislation was transferred to the upper house. And the functions of the governor's council and the upper house were combined, thereby giving one body control over legislative, executive, and judicial matters. These alterations left a lower house of several hundred entitled to a nine-day annual session, and permitted only to approve or reject laws proposed by the council. The assembly could not initiate legislation, elect its own speaker, or decide upon its own adjournment. William Penn had fixed upon a constitutional system which concentrated political power in the hands of the governor and especially his council, and which was far less liberal than the West Jersey Concessions of 1677, the East Jersey Constitution of 1683, or even New York's Charter of 1683.[8]

Why had Penn taken such a conservative position? Evidence is slender, but the most convincing explanation is that he had been persuaded that his early schemes were unworkable and unacceptable to the wealthy men whose backing he sought. As Gary Nash has asked, why should they exchange carefully cultivated estates in England for the uncertainties of a proprietary wilderness unless they were conceded extensive power? Like other Englishmen, the Quakers could comfortably reconcile "spiritual equalitarianism with a traditional view of the natural ordering of social classes. An elective council little threatened the pivotal position which Penn's moneyed supporters expected

---

[8] Gary B. Nash, "The Framing of Government in Pennsylvania. Ideas in Contact with Reality," *William and Mary Quarterly*, ser. 3, XXIII (1966), 194–200. And see *Charter to William Penn, and Laws of the Province of Pennsylvania, 1682 to 1700*, eds. Staughton George, *et al.* (Harrisburg, Pa., 1879).

to occupy." [9] Penn's alterations elicited specific criticisms, however, from his most whiggish friends. Benjamin Furly, a Rotter-
dam merchant, observed that this "divesting of the peoples representatives (in time to come) of the greatest right they have
. . . will lay morally a certain foundation for dissention amongst
our successors." Englishmen, Furly warned, "can never, by any
prescription of time be dispossessed of that naturall right of
propounding laws to be made by their representatives." [1]

Penn's 1682 Frame was never accepted by the colonists. A
convention called, among other purposes, to ratify the document,
rejected it. Whereupon an assembly called early in 1683 to decide
upon a new charter chose to reduce the size of both houses: a
council of 18 rather than 72; an assembly of 36 rather than several
hundred. But while the lower house received the privilege of
conferring with the upper, it was still denied the initiative.
Instead, its members could merely suggest legislation which
"they thought might prevent such Evils and Aggrievances, as
were likely otherwise to fall upon the People of this Province."
Not for a decade, and not without bitter recriminations, would
the initiative be won. A third Frame of Government, passed in
1696 by the assembly, confirmed its right to initiate bills equally
with the council (which had been granted by the Crown during
a brief interlude of royal rule).[2] Although Markham's Frame re-
organized the government, it still did not satisfy many members
of the assembly. Upon Penn's return to his province in 1699, he
permitted still another revision. This one lasted 75 years. In the

[9] Nash, "Framing Government in Pennsylvania," 201–2. See also J. R.
Pole's subtle analysis of Penn's conception of representation at two levels
(*Political Representation in England*, 86–8).

[1] "B[enjamin] F[urly], Abridgment out of Holland and Germany,"
Pennsylvania Magazine of History and Biography, XIX (1895), 297–306.
And see Chester R. Young, "The Evolution of the Pennsylvania Assembly,
1682–1748," *Pennsylvania History*, XXXV (1968), 147–68.

[2] Nash, "Framing Government in Pennsylvania," 205–8; *Votes and Proceedings of the House of Representatives of the Province of Pennsylvania,
Dec. 4, 1682–June 11, 1707* in *Pennsylvania Archives*, ser. 8, I (1931), 42;
Roy N. Lokken, *David Lloyd. Colonial Lawmaker* (Seattle, Wash., 1959),
70–3.

famous Charter of 1701, the legislature acquired all the parliamentary privileges precious to colonial assemblies: the right to choose its own speaker, clerk, and other officers; to appoint its own committees, prepare bills, impeach criminals, judge the qualifications of its own members, determine disputed elections, and decide upon its own adjournment. Thereafter, the unicameral assembly became the only effective branch of the legislature. The appointive council was merely an advisory body to the governor.[3]

The central source of conflict in Pennsylvania during its first two decades was rooted in the assembly's relations with the proprietor and his council. Penn had been so pleased with the first assembly, meeting at Chester late in 1682, because it seemed docile and well behaved, "in a most heavenly manner, like to our general [Quaker] meetings." He regarded the council as the proper colonial legislative organ, however, and by 1688 poured out the frustration of his withered assumptions:

> the Assembly, as they call themselves, is not so, without Gov'r & P[rovincial] Councel, & that noe speaker, clark or [minute] book belong to them[;] that the people have their representatives in ye Pro[vincial] councell to prepare & the Assembly as it is called, has only the power of I or no, yea or nay. If they turn debator, or judges, or complainers you overthrow yr Charter . . . here would be two assemblys, & two representatives, whereas they are but one, so two works, one prepares and promotes, the other assents or Denys the Negative voyce . . . is not a debating, amending, altering, but an accepting or rejecting pow'r [,] minde I entreat you, that all fall not to pieces.[4]

Despite the assembly's assertiveness, and its ability to meet in 1686, 1687, and 1688—when so many colonial legislatures did not—the delegates were apparently inclined against excessive

[3] Bronner, *William Penn's "Holy Experiment,"* 246–9; H. Frank Eshleman, "The Struggle and Rise of Popular Power in Pennsylvania's First Two Decades (1682–1701)," *Pennsylvania Magazine of History and Biography,* XXXIV (1910), 129–61.

[4] Dunn, *William Penn,* 103; Bronner, *Penn's "Holy Experiment,"* 93.

sittings. Between 1684 and 1693 no session of the assembly lasted more than nine days, many were even briefer, and only one special session was convened in addition to the regular annual meeting. After 1683 all sessions gathered in Philadelphia.[5] During these years, the assembly's greatest achievement was simply to expand its purpose beyond its original role and conception: "that all Laws . . . may yet have the more full Concurrence of the Freemen." Thus in 1684, deputies proposed a law "in order that the Freemen of each County might confer with their chosen Members of Assembly, touching in such Matters as they find themselves aggrieved withal, or that they desire to be done at each Assembly." [6] The seed of close attorneyship had fallen upon fertile soil and blossomed.

In Pennsylvania, the Carolinas, and the Jersies—all proprietary colonies—the first decade of political institutions witnessed a conservative tendency, an attempt by elites to shift away from governmental arrangements fully responsive to the people. In Pennsylvania the trend was most vigorously, and successfully, resisted. The reasons are manifold. Pennsylvania showed an abiding concern for precedents established earlier in other colonies. In 1684 a committee was appointed "to inspect the Virginia Laws, and to prepare such things out of them as may be usefull for this Province." Thereafter, the circumstances of other colonies provided examples to avoid as well as to imitate.[7]

In addition, the procedures of the House of Commons were followed closely from the outset. The speaker, like his English

[5] Sister Joan de Lourdes Leonard, "The Composition, Organization, and Legislative Procedure of the Pennsylvania Assembly, 1682–1776" (unpubl. Ph.D. dissertation, University of Pennsylvania, 1947), 123, 133; Illick, *Penn the Politician*, 97 and n.

[6] *Votes and Proceedings of the House of Representatives of Pennsylvania*, I, 58. Throughout this section my discussion owes much to Gary B. Nash, *Quakers and Politics. Pennsylvania, 1681–1726* (Princeton, N.J., 1968), 33, 38–42, 67–70, 72–3, 80–1, 103, 108, 111–14, 123, 203–5, 225, 231–2.

[7] Sister Joan de Lourdes Leonard, *The Organization and Procedure of the Pennsylvania Assembly, 1682–1776* (Philadelphia, Pa., 1949), 36; *Minutes of the Provincial Council of Pennsylvania*, in *Colonial Records of Pennsylvania* (Philadelphia, Pa., 1852–3), II, 278, 285; Andrews, *Colonial Period*, III, 314; Lokken, *David Lloyd*, 168.

counterpart, sought the three privileges of an assembly: access
to executive authority, freedom of speech, and freedom from
arrest. The very first speaker elected in Pennsylvania reminded
the delegates of "those customs practiced in Parliaments, concerning the Duty which each Member owes to each other, and
so to this House." In 1696 Governor Markham was informed
"that in the parliament of England the people had allwise their
privileges granted to them befor they gave anie monie . . . and
tho' wee can pretend to no equalitie with them, being a poor
province, yet we are to proceed in some sense in a parliamentarie
way in our degree." [8] James Logan, who managed Penn's affairs
during his absence, wrote the proprietor in 1704 that "the governor and assembly have clashed so far, notwithstanding all
endeavors have been used on our side to keep matters easy. . . .
They will not allow him the power of dissolving, proroguing,
dismissing for a time, or adjourning them, but claim the privilege
of sitting at all times, as they shall see occasion, like the Parliament in 1641, which they nearly imitate." [9]

◦§ 6 §◦

New Hampshire and New York

New Hampshire, New York, and Delaware all received representative assemblies long after they were first colonized. When
William Penn arrived in New Castle in October 1682, he promised the settlers already there, perhaps 1,000 persons, the same
privileges to be enjoyed in Pennsylvania, including the right to
make their own laws, for which an assembly would be called.
The colonists in the three Lower Counties had been under New
York's jurisdiction, and lacked experience with representative

[8] *Votes and Proceedings of the House of Representatives of Pennsylvania,* I, 17, 36; *Minutes of the Provincial Council,* I, 494; Lokken, *David
Lloyd,* 133.

[9] *Correspondence Between William Penn and James Logan, Secretary
of the Province of Pennsylvania, and Others, 1700–1750,* ed. Edward Arm-
strong (Philadelphia, Pa., 1870–2), I, 344.

bodies. In December 1682, Pennsylvania's first assembly passed
an act of union. Each of the six combined counties was to have
equal representation, both in the provincial council and assembly.
Nevertheless twenty years of conflict ensued, alleviated only partially when Delaware achieved her own legislature in 1704.[1]

Just as Delaware had to be emancipated by Pennsylvania in
order to enjoy representative government, New Hampshire had
to be liberated from the governmental control of Massachusetts.
In May 1679, the Lords of Trade in London ordered the Bay
Colony to withdraw all officials from the territory of Robert
Mason, who claimed the proprietorship of New Hampshire. The
Lords then reached an agreement with Mason that his colony
would be governed by a president, nine councillors, and an
assembly which hopefully would resolve the problem of land
rentals. On March 16, 1680, the first representative body met at
Portsmouth. Eleven delegates attended and legislated. During
the next four years seven assemblies met, and quarreled con-
stantly with Governor Edward Cranfield. Because towns of the
Piscataqua Territory had been represented in the Massachusetts
General Court from 1641 until 1679, New Hampshire's leading
men had acquired considerable experience with both central and
local governance. In many respects, therefore, the colony's assembly was a mature body from the beginning, ready to challenge
the governor and act aggressively, especially in demanding the
initiative and refusing to accept unauthorized taxes and fees.
By the fall of 1692, New Hampshire's assembly was fully developed and empowered. And the twelve deputies were all residents
of the towns they represented.[2]

The pervasive New England experience with political institutions spread south as well as north. But even before Puritans
on Long Island began to clamor for representation, the Dutch

[1] Illick, *William Penn the Politician*, 46–7; Robert W. Johannsen, "The
Conflict Between the Three Lower Counties on the Delaware and the Province of Pennsylvania, 1682–1704," *Delaware History*, V (1952), 96–132.

[2] *Calendar of State Papers, Colonial Series, America and West Indies,
1677–1680*, eds. W. Noel Sainsbury and J. W. Fortescue (London, 1896),
nos. 996, 1036, 1041; William Henry Fry, *New Hampshire as a Royal
Province* (N.Y., 1908), ch. 3.

burghers of New Amsterdam had envied Connecticut's system. "The people [there] have a new election every year," wrote one leader of New Netherland's popular party, "and have the power to make a change . . . and that, they say, is the bridle of their great men." By the time Dutch colonization in North America became active—the middle third of the seventeenth century— representative institutions were well developed at home, where delegates to the States-General were closely bound by instructions.[3]

In New Netherland, by mid-century the citizenry had become accustomed to electing members of various local governing boards and councils. Still, Governor Stuyvesant scoffed at the notion of representative government, and so an agent of the burghers was dispatched to plead their cause at The Hague. As a result Stuyvesant was obliged, in 1653, reluctantly to be sure, to summon delegates from the colony's towns—all except such remote settlements as Fort Orange in the North. Ten delegates were Dutch-speaking; nine English. But they promptly united in insisting to the governor that " 'tis one of our privileges that our consent or that of our representatives is necessarily required in the enactment of such laws and orders." Stuyvesant disagreed and succeeded in preventing additional assemblies for another decade. One met late in 1663, and another in 1664— *eene Laenddagh*. Each of these assemblies was called for a special purpose in a time of crisis in order to discuss provincial affairs and promise support. None of them was entitled to convene a second time. And by 1664 it was too late. The English had conquered and New Netherland became the Duke of York's proprietary. The representative principle had not yet been clearly established.[4]

Richard Nicolls, the first governor under the new regime, did

[3] Ellis L. Raesly, *Portrait of New Netherland* (N.Y., 1945), 94, 102, 121–2, 128; Charles R. Boxer, *The Dutch Seaborne Empire, 1600–1800* (N.Y., 1965), 11–12.

[4] *Narratives of New Netherland 1609–1664*, ed. J. Franklin Jameson (N.Y., 1909), 214, 226, 287, 289, 327, 333, 341; John R. Brodhead, *History of the State of New York* (N.Y., 1859), I, 570–5, 722, 728–31.

much to introduce English political practices; but neither the Duke's charter nor Nicolls's instructions authorized him to call a general assembly. At best he could only draft a body of laws drawn largely from the several New England codes. These so-called Duke's Laws were designed especially for the English population of Long Island. A meeting of 34 deputies from seventeen towns—thirteen English and four Dutch—met at Hempstead in March 1665 to acknowledge their hesitant approval. For another eighteen years, however, the Long Islanders, especially those at the eastern end, expressed continual dissatisfaction with their limited political privileges, and bitterly opposed the imposition of levies without popular consent.[5] Three factors spurred their quest for participatory government: their Puritan intellectual heritage, their full experience with local government by town courts and elected overseers, and the habit of sending delegates to Connecticut's General Court. Such border towns as Rye and Bedford had been settled from New England, and ever since their founding had sent deputies regularly to Hartford. An intercolonial agreement placed these towns under New York's jurisdiction in 1683—just in time to provide a real stimulus for the first legislature.[6]

After New York was recaptured from the Dutch in 1674, the new governor, Major Edmund Andros, received instructions that still included no concession for a popular assembly. He swiftly —on several occasions—conveyed to the Duke of York the widespread unrest caused by this failure. In January, the Duke made his hostile reply:

> unless you had offered what qualifications are usual and proper to such assemblyes, I cannot but suspect they would be of dangerous consequence, nothing being more knowne than the aptness of such

---

[5] Albert E. McKinley, "The Transition from Dutch to English Rule in New York," *American Historical Review*, VI (1900), 693–724; *Documents Relative to the Colonial History of the State of New-York*, ed. Edmund B. O'Callaghan (Albany, N.Y., 1853–87), III, 91; XIV, 564–6; and see Andrews, *Colonial Period*, III, 113n.

[6] See Dixon Ryan Fox, *Caleb Heathcote. Gentleman Colonist* (N.Y., 1926), 46.

bodyes to assume to themselves many priviledges which prove destructive to, or very oft disturbe, the peace of the government wherein they are allowed. Neither do I see any use of them which is not as well provided for, whilst you and your Councell govern according to the laws established.[7]

By 1681, however, the Duke's finances being precarious, and his desire to raise funds for the garrison and government of New York being great, he began to relent. Defense and the need for public revenue would require the inhabitants' cooperation. Consequently Thomas Dongan, Andros's successor, was advised as follows: "I have thought fitt that there shall be a Generall Assembly of all the Freeholders by the person who they shall choose to represent them in order to consulting with yourselfe and the said Councill what laws are fitt and necessary to be made and established for the good weale and government of the said Colony." Laws passed by this assembly had to be approved by both the governor and the Duke. Members could raise money but not spend it. And the governor was authorized to summon, adjourn, and dissolve the body as he saw fit.[8]

Dongan and his council issued the necessary writs on September 13, 1683. On October 17, at Fort James in Manhattan, New York's first assembly met. There were 17 deputies—many of them Dutch—as well as Dongan and five members of the legislative council. They sat for three weeks, followed parliamentary procedure, and met again in 1684. A new election followed the death of Charles II in 1685. Fifty laws plus the famous Charter of Libertyes were passed altogether and approved by James, though the charter was never returned to New York, and was formally disallowed in 1686. By then, with the comprehensive Dominion of New England inaugurated, New York lapsed to its former status of centralized control under executive authority.

[7] *The Glorious Revolution in America. Documents on the Colonial Crisis of 1689*, eds., M. G. Hall, *et al.* (Chapel Hill, N.C., 1964), 93–5.

[8] Edmund B. O'Callaghan, *Origin of Legislative Assemblies in the State of New York* (Albany, N.Y., 1861), 5–24. This pioneering essay must be used with care.

Not until Leisler's Rebellion usurped James's authority in 1689 would another representative body convene. Late in June Leisler sent circular letters instructing the towns to elect delegates to a committee to meet in New York to consider how best to sustain the coup. Nine towns responded, 18 men were chosen, 13 actually appeared and sat for seven weeks, issuing orders and caring for the colony's finances. This anomalous body was as shortlived as Leisler's Rebellion. When New York reverted to royal control, an assembly was called in April 1691, for the first time under the direct authority of the English Crown.[9]

By the time New York knew her first assembly in 1683, every other English colony then in existence already had one. Although this fact unquestionably intensified the demands of restless colonists under the Duke of York, the standard to which they most frequently appealed was the English Parliament. Nevertheless, many of the practices early adopted were peculiarly American. The Leislerians, for example, had insisted that representatives be residents of their constituencies. An act passed in 1699 reaffirmed this requirement, and it withstood the political manipulations of the De Lancey faction half a century later. New York's legislature matured rapidly during the eighteenth century, and protoparties flourished there earlier than in most other colonies.[1]

During the middle third of the eighteenth century, a miscellaneous gaggle of colonies got representative assemblies: the Bahamas in 1729; Georgia in 1755; Nova Scotia in 1758; and West Florida in 1766. In each case, the particular circumstances and influences differed. The Bahamas benefited from Bermuda's experience. Georgia was affected by practices in her Carolina neighbor, while Nova Scotia learned much from New England's Mother of Parliaments in Massachusetts Bay. Nonetheless, the results were swiftly and strikingly similar.[2] Patterns and prece-

[9] David S. Lovejoy, "Equality and Empire. The New York Charter of Libertyes, 1683," *William and Mary Quarterly*, ser. 3, XXI (1964), 493–515; Andrews, *Colonial Period*, III, 127, 137.

[1] Charles W. Spencer, *Phases of Royal Government in New York 1691–1719* (Columbus, Ohio, 1905), ch. 3; Fox, *Heathcote*, 29, 42 and n. 64; Bailyn, *Origins of American Politics*, 112–13.

[2] See Michael Craton, *A History of the Bahamas* (London, 1962), 112–

dents had previously emerged that would shape, not only American institutions, but an indigenous ideology as well. Just what were those patterns, and how had the precedents been established?

19; Bryan Little, *Crusoe's Captain. Being the Life of Woodes Rogers, Seaman, Trader, Colonial Governor* (London, 1960), 213–19; E. Merton Coulter, *Georgia. A Short History* (2nd ed., Chapel Hill, N.C., 1960), 81–5; J. B. Brebner, *New England's Outpost: Acadia Before the Conquest of Canada* (N.Y., 1927), 135–7, 235, 252–62; Clinton N. Howard, *The British Development of West Florida, 1763–1769* (Berkeley and Los Angeles, Calif., 1947), 43–7.

❧ III ❧

Summary Analysis

ANY appraisal of the origins of representative government in British North America must keep in balance two counterpointed emphases: on the one hand, continuities and common origins; on the other, change and the need for chronological clarity. The several colonial societies were new in nature, varied in structure, and their general beginnings differed decade by decade. Add the rapidity of change in English political thought as the seventeenth century progressed, and it becomes clear that precise periodization is necessary if we are to understand the particular configuration of circumstances central to each successive establishment of representative institutions.

In 1932 Andrew C. McLaughlin performed an outstanding service by pointing out that "representation was not gathered from the air; it was not some vague though luminous theory of right and liberty, but a convenient method of exercising fully legal right in a corporation." [1] By the seventeenth century, such bodies as the Merchant Adventurers of England concentrated their central administrative and governmental offices in whatever market city was currently most vital. When Hamburg acquired such importance, for example, the Adventurers established, in effect, a distinct colonial outpost there.[2] The nature of these organizations was corporate; their structure was commonly elective and representative. Not surprisingly, then, the argument at Jamestown in 1619 against seating the two delegates from Martin's Brandon hinged upon the fact that Captain John Martin's

---

[1] McLaughlin, *Foundations of American Constitutionalism*, 50.
[2] William E. Lingelbach, *The Internal Organisation of the Merchant Adventurers of England* (Philadelphia, Pa., 1903), 27–38.

patent was of an early and peculiar sort. It did not oblige Martin to obey the laws of Virginia except in time of war. The other 20 burgesses complained that Martin and his men "might deride the whole company & chuse whether they would obey the same or not." Martin and the members of his plantation simply were not proper adventurers in the Company, and therefore did not deserve to vote with the generality or help to govern them.[3]

"I have intimated, even if I have not demonstrated," McLaughlin remarked, "the connection between the corporation, as a quasi-body-politic, and the beginnings of representation, by deputies and proxies." McLaughlin was more careful than many of his successors, who have casually assumed some deterministic causal connection between the structure of chartered commercial companies and colonial representation. Only *certain* company charters, specifically those which envisioned large-scale colonization, led to the development of representative systems. The Newfoundland Company's charter, for example, mentions colonization; but that end is clearly subordinated to securing the coastal fishing trade.[4] Moreover, French overseas joint stock companies closely resembled the chartered organization of their English counterparts. Yet a representative assembly never flowered in New France, simply because other variables were determinative: the involvement of the Crown in running the trading companies and supervising the colonization process.[5] The Dutch West India Company was managed at home by five chambers (located regionally throughout the Dutch republic), which delegated their governmental powers to a board of 19 at Amsterdam,

[3] McIlwaine, *Journals of the House of Burgesses of Virginia, 1619–1658,* 5.

[4] McLaughlin, *Foundations of American Constitutionalism,* 58; *Select Charters of Trading Companies, A.D. 1530–1707,* ed. Cecil T. Carr, *Publications of the Selden Society,* XXVIII (London, 1913), 51.

[5] See H. P. Biggar, *The Early Trading Companies of New France* (Toronto, 1901); Gustave Lanctot, "Un parlement colonial au temps de Louis XIV (1647–1663)," *Revue d'histoire des colonies,* XLII (1955), 277–90; Allana G. Reid, "Representative Assemblies in New France," *Canadian Historical Review,* XXVII (1946), 19–26. See also Lesley B. Simpson, *et al.,* "Representative Institutions in the Spanish Empire in the Sixteenth Century," *The Americas,* XII (1955–6), 223–57.

made up of representatives from each chamber. This group of
19 served the Company as a general assembly, and its orders
were binding upon all the chambers. Although the Company was
legally in the same class with the Virginia and Somers Island
Companies, a representative assembly was never permanently
established in New Netherland.[6] Clearly, then, there is much
more to the origins of representative government in British
North America than the charters and structures of commercial
corporations.

KEY

In the preceding section I tried to indicate some of the
more important variations that accompanied the emergence of
colonial assemblies decade by decade after 1619. It should therefore be clear that the traditional view—epitomized by Professor
De Grazia: "on the whole . . . the colonial representative systems were modeled after the English law"—is simplistic and
perhaps misleading.[7] Scholars have assumed that ideas and events
in England, especially during the Civil War and Commonwealth,
did much to shape colonial legislative bodies. But by 1640 eight
American assemblies had already been established, six of them
during the eleven years when Charles I ruled *without* a Parliament;[8] and including two which deserve to be called the parents
of American parliaments: Massachusetts and Barbados. The
former helped shape subsequent assemblies in Connecticut,
Plymouth, and indirectly in New Haven, East New Jersey, New
Hampshire, New York, and Nova Scotia; while Barbadians would
influence the origins of legislatures in all four Leeward Islands,
Jamaica, and South Carolina.

Although circumstances of the English Interregnum contributed to the development of bicameralism in Virginia and
Maryland, the 1644 division in Massachusetts grew out of a long-

---

[6] *Documents Relating to New Netherland 1624–1626 in the Henry E.
Huntington Library*, ed. A. J. F. van Laer (San Marino, Calif., 1924), 2–18;
Andrews, *Colonial Period*, III, 75.

[7] De Grazia, *Public and Republic*, 54, and see 21–8.

[8] There is marvelous irony in the timing of Charles I. In January 1639,
after a decade of personal rule at home, he finally gave formal approval to
the representative assembly in Virginia, and thereby perhaps lent tacit sanc-
tion to the several assemblies of New England as well!

standing issue there over the negative voice. In Virginia between 1652 and 1660 the burgesses stood as the ultimate source of authority, empowering both the governor and his council. Yet the actual leverage of the Virginia assembly was largely exerted *against* the leading colonial spokesmen of the parliamentary cause in England.[9] A similar paradox appeared in Barbados. It is noteworthy also that the eight colonial assemblies established before 1641 survived in the years after 1660 much better than those five founded between 1642 and the Restoration. By the mid-1640's, the Long Parliament was already becoming a less representative body, and after the accession of Charles II theorists of representation remained quiescent for a while.[1] One might indeed argue that English politics at mid-century were as much influenced by New Englanders or men with strong connections there, such as young Henry Vane and Richard Hutchinson, who had cut their parliamentary teeth in Massachusetts during the 1630's.[2]

Following the Restoration there occurred a considerable amount of model building and speculation about the ideal structure of colonial governments. Except perhaps for the efforts of Sir Edwin Sandys—a committed parliamentarian and political theorist who may have helped shape the first assemblies in Virginia and Bermuda[3]—this was a rather new departure. Not surprisingly the constitutional schemes of the 1660's, 1670's, and early 1680's were often unworkable, and underwent endless alterations and revisions. In addition, the early history of those colonial assemblies established after 1660 was much more stormy than their earlier prototypes. Acrimony between the executive and young legislatures was intensified because most colonies develop-

[9] Craven, *Southern Colonies in the Seventeenth Century,* 262–3.

[1] Brown, "Ideas of Representation from Elizabeth to Charles II," 33, 38. See also Philip A. Gibbons, *Ideas of Political Representation in Parliament, 1660–1832* (Oxford, 1914), part 1.

[2] See James E. Farnell, "The Usurpation of Honest London Householders: Barebone's Parliament," *English Historical Review,* LXXXII (1967), 28, 38.

[3] See Frederick G. Marcham, "Sir Edwin Sandys and the Growth of the Opposition in the House of Commons, 1604–1610" (unpubl. Ph.D. dissertation, Cornell University, 1926); McLaughlin, *Foundations of American Constitutionalism,* 44.

ing under Charles II were proprietary or royal, so that the executive's existence *preceded* the assembly, confronting it with an inflexible and established prerogative.

During the final third of the seventeenth century, English exponents of New World colonization vacillated ambiguously between their desire to keep close control of their expensive overseas ventures, and the need to attract colonists with generous terms. The historian of representative institutions is tempted to argue that colonial self-government through elected assemblies was the most important inducement offered immigrants during these decades. In fact, however, freedom of conscience and religious toleration was at least equally magnetic, and perhaps even more so. Just as the Virginia Company's new land policies in 1618–19 were then regarded as the heart of "the greate charter," even more important than convening an assembly, so the longest section of New York's Charter of Libertyes in 1683 was devoted to religious considerations, rather than representative government.[4] A cursory glance at the history of the Carolinas, Jersies, Pennsylvania, and New York in this period would suggest that many settlers there wanted to be left alone even more than they wanted to participate in public affairs. The proprietors' political thinking and behavior both affected and reflected that inclination.[5]

By the later 1670's, imperial officials nonetheless felt troubled by the growing assertiveness of colonial legislatures. As William Blathwayt observed, American assemblies "by declaring . . . that the revenue ought to arise from them and that the disposall of it and the power of receiving the accounts is belonging to them . . . have left his Majesty but a small share of the Sovereignty and may as well question that which remains." One aim of the comprehensive Dominion of New England, established in 1686, was therefore to eliminate representative assemblies and

[4] Craven, *Southern Colonies in the Seventeenth Century*, 127; Lovejoy, "The New York Charter of Libertyes," 505–6.

[5] Leaming and Spicer, *The Grants, Concessions, and Original Constitutions of New Jersey*, 15; Craven, *The Colonies in Transition*, 178–9, 187–8, 195–6, 282–4; Nash, "The Framing of Government in Pennsylvania," 185, 187, 204.

instead concentrate political power in a viceroy advised by a privy council.[6] The Dominion failed, of course, and its overthrow in 1689 owed much to American anxieties over the status and future of their cherished assemblies. The tumultuous events of 1687–9 in New England and New York helped to give form and substance to hitherto scattered feelings about the value of representative government. As the town meeting of newly formed Chebacco Parish in Massachusetts insisted, it "was not the townes Duties any wayes to assist those ill Methods of Raising money without a General Assembly."[7]

Beginning with the 1690's, the representative assembly can be said to have become a fixed feature of English colonial administration. In addition, provincial lower houses had largely shed their early exercise of broad judicial powers, and become essentially legislative assemblies. Only now, moreover, in the last two decades of the seventeenth century, did the tendency become pervasive to imitate the House of Commons in London and insist upon every jot and tittle of parliamentary privilege.[8] In those colonies involved in King William's and Queen Anne's wars at the turn of the century, assemblymen had to be consulted about any expensive or dangerous enterprise requiring community cooperation. Repeated consultations between governors and their assemblies over troops, strategies, military leadership, and finance simply confirmed and reinforced the steady growth of representative institutions in British North America.[9]

[6] Stephen S. Webb, "William Blathwayt, Imperial Fixer: From Popish Plot to Glorious Revolution," *William and Mary Quarterly*, ser. 3, XXV (1968), 7; Webb, "The Strange Career of Francis Nicholson," *ibid.*, XXIII (1966), 522; and John C. Rainbolt, "A New Look at Stuart 'Tyranny': The Crown's Attack on the Virginia Assembly, 1676–1689," *Virginia Magazine of History and Biography*, LXXV (1967), 387–406.

[7] Perry Miller, *The New England Mind from Colony to Province* (Cambridge, Mass., 1953), 156–7; *Calendar of State Papers, Colonial Series, America and West Indies, 1685–1688*, no. 1534, iv, v.

[8] Clarke, *Parliamentary Privilege in American Colonies, passim*. Not until the end of the century, for example, were such compilations available as John Rushworth's *Historical Collections of Private Passages of State, Weighty Matters in Law, Remarkable Proceedings . . . 1618 . . . 1648* (8 vols., London, 1680–1701).

[9] Craven, *Colonies in Transition*, 320, 322.

As the eighteenth century opened, with bicameralism everywhere established, it was not especially surprising that Pennsylvania's new Frame of 1701 provided for a unique unicameral legislature with extensive rights and privileges. Partially the decision grew out of two decades of legislative-proprietary bickering, in which the council committed itself as part of the proprietary interest. The concept of mixed government was simply irrelevant here. Even more, the decision taken in 1701 symbolized the advent of exactly two centuries of legislative domination in American life. There would occasionally be strong governors, and later strong presidents. Nevertheless, most Americans would long regard their elected assemblies as watchdogs of the common weal.[1]

→ cf. Heale

There was, to be sure, a conscious and cumulative colonial experience with representative institutions throughout the seventeenth century. Yet despite the rapidity of change, decade by decade, and despite diversity of constitutional origins, the American assemblies all moved swiftly in similar directions. Virginia's emerged from the needs of a commercial company, Maryland's from a medieval proprietary charter, and Connecticut's from a body politic literally in a state of nature. Yet within a few decades, their structural and functional resemblances were remarkable.[2] The birth of representative government in corporate colonies was accompanied by greater flexibility for experimentation, in company colonies by surprising stability and continuity, and in proprietary colonies by agonizing labor pains. In all of them, however, the time-honored clichés about counsel and consent, advice and

[1] Cf. the very interesting letter from James Alexander to Governor William Burnet, January 27, 1729, in *Documents Relating to the Colonial History of the State of New Jersey*, ed. William A. Whitehead (Newark, N.J., 1882), V, 230–3; and James Sterling Young, *The Washington Community, 1800–1828* (N.Y., 1966), especially parts 3 and 4.

[2] Winthrop Jordan has observed the same phenomenon with another very different American institution: chattel slavery. See *White Over Black. American Attitudes Toward the Negro, 1550–1812* (Chapel Hill, N.C., 1968), 83 ff.

assent, taxation and representation have astonishing validity. And so we must, for a moment, look at the overwhelming weight of those sustained affirmations.

We have already noted that both the Virginia and Somers Island Companies inaugurated colonial assemblies in order to win the consent of planters to plans for economic reform, law enforcement, and tax levies. The Orders and Constitutions of Bermuda, passed in February 1622 and derived from the Virginia Company promulgation of 1619, declared that "the Governour shall not lay any taxes or Impositions upon the Lands in the *Summer Islands*; or upon the people or Commodities, otherwise then by the authority of the generall Assembly; to be levied and imployed as the said Assembly shall appoynt." [3] In Massachusetts the Watertown protest of 1632, even before the proper establishment of representative government, forced Governor John Winthrop to concede that thereafter two freemen from every town should be selected "to conferre with the Courte about raiseing of a publique stock, so as what they should agree upon should bind all." The phraseology brings to mind the frequent medieval demand: *Quod omnes tangit ab ominbus approbetur.* By 1637, Winthrop's concern for first principles elicited his insistence that "no common weale can be founded but by free consent. The persons so incorporating have a public and relative interest in each other . . . so as none other can claime priviledge with them but by free consent." [4]

In Maryland, the governor's commission of 1637 authorized him to assemble the freemen or their deputies, and to issue laws only with their advice and consent. Five years later, influenced by the Long Parliament in England, Maryland's assembly resolved that it could not be adjourned except by its own consent. The decision to establish representative government in Plymouth in 1638 was made with the relationship between taxation, repre-

---

[3] *Memorials of the Discovery and Early Settlement of the Bermudas or Somers Islands, 1515–1685,* ed. J. Henry Lefroy (London, 1877), I, 209–10.

[4] Haskins, "Representative Government in Early New England," *Liber Memorialis Sir Maurice Powicke,* 91; Winthrop, *Life and Letters of John Winthrop,* II, 182–3.

sentation, and citizenship clearly in mind. And in Connecticut,
impending war against the Pequots "demanded that what so
intimately concerned all should be approved by all," though the
precise meaning of consent was only made clear through actual
practice over a period of years. In Rhode Island, the immediate
origins of representation were also tied closely to the concept of
consent.[5] On St. Christopher in 1642, rebels asserted that laws
could not be made without the people's consent, asked that laws
passed by executive authority be revoked, and new ones made
only "with the consent of the commons." In Barbados a year later,
the same hue and cry: "Nothing would bee done or Consented
unto without a general Assembly." By 1645 all parties there,
including the governor, had fully agreed that "the vote and consent of the whole country [was] required in the buisiness." In
Jamaica the principle was established from the outset in 1664.[6]

William Berkeley's commission as governor of Albemarle in
1663 empowered him and his councillors to make laws "by and
with the advice and consent of the freeholders or freemen . . .
their deputies or delligates," thereby confirming Provision 4 of
the proprietors' Declaration and Proposals of August 1663. Here
representation, advice, and assent were becoming part of the very
essence of a colonization scheme.[7] In East New Jersey settlers
early made their consent a fundamental issue, while in West
Jersey William Penn and five other trustees in 1676 "lay a foundation for after ages to understand their liberty as men and chris-
tians, that they may not be brought in bondage, but by their
own consent." In 1681 the first act of the first assembly defined
the status and powers of the executive, and made it crystal clear
that he was to do nothing without the representatives' approbation.[8] When William Penn made conservative revisions in his

[5] Andrews, *Colonial Period,* II, 92, 106, 300–1; Langdon, *History of New Plymouth,* 86; Osgood, *Colonies in the Seventeenth Century,* I, 355, 357.

[6] Bennett, "English Caribbees in the Period of the Civil War," 362, 369, 373; Andrews, *Colonial Period,* II, 269.

[7] Saunders, *Colonial Records of North Carolina,* I, 45, 48–50.

[8] Leaming and Spicer, *The Grants, Concessions, and Original Constitu-tions of New Jersey,* 20; Andrews, *Colonial Period,* III, 151n., 169; *Docu-*

drafts for the Frame of Government in 1682, the one right he dared not take from the lower chamber was that of consent, for his charter (like Maryland's and the Carolinas') provided that laws were to be made by the proprietor "with the advice, assent, and approbation of the freemen." [9] In New Netherland, as early as 1653 a discontented Dutch populace insisted that " 'tis one of our privileges that our consent or that of our representatives is necessarily required in the enactment of such laws and orders." After 1664 this became a major grievance of both Dutch and English subjects, so that the Charter of Libertyes passed in 1683 included a paragraph from the famous 1628 Petition of Right, thereby protecting New Yorkers against taxation without representation. In 1684 this very issue became a burning concern in New Hampshire, and the people simply refused to pay.[1]

Professor W. F. Craven has wisely observed that "the concept of government by consent . . . has a very deep rootage in the American experience." It is questionable, however, whether "the seventeenth-century assembly had been basically a consultative body in which *the elected delegates were expected to give their consent* to what was proposed by the established leadership of the colony, and *in normal circumstances usually did*." [2] Firmly rooted by the second quarter of the century, the concept of consent in colonial America did not denote a *pro forma* gesture on the part of the people. Moreover, their essential Protestantism, and in many places Congregational theory specifically, held that a free Christian community could be bound together only by true consent. For the Mathers and other apologists of the covenant theology, one principle of Protestantism remained inviolate: "that the consent of a believer is an essential part of belief." [3]

---

ments Relating to the Colonial History of New Jersey (Newark, N.J., 1880), I, 228.

[9] Nash, "Framing of Government in Pennsylvania," 199, 207–8.

[1] Raesly, *Portrait of New Netherland,* 122; Andrews, *Colonial Period,* III, 113n; Lovejoy, "New York Charter of Libertyes," 505; Osgood, *Colonies in the Seventeenth Century,* III, 355–6.

[2] Craven, *Colonies in Transition,* 29, 263 (italics mine); cf. Haskins, *Growth of English Representative Government,* 59–61.

[3] See Miller, *New England Mind from Colony to Province,* 255–6, 259.

Historians have traditionally assumed that seventeenth-century assemblies "were still in a position of subordination, slowly groping for the power to tax and the right to sit separately from the council and to initiate laws." Consequently, students have viewed the so-called "rise of the assembly" as a characteristic phenomenon of the first half of the *eighteenth* century, beginning perhaps in 1691 or so.[4] It is true that some early representatives could be remarkably deferential and diffident on occasion; often they were quite happy to adjourn after a session lasting only a few days. But much more striking are the aggressive and demanding qualities of these bodies. All of them were engaged in continuous struggles against local executives, proprietors, or the Crown, and usually from their very first meetings. A few illustrations should suffice.

In Virginia as early as 1624, when the assembly anticipated the end of company rule, it urged the Privy Council to limit the authority of future governors, and actually passed a bill stating that "the governor shall not lay any taxes or ympositions upon the colony, their lands or commodities other way than by the authority of the General Assembly." During the next fifteen years, the burgesses became increasingly self-confident and assertive. In Massachusetts, as Professor Haskins has shown, "almost at once, the deputies became particularly active in legislation, which became a progressively more important source of positive law in the colony. Most deputies served for successive terms, and by 1650 there were among them veteran legislators with extensive committee experience."[5] In Barbados the assembly became extraordinarily assertive early in the 1640's, just a few years after its creation. It insisted that no new land rents might be

[4] Cf. Jack P. Greene, "The Role of the Lower Houses of Assembly in Eighteenth-Century Politics," *Journal of Southern History*, XXVII (1961), 454; Craven, *Colonies in Transition*, 326.

[5] McIlwaine, *Journals of the House of Burgesses of Virginia, 1619–1658,* 27; *The Statutes at Large; Being a Collection of All the Laws of Virginia, from the First Session of the Legislature, in the Year 1619,* ed. William W. Hening (Richmond, Va., 1819–23), I, 124; Haskins, "Representative Government in Early New England," *Liber Memorialis Sir Maurice Powicke,* 92–3.

imposed or collected without its prior approval, and that it would withold approval until certain conditions were met. Similar circumstances obtained at Antigua in 1645, and Jamaica in 1664.[6]

Owen's Parliament, convened in South Carolina in 1670, could hardly have been more aggressive; and by 1682 the provincial assembly's role had increased immeasurably.[7] To the north, in East New Jersey, Philip Carteret was continually defied after 1668 by contentious Puritan deputies concerned about quit rents, tax rates, and the proper basis of representation. In West Jersey, the assembly's seizure of power by 1683 was altogether revolutionary.[8] Pennsylvania's first assembly had no sooner met in 1682 than it organized various committees, one a "Committee of Foresight, for the Preparation of Provincial Bills." This and other actions taken were contrary to the first Frame of Government, which denied the assembly's right to initiate legislation. When William Penn added 50 laws to the 40 already agreed upon in England, the assembly rejected 19 of them as well as the Frame of 1682 and the charter of the Free Society of Traders. By 1685, in response to an aggressive assembly, the frustrated Penn pleaded that "for the love of God, me and the poor country, be not so governmentish, so noisy and open in your dissatisfactions." They would not be pacified, however, and the conflict endured. As the lower house characteristically remarked in 1694 (while fighting the lieutenant governor's effort at dissolution): that we are to adjourn "before we can accomplish the Country's Business . . . we conceive to be . . . inconsistent with the Tenor of the said Writs, and the necessary Privileges of a legislative Authority." [9] By 1683, when New Hampshire's assembly met

[6] Bennett, "English Caribbees in the Period of the Civil War," 368; Harlow, *History of Barbados*, 100–2; Whitson, *Development of Jamaica*, 23–6.

[7] Andrews, *Colonial Period*, III, 229; Sirmans, *Colonial South Carolina*, 37.

[8] Andrews, *Colonial Period*, III, 144, 146–9; Richard P. McCormick, *The History of Voting in New Jersey* (New Brunswick, N.J., 1953), 27–30; Pomfret, *West New Jersey*, 135–6.

[9] George, *Charter to William Penn, and Laws of the Province of Pennsylvania*, 107–23, 472–81; Nash, "Framing of Government in Pennsylvania,"

for its second session, it refused to pass the governor's revenue bill, insisted upon originating all bills, establishing courts, and nominating judges. When the governor retaliated by dissolving the legislature, an attempted insurrection almost became general. The next assembly, called a year later, was even more passionately embroiled.[1]

Among all the factors stimulating the aggressiveness of these seventeenth-century assemblies, none was more important than their desire to initiate legislation. In Virginia, Bermuda, and Plymouth they could do so from the very outset, and fought tenaciously to preserve the right. In the Carolinas it had been promised early in the 1660's, was taken away by the Fundamental Constitutions in 1669–70, and not really secured again until 1692. In Pennsylvania the right to initiate legislation provided a central source of acrimony throughout the 1680's, but was not achieved until 1693. Paradoxically perhaps, the problem of legislative initiative appears to have been a touchier matter in the New World after 1660 than before.

Professor J. S. Roskell has recently offered an important and provocative essay which is quite relevant to our concerns here. Indeed, it places the problem of gauging maturity in colonial assemblies in a fresh perspective. Although he is a medievalist, Roskell asserts that the "great divide" in the history of Parliament, and especially the House of Commons, occurred in the late seventeenth century. No matter how aggressive the Commons might be, no matter how elected, composed, or privileged, so long as they were dependent upon the king's will for their very existence, they did not yet constitute a mature institution. The basic precondition of governmental control by the Commons was that Parliament should meet regularly. In practice, the annual need after 1689 to pass a Mutiny Act, and also to make appropriation of supply, ensured that Parliament would meet on

---

206–9; Dunn, *William Penn,* 104, 151–2; Bronner, *Penn's "Holy Experiment,"* 93, 106; *Votes and Proceedings of the House of Representatives of Pennsylvania,* I, 156–7.

[1] Osgood, *Colonies in the Seventeenth Century,* III, 349–50; Phillips, *Development of a Residential Qualification,* 48.

a yearly basis. But there also had to be some limitation of the king's right to dissolve Parliament at his discretion, and some restraint upon the maximum life of Parliament. A "standing parliament" such as the Cavalier Parliament of Charles II was obviously quite vulnerable to corruption and royal control. Hence the importance of the Triennial Act of 1694 in providing a solution to the problem of a statutory interval between Parliaments.[2]

Roskell's well-argued claim that Parliament did not become a *regularized* part of the constitution until the 1690's is an interpretation that will not go unchallenged (especially by the Tudor specialists). But his criteria of institutional maturity—independence, duration, and regularity in meeting—cast the seventeenth-century American experience in a different perspective; for they make the early colonial assemblies seem less primitive in comparison with a fully established and arbitrarily normative Stuart standard. Not until 1678 did the House of Commons finally make good its claim that money bills must originate therein. Those historians who would minimize the importance of seventeenth-century colonial bodies because they met infrequently and briefly, should note that under Elizabeth I, when the House of Commons was embarked upon its famous seizure of the initiative, only ten parliaments with a total of thirteen sessions met, averaging less than ten weeks each in duration, and with an average gap of more than three years between each session.[3]

The seventeenth-century experience with representative bodies in England and in her colonies was distinctly pre-modern, although in divergent ways. In England, the gentry seeking parliamentary seats had to find them in an existing system, "and their ambitions have to wrestle with a structure that is already firmly embedded," as J. R. Pole has observed. Therefore the "carpetbagger" representation of both boroughs and shires was the result of a clash between old values and new social

[2] J. S. Roskell, "Perspectives in English Parliamentary History," *Bulletin of the John Rylands Library*, XLVI (1964), 452–5.
[3] *Ibid.*, 459, 461, 470.

and political drives.[4] In the young colonies, such drives and the
system of representation developed *pari passu,* thereby reducing
certain traditional frictions and patterns but introducing others.
It is precisely because of this absence of parliamentary experience and structures in seventeenth-century America that the
circumstances of fourteenth-century England are so relevant
and illuminating.

Before offering a final analysis, it is appropriate at least to
acknowledge some difficult but as yet unanswerable questions. If
plena potestas, that is, full powers for deputies (the fact rather
than the concept), was so firmly established in England by the
end of Elizabeth's reign, then it is not at all clear why early
colonial representation reverted to the medieval pattern of attorneyship. Perhaps the answer lies in a sense of foreboding shared
by many Englishmen in Stuart times that representative institutions were severely threatened all over western Europe. In England between 1610 and 1640, it became apparent that executive
administration could be sustained and the royal budget (barely)
balanced without parliamentary taxation so long as the government remained free from foreign wars. The French Estates General met in 1614 for the last time before 1789. And in Naples
and Spain, authoritarian states became much less sensitive to
the people's elected representatives.[5]

Nor is it clear whether there is any pattern or historical significance in the particular time lag (or lack thereof) between
initial colonization/settlement and the formal origins of representative government in each colony. The gap would seem generally to shorten as the seventeenth century progressed; yet New
Hampshire, New York, Delaware, the Bahamas, Georgia, and
Nova Scotia appear to reverse the trend—in each case, one might
argue, for special reasons.

Did large colonies feel the need for representative institutions earlier than small ones? To be sure, it was more diffi-

[4] I am deeply indebted to Dr. Pole for his lengthy, thoughtful, and
incisive letter of July 26, 1968.
[5] See Christopher Hill, *The Century of Revolution, 1603–1714* (Edin-
burgh, 1961), 72–3.

cult to administer a large area without consent; and the problem of population dispersal would undercut direct government more seriously in a large area. Yet Plymouth, a rather small colony, was nonetheless obliged to abandon its primary assembly because of a scattering populace. Finally, we have no clear perception of the way governors' councils changed during the seventeenth century in response to the growth of representative government. Many of those originally elected became appointed bodies once the lower houses became aggressive attorneys for popular constituencies. But detailed knowledge on this political and constitutional question is still lacking.[6]

What then can be concluded with certainty? Just as burgess standing was used by the Normans to attract English peasants to Ireland in the twelfth century, so representative government was an important inducement to successful English colonization in the seventeenth.[7] Yet the special economic and demographic circumstances of Stuart settlements in the New World, as well as the ideological ferment then in progress, caused colonial representation to differ from its English prototype. Here elections were more frequent, residential requirements were common, deputies were (nominally) paid, often instructed, and sometimes prevented from holding appointive places.[8] Just as constituencies in developing nations today are more concerned with local needs than national issues, so representatives then tended to be more sensitive to parochial than provincial concerns.[9]

The causes, origins, and early stimuli of representative institutions in British North America were, I believe, manifold and varied: (1) the organization and economic imperatives of

[6] See James LaVerne Anderson, "The Governors' Councils of Colonial America. A Study of Pennsylvania and Virginia, 1660–1776" (unpubl. Ph.D. Dissertation, University of Virginia, 1967).

[7] See Jocelyn Otway-Ruthven, "The Character of Norman Settlement in Ireland," *Historical Studies*, V (London, 1965), 79.

[8] Cf. *Acts of Assembly, Passed in the Island of Barbadoes, from 1648, to 1718* (London, 1721), 11; Leaming and Spicer, *The Grants, Concessions, and Original Constitutions of New Jersey*, 405–6; R. C. Latham, "Payment of Parliamentary Wages—the Last Phase," *English Historical Review*, LXVI (1951), 27–50.

[9] Cf. Notestein, *Winning of the Initiative by the House of Commons*, 43.

English commercial companies involved in the colonization process; (2) clauses inserted by the Privy Council in proprietary charters; (3) the necessity of luring emigrants to the New World; (4) the relationship between economic opportunities and early provincial politics; (5) the gradual dispersion of settlement within Virginia, Bermuda, Massachusetts, and Plymouth; (6) English parliamentary traditions and ideas, especially after 1640; (7) the early existence and experience with local government; (8) Puritan and Quaker thought and social organization; (9) colonial autonomy during the English Civil War and Interregnum; and finally, (10) the far-reaching influence of settlers migrating from Massachusetts Bay and Barbados.

I remarked earlier that despite diverse constitutional origins, representative institutions in all of the English settlements quickly—within a generation as a rule—came to resemble one another to a startling degree. The reason is that while no colony partook of all ten factors mentioned above, every colony shared several if not many of them. It is this overlap, this fact of their all drawing heavily upon a common pool of crucial elements, that explains the unity born of diversity and the strikingly ubiquitous presence early on of representative government in British North America.

᭤ Part Two ᭥

THE SOURCES:
A Documentary Selection

A Note on the Texts

In seventeenth-century times the new year did not officially begin on January 1, but on March 25. Consequently dates occurring between those two points were usually written in a hyphenated manner. I have modernized those citations to conform with the modern calendar, so that February 13, 1682/83, for example, would appear in these documents as February 13, 1683.

The modernization of orthography and punctuation is more complicated and less consistent. Where a well-established modern version of a text is available, I have used it for two reasons: it is the most accurate and it is the one students would most likely find in consulting the complete source or its context. Where a twentieth-century text is lacking, I have followed the guidelines used by Julian P. Boyd, Lyman H. Butterfield, and Leonard W. Labaree in editing the papers of Jefferson, Adams, and Franklin: that is, to follow a "middle course" between "exact reproduction" and "complete modernization" of the text. "The purpose," as Franklin's editors wrote, "is to preserve as faithfully as possible the form and spirit in which the authors composed their documents, and at the same time to reproduce their words in a manner intelligible to the present-day reader and within the normal range of modern typographical equipment and techniques."

The Colonial Inheritance: *The House of Commons in Jacobean England*

THE Apology and Satisfaction of the House of Commons, 1604 (Doc. 1), is one of the most significant constitutional documents from the reign of James I, for it reveals Parliament's own conception of its role in English government. Two statements in the Apology are especially noteworthy. The first concerns the Commons' capacity and right, as representatives *vox* of the realm, to discuss and determine all matters pertaining to *populi* the common weal. The second, that "the voice of the people in *Key* things of their knowledge is said to be as the voice of God," seeks to claim for Parliament the equivalent of divine right. The House of Commons Petition Respecting Impositions, 1610 (Doc. 2) was not really an attack upon the Crown's right to place financial impositions. Such imposts, as part of the King's ancient prerogative, were still invulnerable in 1610. Nonetheless, the Petition extended the Apology of 1604 to include Parliament's right to a greater voice in matters of extra-parliamentary Crown income. The Commons believed they could demand that the Crown clarify the full extent of its prerogative in money matters. From there it would be only a short step to discussing parliamentary rights in general.

By 1621, relations between King and Commons were taut. Warfare on the continent had made manifest their widely divergent views on foreign policy. Then the proposed marriage between Prince Charles and a Spanish princess intensified domestic fears of foreign intrigue and possible intervention in English affairs. James refused to debate his every policy and decision with Parliament, and his threatening statement of that refusal (Doc. 3) drew an immediate response from the Commons: their Protestation of 1621 (Doc. 4). The Protestation explicitly denied the King's right to censure the House of Commons for its debates or molest any individual member for actions or words in the House. Parliament thereby attempted to eliminate all limitations upon its privilege of free speech. Subsequently, however, James angrily tore the Protestation from the House Journal, and declared it void. Actually the document did not extend Parliament's claims beyond those already recorded in the Apology of 1604. The defiant mood in which the Protestation was written had more significance for constitutional controversy and development than its actual substance would suggest.

Certain judicial decisions rendered early in the reign of Charles I affirmed that the King had the right to commit men to prison without cause shown, and made it clear to Parliament that the courts, allied with the Crown, would interpret laws so as to defeat parliamentary purposes. Therefore, the House of Commons devised the Petition of Right, 1628 (Doc. 5) in order to establish that the King was bound by the law, that judges must enforce the law, and that therefore Parliament must make the law concrete by giving it statutory form and obliging the King to accept it. With this in mind, the parliamentarians were careful in the Petition not to render another loosely constructed document such as the Apology of 1604. Instead, they paid close attention to compiling legal precedents and sound arguments against arbitrary imprisonment and taxation without consent.

The Petition of Right is traditionally regarded, along with Magna Carta and the Bill of Rights, as one of the three most important English constitutional documents limiting the power of the monarch. In fact, Parliament was more concerned with protecting traditional rights and liberties than with establishing radical limitations on the power of the King.

⊷§ 1 §⊷

The Apology and Satisfaction of the House of Commons, June 20, 1604

To the King's most excellent Majesty: From the House of Commons assembled in Parliament.

Most gracious Sovereign, we cannot but with much joy and thankfulness of mind acknowledge your Majesty's great graciousness in declaring lately unto us by the mouth of our Speaker that you rested now satisfied with our doings.

Which satisfaction notwithstanding, though most desired and dear unto us, yet proceeding merely from your Majesty's most gracious disposition and not from any justification which on our behalf hath been made, we found this joy intermingled with no small grief, and could not, dread Sovereign, in our dutiful love to your Majesty and in our ardent desire of the continuance of your favor towards us, but tender in humble sort this farther satisfaction, being careful to stand right not only in the eye of your Majesty's Grace but also, and that much more, in the balance of your princely judgment, on which all assuredness of love and grace is founded. Into which course of proceedings we have not been rashly carried by vain humor of curiosity, of contradiction, of presumption, or of love of our own devices or doings; unworthy affections in a Council of Parliament, and more unworthy in subjects towards their Lord and Sovereign. . . .

With these minds, dread Sovereign, your Commons of England, represented in us their knights, citizens, and burgesses, do come with this humble declaration to your Highness, and in great affiance of your most gracious disposition, that your Majesty, with benignity of mind correspondent to our dutifulness, will be pleased to pursue it. . . .

But now, no other help or redress appearing, and finding those misinformations to have been the first, yea, the chief and

From "The Apology Directed, To the King's Most Excellent Majesty: From the House of Commons, Assembled in Parliament," in William Petyt, *Jus Parliamentarium* (London, 1739), 227–43.

almost the sole cause of all the discontentful and troublesome proceedings so much blamed in this Parliament, and that they might be again the cause of like or greater discontents and troubles hereafter . . . we have been constrained, as well in duty to your royal Majesty whom we serve as to our dear native country for which we serve in this Parliament, to break our silence, and freely to disclose unto your Majesty the truth of such matters concerning your subjects the Commons as hitherto by misinformation hath been suppressed or perverted. . . .

. . . We could not in duty as well unto your Majesty as to our country, cities, bouroughs, who hath sent us hither not ignorant or uninstructed of their griefs, of their desires, and hopes, but according to the ancient use and liberty of Parliaments, present our several humble petitions to your Majesty of different nature, some for right and some for grace, to the easing and relieving of us of some just burdens and of other some unjust oppressions, wherein what due care and what respect we have had that your Majesty's honor and profit should be enjoyed with the content and satisfaction of your people, shall afterwards in their several due places appear.

Now concerning the ancient rights of the subjects of this realm, chiefly consisting in the privileges of this House of Parliament, the misinformation openly delivered to your Majesty hath been in three things:

First, that we held not privileges of right, but of grace only, renewed every Parliament by way of donature [the King's gift] upon petition, and so to be limited.

Secondly, that we are no Court of Record, nor yet a Court that can command view of records, but that our proceedings here are only to acts and memorials, and that the attendance with the records is courtesy, not duty.

Thirdly, that the examination of the return of writs for knights and burgesses is without our compass, and due to the Chancery.

Against which assertions, most gracious Sovereign, tending directly and apparently to the utter overthrow of the very fundamental privileges of our House, and therein of the rights and liberties of the whole Commons of your realm of England which they and their ancestors from time immemorable have undoubtedly enjoyed under your Majesty's most noble progenitors, we, the knights, citizens, and burgesses of the House of Commons assembled in Parliament, and in the name of the whole commons of the realm of England, with uniform consent for ourselves and our posterity, do expressly protest, as being derogatory in the highest degree to the true dignity, liberty, and authority of your Majesty's high Court of Parliament, and consequently to the rights of all your Majesty's said subjects and the whole body of this your kingdom; and desire that this our protestation may be recorded to all posterity.

And contrariwise, with all humble and due respect to your Majesty our Sovereign Lord and Head, against those misinformations we most truly avouch:

First, that our privileges and liberties are our right and due inheritance, no less than our very lands and goods.

Secondly, that they cannot be withheld from us, denied, or impaired, but with apparent wrong to the whole state of the realm.

Thirdly, and that our making of request in the entrance of Parliament to enjoy our privilege is an act only of manners, and doth weaken our right no more than our suing to the King for our lands by petition. . . .

Fourthly, we avouch also, that our House is a Court of Record, and so ever esteemed.

Fifthly, that there is not the highest standing court in this land that ought to enter into competition, either for dignity or authority, with this High Court of Parliament, which with your Majesty's royal assent gives laws to other courts but from other courts receives neither laws nor orders.

Sixthly, we avouch that the House of Commons is the sole proper judge of returns of all such writs and of the election of all such members as belong to it, without which the freedom of election were not entire, and that the Chancery, though a standing court under your Majesty, be to send out those writs and receive the returns and to preserve them, yet the same is done only for the use of the Parliament, over which neither the Chancery nor any other court ever had or ought to have any manner of jurisdiction.

From these misinformed positions, most gracious Sovereign, the greatest part of our troubles, distrusts, and jealousies have risen; having apparently found that in the first Parliament of the happy reign of your Majesty the privileges of our House, and therein the liberties and stability of the whole kingdom, have been more universally and dangerously impugned than ever, as we suppose, since the beginnings of Parliaments. For although it may be true that in the latter times of Queen Elizabeth some one privilege now and then were by some particular act attempted against . . . yet was not the same ever by so public speech nor by positions in general denounced against our privileges.

Besides that in regard of her sex and age which we had great cause to tender, and much more upon care to avoid all trouble which by wicked practice might have been drawn to impeach the quiet of your Majesty's right in the succession, those actions were then passed over which we hoped, in succeeding times of freer access to your Highness of renowned grace and justice, to redress, restore, and rectify. Whereas contrariwise in this Parliament which your Majesty in great grace . . . intended to be a precedent for all Parliaments that should succeed, clean contrary to your Majesty's so gracious desire, by reason of these misinformations not privileges but the whole freedom of the Parliament and realm have from time to time upon all occasions been mainly hewed at;

First, the freedom of persons in our election hath been impeached,

Secondly, the freedom of our speech prejudiced by often reproofs,

Thirdly, particular persons noted with taunt and disgrace who have spoken their consciences in matters proposed to the House, but with all due respect and reverence to your Majesty. . . .

What cause we your poor Commons have to watch over

our privileges is manifest in itself to all men. The prerogatives of princes may easily and do daily grow; the privileges of the subject are for the most part at an everlasting stand. They may be by good providence and care preserved, but being once lost are not recovered but with much disquiet. If good kings were immortal as well as kingdoms, to strive so for privilege were but vanity perhaps and folly; but seeing the same God who in his great mercy hath given us a wise King . . . doth also sometimes permit hypocrites and tyrants in his displeasure and for the sins of the people, from hence hath the desire of rights, liberties, and privileges, both for nobles and commons, had its just original, by which an harmonious and stable State is framed, each member under the Head enjoying that right and performing that duty which for the honor of the Head and happiness of the whole is requisite. . . .

The right of the liberties of the Commons of England consists chiefly in these three parts:

First, that the shires, cities, and boroughs of England, by representation to be present, have free choice of such persons as they shall put in trust to represent them.

Secondly, that the persons chosen, during the time of the Parliament as also of their access and recess, be free from restraint, arrest, and imprisonment.

Thirdly, that in Parliament they may speak freely their consciences without check and controlment, doing the same with due reverence to the Sovereign Court of Parliament, that is, to your Majesty and both the Houses, who all in this case make but one politic body whereof your Highness is the Head. . . .

For matter of religion, it will appear by examination of truth and right that your Majesty should be misinformed if any man should deliver that the Kings of England have any absolute power in themselves either to alter Religion . . . or to make any laws concerning the same otherwise than in temporal causes, by consent of Parliament. We have and shall at all times by our oaths acknowledge that your Majesty is Sovereign Lord and Supreme Governor in both. Touching our own desires and proceedings therein, they have not been a little misconceived and misreported. We have not come in any Puritan or Brownist spirit, to introduce their party [represent radical religious causes] or to work the subversion of the state ecclesiastical as now it standeth; things so far and so clearly from our meaning as that with uniform consent in the beginning of this Parliament we committed to the Tower a man who out of that humor in a petition exhibited to our House had slandered the Bishops. But according to the tenor of your Majesty's writ of summons directed to the counties from whence we came, and according to the ancient and long continued use of Parliaments as by many records from time to time appeareth, we came with another spirit, even with the spirit of peace. We disputed not of matters of faith and doctrine; our desire was peace only and our device of unity, how this lamentable and longlasting dissension amongst the ministers, from which both atheism, sects, and all ill life have received such encouragement and so dangerous increase, might at length, before help came too late, be extinguished. And for the ways of this peace, we are not all addicted to our own inventions but ready to embrace any fit way that may be offered; neither desire we so much that any man in regard of weakness of conscience may be exempted by Parliament from obedience unto laws established, as that in this Parliament such laws may be enacted as by the relinquishment of some few ceremonies of small importance, or by any way better, a perpetual uniformity may be enjoined and observed. . . .

There remaineth, dread Sovereign, yet one part of our duty at this present. . . . We stand not in place to speak or do things pleasing; our care is and must be to confirm the love and tie the hearts of your subjects the commons most firmly to your Majesty. Herein lieth the means of our well deserving of both. . . . Let your Majesty be pleased to receive public information from your Commons in Parliament as to the civil estate and government, for private informations pass often by practice: the voice of the people, in the things of their knowledge, is said to be as the voice of God. And if your Majesty shall vouchsafe, at your best pleasure and leisure, to enter into your gracious consideration of our petition for the ease of these burdens under which your whole people have of long time mourned, hoping for relief by your Majesty, then may you be assured to be possessed of their hearts, and if of their hearts, of all they can do or have.

◄§ 2 §►

The House of Commons Petition Respecting Impositions, May 23, 1610

To the King's most Excellent Majesty.

Most gracious Sovereign, whereas your Majesty's most humble subjects the Commons assembled in Parliament have received, first by message and since by speech from your Majesty, a commandment of restraint from debating in Parliament your Majesty's right of imposing upon your subjects' goods exported or imported out of or into this realm, yet allowing us to examine the grievance of those impositions in regard of quantity, time, and other circumstances of disproportion thereto incident; we your said humble subjects, nothing doubting but that your Majesty had no intent by that commandment to infringe the ancient and fundamental right of the liberty of the Parliament in point of exact discussing of all matters concerning them and their possessions, goods, and rights whatsoever, which yet we cannot but conceive to be done in effect by this commandment; do with all humble duty make this remonstrance to your Majesty.

First, we hold it an ancient, general, and undoubted right of Parliament to debate freely all matters which do properly concern the subject and his right or state; which freedom of debate being once foreclosed, the essence of the liberty of Parliaments is withal dissolved.

And whereas in this case the subjects' right on the one side and your Majesty's prerogative on the other cannot possibly be served in debate of either, we allege that your Majesty's prerogatives of that kind concerning directly the subject's right and interest are daily handled and discussed in all Courts at

From *Journals of the House of Commons* [1547–1628] (London, 1803), I, 431–2.

Westminster, and have been ever freely debated upon all fit occasions, both in this and all former Parliaments, without restraint: which being forbidden, it is impossible for the subject either to know or to maintain his right and property to his own lands and goods, though never so just and manifest.

It may further please your most excellent Majesty to understand that we have no mind to impugn, but a desire to inform ourselves of, your Highness's prerogative in that point, which, if ever, is now most necessary to be known; and though it were to no other purpose, yet to satisfy the generality of your Majesty's subjects, who finding themselves much grieved by these new impositions do languish in much sorrow and discomfort.

These reasons, dread Sovereign, being the proper reasons of Parliament, do plead for the upholding of this our ancient right and liberty. Howbeit, seeing it hath pleased your Majesty to insist upon that judgment in the Exchequer as being direction sufficient for us without further examination, upon great desire of leaving your Majesty unsatisfied in no one point of our intents and proceedings, we profess touching that judgment that we neither do nor will take upon us to reverse it; but our desire is, to know the reasons whereupon the same was grounded, and the rather for that a general conceit is had that the reasons of that judgment may be extended much further, even to the utter ruin of the ancient liberty of this kingdom and of your subjects' right of property of their lands and goods.

Then for the judgment itself, being the first and last that ever was given in that kind, for ought appearing unto us, and being only in one case and against one man, it can bind in law no other but that person, and is also reversible by writ of error granted heretofore by Act of Parliament, and neither he nor any other subject is debarred by it from trying his right in the same or like case in any of your Majesty's Courts of Record at Westminster.

Lastly, we nothing doubt but our intended proceeding in a full examination of the right, nature, and measure of these new impositions (if this restraint had not come between) should have been so orderly and moderately carried, and so applied to

the manifold necessity of these times, and given your Majesty
so true a view of the state and right of your subjects, that it
would have been much to your Majesty's content and satisfaction . . . and removed all cause of fears and jealousies from the
loyal hearts of your subjects, which is . . . our careful endeavor;
whereas, contrariwise, in that other way directed by your Majesty
we cannot safely proceed without concluding forever the right
of the subject, which without due examination thereof we may
not do.

We therefore, your Highness's loyal and dutiful Commons,
not swerving from the approved steps of our ancestors, most
humbly and instantly beseech your gracious Majesty that without offence to the same we may, according to the undoubted
right and liberty of Parliament, proceed in our intended course
of a full examination of these new impositions; that so we may
cheerfully pass on to your Majesty's business, from which this
stop hath by diversion so long withheld us. And we your Majesty's
most humble, faithful, and loyal subjects shall ever, according
to our bounden duty, pray for your Majesty's long and happy
reign over us.

☙ 3 ❧

A Letter from James I to the House of Commons, December 3, 1621

Mr. Speaker:

We have heard by divers reports, to our great grief, that
our distance from the Houses of Parliament, caused by our
indisposition of health, has emboldened some fiery and popular
spirits of some of the House of Commons to argue and debate
publicly of the matters far above their reach and capacity,
tending to our high dishonor and breach of prerogative royal.
These are therefore to command you to make known, in our
name, unto the House that none therein shall presume hence-

From John Rushworth, *Historical Collections of Private Passages of
State, Weighty Matters in Law, Remarkable Proceedings . . . 1618 . . .
1648* (8 vols., London, 1680–1701), I, 43.

forth to meddle with anything concerning our government or deep matters of State; and, namely, not to deal with our dearest son's match with the daughter of Spain, nor to touch the honor of that King or any other our friends and confederates, and also not to meddle with any man's particulars which have their due motion in our ordinary courts of justice. And whereas we hear they have sent a message to Sir Edwin Sandys to know the reasons of his late restraint, you shall in our name resolve them that it was not for any misdemeanor of his in Parliament. But, to put them out of doubt of any question of that nature that may arise among them hereafter, you shall resolve them, in our name, that we think ourself very free and able to punish any man's misdemeanors in Parliament, as well during their sitting as after: which we mean not to spare hereafter upon any occasion of any man's insolent behavior there that shall be ministered unto us. And if they have already touched any of these points, which we have forbidden, in any petition of theirs which is to be sent unto us, it is our pleasure that you shall tell them that, except they reform it before it come to our hands, we will not deign the hearing nor answering of it.

◅ 4 ▻

The Protestation of the House of Commons, December 18, 1621

The Commons now assembled in Parliament, being justly occasioned thereunto concerning sundry liberties, franchises, and privileges of Parliament, amongst others here mentioned, do make this Protestation following:

That the liberties, franchises, privileges, and jurisdictions of Parliament are the ancient and undoubted birthright and inheritance of the subjects of England; and that the arduous and urgent affairs concerning the King, State, and defence of the Realm and of the Church of England, and the maintenance

From Rushworth, *Historical Collections of Private Passages of State, Weighty Matters in Law, Remarkable Proceedings . . . 1618 . . . 1648,* I, 53.

and making of laws, and redress of mischiefs and grievances which daily happen within this Realm, are proper subjects and matter of counsel and debate in Parliament; and that in the handling and proceeding of those businesses every member of the House of Parliament hath, and of right ought to have, freedom of speech to propound, treat, reason, and bring to conclusion the same; and that the Commons in Parliament have like liberty and freedom to treat of these matters in such order as in their judgments shall seem fittest; and that every member of the said House hath like freedom from all impeachment, imprisonment, and molestation (other than by censure of the House itself) for or concerning any speaking, reasoning, or declaring of any matter or matters touching the Parliament or Parliament-business; and that if any of the said members be complained of and questioned for anything done or said in Parliament, the same is to be showed to the King by the advice and assent of all the Commons assembled in Parliament, before the King give credence to any private information.

◄§ 5 §►

The Petition of Right, 1628

The Petition exhibited to his Majesty by the Lords Spiritual and Temporal, and Commons in this present Parliament assembled, concerning divers rights and liberties of the subjects. . . .

To the King's most excellent Majesty:

Humbly show unto our Sovereign Lord the King the Lords Spiritual and Temporal, and Commons in Parliament assembled, that, whereas it is declared and enacted by a statute made in the time of the reign of King Edward I, commonly called *Statutum de Tallagio non Concedendo,* that no tallage or aid should be laid or levied by the King or his heirs in this Realm without the goodwill and assent of the archbishops, bishops, earls, barons, knights, burgesses, and other the freemen of the commonalty of this Realm; and, by authority of Parliament holden in the five and twentieth year of the reign of King Edward III, it is

From *The Statutes of the Realm* (London, 1810–22), V, 23–4.

declared and enacted that from thenceforth no person should be compelled to make any loans to the King against his will, because such loans were against reason and the franchise of the land; and by other laws of this Realm it is provided that none should be charged by any charge or imposition, called a benevolence, or by such like charge; by which the statutes before mentioned, and other the good laws and statutes of this Realm, your subjects have inherited this freedom, that they should not be compelled to contribute to any tax, tallage, aid, or other like charge not set by common consent in Parliament; yet, nevertheless, of late divers commissions directed to sundry commissioners in several counties with instructions have issued, by means whereof your people have been in divers places assembled and required to lend certain sums of money unto your Majesty; and many of them, upon their refusal to do so, have had an oath administered unto them, not warrantable by the laws or statutes of this Realm, and have been constrained to become bound to make appearance and give attendance before your Privy Council and in other places; and others of them have been therefor imprisoned, confined, and sundry other ways molested and disquieted; and divers other charges have been laid and levied upon your people in several counties by lord lieutenants, deputy lieutenants, commissioners for musters, Justices of Peace, and others, by command or direction from your Majesty or your Privy Council, against the laws and free customs of this Realm.

And where also, by the statute called the Great Charter of the Liberties of England, it is declared and enacted that no freeman may be taken or imprisoned, or be disseised of his freehold or liberties or his free customs, or be outlawed or exiled or in any manner destroyed, but by the lawful judgment of his peers or by the law of the land; and in the eight and twentieth year of the reign of King Edward III it was declared and enacted by authority of Parliament that no man, of what estate or condition that he be, should be put out of his land or tenements, nor taken, nor imprisoned, nor disherited, nor put to death, without being brought to answer by due process of law:

Nevertheless, against the tenor of the said statutes and other the good laws and statutes of your Realm to that end provided, divers of your subjects have of late been imprisoned without any cause showed; and when for their deliverance they were brought before your Justices by your Majesty's writs of *habeas corpus*, there to undergo and receive as the court should order, and their keepers commanded to certify the causes of their detainer, no cause was certified, but that they were detained by your Majesty's special command, signified by the Lords of your Privy Council; and yet were returned back to several prisons, without being charged with anything to which they might make answer according to the law. . . .

They do therefore humbly pray your most excellent Majesty that no man hereafter be compelled to make or yield any gift, loan, benevolence, tax, or such like charge without common consent by act of Parliament, and that none be called to make answer, or take such oath, or to give attendance, or be confined, or otherwise molested or disquieted concerning the same, or for refusal thereof; and that no freeman, in any such manner as is before mentioned, be imprisoned or detained; and that your Majesty would be pleased to remove the said soldiers and mariners; and that your people may not be so burdened in time to come; and that the foresaid commissions for proceeding by martial law may be revoked and annulled; and that hereafter no commissions of like nature may issue forth to any person or persons whatsoever, to be executed as aforesaid, lest by color of them any of your Majesty's subjects be destroyed or put to death, contrary to the laws and franchise of the land . . . and that your Majesty would also vouchsafe and declare that the awards, doings, and proceedings to the prejudice of your people in any of the premises shall not be drawn hereafter into consequence or example; and that your Majesty would be also graciously pleased, for the further comfort and safety of your people, to declare your Royal will and pleasure that in the things aforesaid all your officers and ministers shall serve you according to the laws and statutes of this Realm, as they tender the honor of your Majesty and the prosperity of this kingdom.

Jamestown Genesis:
The First American Assembly

T HE Virginia Company charter of 1612 (Doc. 6) was
typical of an English trading company. Governor and
council would be elected by a majority vote of the stockholders
and would conduct the daily affairs of the company. To consider
larger decisions, however, the stockholders would meet in four
great and general courts each year. These had the power to make
laws and ordinances for the Company and colony so long as
they "shall not be contrary to the laws and statutes of our
realm of England." With this charter of 1612 the Crown aban-
doned its attempt at direct control of the Company and colony
in Virginia. Thereafter, the third Virginia charter set the pattern
for most subsequent trading company charters, notably the one
granted to the Massachusetts Bay Company in 1629 (Doc. 10).

In 1618, following six hard and tumultuous years, the Virginia Company ratified the so-called Great Charter, which authorized the calling of an assembly in 1619. Although that document has been lost, historians assume that the Ordinance and
Constitution of 1621 (Doc. 7) was essentially the same in most
respects.

On April 17, 1619, Sir George Yeardley arrived at Jamestown as governor to make the Great Charter operative. Martial
law and communism were abolished; lands were assigned to
the settlers; four corporations were created; and the various
settlements were invited to send delegates to Jamestown in
July to help the Company make laws. When the first legislative

assembly in America convened, John Pory, secretary of the colony, was elected speaker. His Report of the Proceedings of the first American assembly (Doc. 8), an invaluable and interesting document, was sent to the Company in England. Pory was born about 1570, studied at Cambridge, and was especially influenced by Richard Hakluyt. From 1605 until 1611, he sat as a member of the House of Commons. During the next seven years he traveled extensively in Europe and the East, where he was attached to several English embassies. In January 1619, he sailed to Virginia to be the colonial secretary. As speaker of the initial assembly, his parliamentary experience at home became exceedingly valuable to the members. Thereafter Pory remained in Virginia for another thirteen months, making exploratory trips, writing, and serving usefully in public affairs. In October 1623, he returned to Virginia as one of the commissioners to inquire into the sagging state of the colony.

Participants in the 1619 assembly realized fully the speaker's important role in preparing the meeting, its agenda, and format. In reading Pory's comprehensive report, one notes the variety of concerns considered: the importance of the issue of Martin's Brandon, the various judicial cases heard, the nature of the laws passed, and the critical interest in decisions affecting real estate. One senses also from Pory's report how desperately a stable, ordered government was needed in order to stave off licentiousness and anarchy.

≈§ 6 §≈

The Third Charter of the Virginia
Company, March 12, 1612

And we do hereby ordain and grant by these Presents, that the said Treasurer and Company of Adventurers and Planters aforesaid, shall and may, once every week, or oftener, at their Pleasure, hold, and keep a Court and Assembly for the better Order

From Francis Newton Thorpe, ed., *The Federal and State Constitutions, Colonial Charters, and Other Organic Laws* . . . (7 vols., Washington, D.C., 1909), VII, 3802–5.

and Government of the said Plantation, and such Things as shall concern the same; And that any five Persons of our Council for the said first Colony in *Virginia,* for the Time being, of which Company the Treasurer, or his Deputy, to be always one, and the Number of fifteen others, at the least, of the Generality of the said Company, assembled together in such Manner, as is and hath been heretofore used and accustomed, shall be said, taken, held, and reputed to be, and shall be a *sufficient Court* of the said Company, for the handling and ordering, and dispatching of all such casual and particular Occurrences, and accidental Matters, of less Consequence and Weight, as shall from Time to Time happen, touching and concerning the said Plantation.

And that nevertheless, for the handling, ordering, and disposing of Matters and Affairs of greater Weight and Importance, and such as shall or may, in any Sort, concern the Weal Publick and general Good of the said Company and Plantation, as namely, the Manner of Government from Time to Time to be used, the ordering and Disposing of the Lands and Possessions, and the settling and establishing of a Trade there, or such like, there shall be held and kept every Year, upon the last *Wednesday,* save one, of *Hillary* Term, *Easter, Trinity,* and *Michaelmas* Terms, for ever, one great, general, and solemn Assembly, which four Assemblies shall be stiled and called, *The four Great and General Courts of the Council and Company of Adventurers for Virginia;* In all and every of which said Great and General Courts, so assembled, our Will and Pleasure is, and we do, for Us, our Heirs and Successors, for ever, Give and Grant to the said Treasurer and Company, and their Successors for ever, by these Presents, that they, the said Treasurer and Company, or the greater Number of them, so assembled, shall and may have full Power and Authority, from Time to Time, and at all Times hereafter, to elect and chuse discreet Persons, to be of our said Council for the said first Colony in *Virginia,* and to nominate and appoint such Officers as they shall think fit and requisite, for the Government, managing, ordering, and dispatching of the Affairs of the said Company; And shall likewise have full

Power and Authority, to ordain and make such Laws and Ordinances, for the Good and Welfare of the said Plantation, as to them from Time to Time, shall be thought requisite and meet: *So always,* as the same be not contrary to the Laws and Statutes of this our Realm of *England:* And shall, in like Manner, have Power and Authority, to expulse, disfranchise, and put out of and from their said Company and Society for ever, all and every such Person and Persons, as having either promised or subscribed their Names to become Adventurers to the said Plantation, of the said first Colony in *Virginia,* or having been nominated for Adventurers in these or any other our Letters-Patents, or having been otherwise admitted and nominated to be of the said Company, have nevertheless either not put in any adventure at all for and towards the said Plantation, or else have refused or neglected, or shall refuse and neglect to bring in his or their Adventure, by Word or Writing, promised within six Months after the same shall be so payable and due. . . . And We do, for Us, our Heirs and Successors, further give and grant to the said Treasurer and Company, or their Successors forever, that the said Treasurer and Company, or the greater Part of them for the Time being, so in a full and general Court assembled as aforesaid, shall and may from Time to Time, and at all times forever hereafter, elect, choose and admit into their Company, and Society, any Person or Persons, as well Strangers and Aliens born in any Part beyond the Seas wheresoever, being in Amity with us, as our natural Liege Subjects born in any our Realms and Dominions: And that all such Persons so elected, chosen, and admitted to be of the said Company as aforesaid, shall thereupon be taken, reputed, and held, and shall be free Members of the said Company, and shall have, hold, and enjoy all and singular Freedoms, Liberties, Franchises, Privileges, Immunities, Benefits, Profits, and Commodities whatsoever, to the said Company in any Sort belonging or appertaining, as fully, freely and amply as any other Adventurers now being, or which hereafter at any Time shall be of the said Company, hath, have, shall may, might, or ought to have and enjoy the same to all Intents and Purposes whatsoever.

ᵈᔓ 7 ᔓᵉ

An Ordinance and Constitution from the Treasurer and Company in England Calling for a Council and Assembly in Virginia [1618?], July 24, 1621

To all people to whom these presents shall come, bee seen, or heard, the Treasuror, Council and Company of Adventurers and planters of the Citty of London for the first Collony in Virginia send greeting. Knowe yee That wee the said Treasuror Counsell and Company takeing into our Carefull Consideration the present state of the said Colony in Virginia: And intending by the devine assistance to settle such a forme of government ther as may bee to the greatest benifitt and comfort of the people and whereby all Injustice grevance and oppression may bee prevented and kept off as much as is possible from the said Colony, have thought fitt to make our Entrance by ordayning & establishing such supreame Counsells as may not only bee assisting to the Governor for the time being in administration of Justice, and the executing of other duties to his office belonging, but also by ther vigilent Care & prudence may provide as well for remedy of all inconvenyencies groweing from tyme to tyme, As also for the advancing of Encrease strength stabillitie and prosperytie of the said Colony

Wee therfore the said Treasuror Counsell and Company, by authoritie directed to us from his Majestie under his great seale upon mature deliberation doe hereby order & declare, That from hence forward ther bee two Supreame Counsells in Virginia for the better government of the said Colony as aforesaid. The one of which Counsells to bee called the Counsell of State and whose office shall Cheiflie bee assisting with ther Care advise & circomspection to the said Governor shall be Chosen nominated placed and displaced from tyme to tyme by us the said Treasurer Counsell & Company and our successors, which Counsell of State shall Consiste for the present onlie of those persons whose

From Susan Myra Kingsbury, ed., *The Records of the Virginia Company of London* (4 vols., Washington, D.C., 1906–35), III, 482–4.

names are here inserted, vizt Sr Francis Wyatt governor of Virginia, Captaine Francis West, Sr George Yeardly knight, Sr William Newce knight, Marshall of Virginia, Mr George Sandys Tresuror, Mr George Thorpe deputy of the Colledge, Captaine Thomas Newce deputy for the Company, Mr Christopher Davison secretarie, Doctor Potts phisition to the Company, Mr Paulet, Mr Leech, Captaine Nathaniell Powell, Mr Roger Smith, Mr John Berkley, Mr John Rolfe, Mr Ralfe Hamer, Mr John Pountus, Mr Michael Lapworth, Mr Harwood, Mr Samuel Macocke. Which said Counsellors and Counsell wee Earnestlie pray & desier, and in his Majestie's name strictlie charge and Comand, That all factious parcialties and sinester respects laid aside they bend ther care and Endeavors to assist the said Governor first and principallie in advancement of the honor and service of almightie god, and the Enlargement of his kingdome amongste those heathen people, And next in the erecting of the said Colonie in one obedience to his Majestie and all lawfull Authoritie from his Majestie dirived, And lastlie in mayntayning the said people in Justice and Christian Conversation among themselves and in strength and habillytie to with stand ther Ennimies, And this Counsell is to bee alwaies or for the most part residing about or neere the said Governor. The other Counsell, more generall, to bee called by the Governor and yeerly of Course & no oftener but for very extreordynarie & Important occasions shall consist for present of the said Counsell of State and of Two Burgesses out of every towne, hunderd and other particuler plantation to bee espetially Chosen by the inhabitants. Which Counsell shal bee called the generall Assemblie, wherin as also in the said Counsell of State, all matters shall be decyded, determined & ordred by the greater part of the voyces then present, Reserveing alwaies to the Governor a negative voyce, And this generall assembly shall have free power, to treat Consult & conclude as well of all emergent occasions concerning the publique weale of the said colony and everie parte therof, as also to make, ordeine & enact such generall lawes & orders for the behoof of the said colony and the good government thereof as shall time to tyme appeare necessarie or requisite. Wherin as in all other things wee

requier the said gennerall Assembly, as also the said Counsell of
State to imitate and followe the policy of the forme of government, Lawes, Custome manners of loyall and other administration
of Justice used in the Realme of England as neere as may bee
even as ourselves by his Majestie's Lettres patent are required.
Provided that noe lawes or ordinance made in the said generall
Assembly shal be and continew in force and validytie, unlese the
same shal be sollemlie ratified and Confirmed in a generall greater
Court of the said Court here in England and so ratified and returned to them under our seale. It being our intent to affoord the
like measure also unto the said Colony that after the government
of the said Colony, shall once have been well framed & settled
accordingly, which is to be done by us as by authoritie derived
from his Majestie and the same shall have bene soe by us declared,
No orders of our Court afterwarde shall binde the said colony
unles they bee ratified in like manner in ther generall Assembly.

In wittnes wherof wee have hereunto sett our Comon seale the
24th day of July 1621, and in the yeare of the raigne of our governour Lord James by the grace of God of England Scotland
France & Ireland King defendor of the   vizt of England
France and Scotland the Nyneteenth and of Scotland the four
and fiftieth.

◄§ 8 §►

John Pory's Report of the Proceedings of the First Assembly in Virginia, July 30 to August 4, 1619

*A Reporte of the manner of proceeding in the General assembly
convened at James citty in Virginia, July 30, 1619, consisting of
the Governor, the Counsell of Estate and two Burgesses elected out
of eache Incorporation and Plantation, and being dissolved the 4th
of August next ensuing*

FIRST. Sir George Yeardley, Knight, Governor and Captaine general of Virginia, having sent his sumons all over the Country, as

From Kingsbury, ed., *The Records of the Virginia Company of London,*
III, 153–77.

well to invite those of the Counsell of Estate that were absent as also for the election of Burgesses, there were chosen and appeared. . . . [22 names follow]

The most convenient place we could finde to sitt in was the Quire of the Churche Where Sir George Yeardley, the Governor, being sett downe in his accustomed place, those of the Counsel of Estate sate nexte him on both hands excepte onely the Secretary then appointed Speaker, who sate right before him, John Twine, clerke of the General assembly, being placed nexte the Speaker, and Thomas Pierse, the Sergeant, standing at the barre, to be ready for any service the Assembly shoulde comaund him. But forasmuche as men's affaires doe little prosper where God's service is neglected, all the Burgesses tooke their places in the Quire till a prayer was said by Mr. Bucke, the Minister, that it would please God to guide and sanctifie all our proceedings to his owne glory and the good of this Plantation. Prayer being ended, to the intente that as we had begun at God Almighty, so we might proceed with awful and due respecte towards the Lieutenant, our most gratious and dread Soveraigne, all the Burgesses were intreatted to retyre themselves into the body of the Churche, which being done, before they were fully admitted, they were called in order and by name, and so every man (none staggering at it) tooke the oathe of Supremacy, and entred the Assembly. . . .

An order concluded by the General assembly concerning Captaine Warde, July 30th, 1619, at the opening of the said Assembly

At the reading of the names of the Burgesses, Exception was taken against Captaine Warde as having planted here in Virginia without any authority or comission from the Tresurer, Counsell and Company in Englande. But considering he had bene at so great chardge and paines to augmente this Colony, and adventured his owne person in the action, and since that time had brought home a good quantity of fishe, to relieve the Colony by waye of trade, and above all, because the Comission for authorising the General Assembly admitteth of two Burgesses out of every plantation without restrainte or exception, Upon all these considerations, the Assembly was contented to admitt of him and his Lieutenant (as members of their body and Burgesses) into their society. Provided, that the said Captaine Warde with all expedition, that is to saye between this and the nexte general assembly (all lawful impediments excepted), should procure from the Tresurer, Counsell and Company in England a comission lawfully to establish and plant himselfe and his Company as the Chieffs of other Plantations have done. And in case he doe neglect this he is to stande to the censure of the nexte general assembly. To this Captaine Warde, in the presence of us all, having given his consente and undertaken to performe the same was, together with his Lieutenant, by voices of the whole Assembly first admitted to take the oath of Supremacy, and then to make up their number and to sitt amongst them.

This being done, the Governor himselfe alledged that before we proceeded any further it behooved us to examine whither it were fitt, that Captaine Martin's Burgesses shoulde have any place in the Assembly, forasmuche as he hath a clause in his Patente which doth not onely exempte him from that equality and uniformity of lawes and orders which the great charter saith are to extende over the whole Colony, but also from diverse such lawes as we must be enforced to make in the General Assembly. That clause is as followeth: Item. That it shall and may be lawfull to and for the said Captain John Martin, his heirs, executours and assignes to governe and comaunde all suche person or persons as at this time he shall carry over with him, or that shal be sente him hereafter, free from any comaunde of the Colony, excepte it be in ayding and assisting the same against any forren or domestical enemy.

Upon the motion of the Governor, discussed the same time in the assembly, ensued this order following:

An order of the General Assembly touching a clause in
Captain Martin's Patent at James Citty, July 30, 1619

After all the Burgesses had taken the oath of Supremacy and were admitted into the house and all sett downe in their places, a Copie of Captain Martin's Patent was produced by the Governor out of a Clause whereof it appeared that when the general assembly had made some kinde of lawes requisite for the whole Colony, he and his Burgesses and people might deride the whole company and chuse whether they would obay the same or no. It was therefore ordered in Courte that the foresaid two Burgesses should withdraw themselves out of the assembly till suche time as Captaine Martin had made his personall appearance before them. At what time, if upon their motion, if he would be contente to quitte and give over that parte of his Patente, and contrary thereunto woulde submitte himselfe to the general forme of governement as all others did, that then his Burgesses should be readmitted; otherwise they were to be utterly excluded as being spies rather than loyal Burgesses, because they had offered themselves to be assistant at the making of lawes which both themselves and those whom they represented might chuse whether they would obaye or not. . . . These obstacles removed, the Speaker, who for a long time has bene extreame sickly, and therefore not able to passe through long harangues, delivered in briefe to the whole assembly the occasions of their meeting. Which done he read unto them the commission for establishing the Counsell of Estate and the general Assembly, wherein their duties were described to the life.

Having thus prepared them he read over unto them the greate Charter, or commission of privileges, orders and laws, sent by Sir George Yeardley out of Englande. Which for the more ease of the Committies, having divided into fower books, he read the former two the same forenoon for expeditions sake, a second time over, and so they were referred to the perusall of two Committies, which did reciprocally consider of either, and accordingly brought in their opinions. But some may here objecte to what ende we should presume to referre that to the examination of Committies which the Counsell and Company in England had already resolved to be perfect, and did expect nothing but our assente thereunto. To this we answere, that we did it not to the ende to correcte or controll anything therein contained, but onely in case we should finde ought not perfectly squaring with the state of this Colony or any lawe which did presse or binde too harde, that we might by waye of humble petition, seeke to have it redressed, especially because this great Charter is to bind us and our heirs for ever. . . .

After dinner the Governour and those that were not of the Committies sate a second time, while the said Committies were employed in the perusall of those two bookes. And whereas the Speaker had propounded four severall objects for the Assembly to consider on: namely, first the great charter of orders, lawes and privileges; Secondly, which of the instructions given by the Counsel in England to my Lord de La Warre, Captain Argall or Sir George Yeardley, might conveniently putt on the habite of lawes; Thirdly, what lawes might issue out of the private conceite of any of the Burgesses, or any other of the Colony; and lastly, what petitions were fitt to be sente home for England. It pleased the Governour for expedition sake to have the second objecte of the four to be examined and prepared by himselfe and the Non-Committies. Wherein after having spente some three hours conference, the two Committies brought in their opinions concerning the two former bookes, (the second of which beginneth at these wordes of the charter: And forasmuche as our intente is to establish one equall and uniforme kinde of government over all Virginia &c.,) which the whole Assembly, because it was late, deferred to treatt of till the next morning. . . .

James citty out of the said General Assembly, July 31, 1619

At the same the Instructions convertible into lawes were referred to the consideration of the above named Committies, viz., the general Instructions to the first Committie and the particular Instructions to the second, to be returned by them into the assembly on Munday morning.

Sunday, Aug. 1

Mr. Shelley, one of the Burgesses, deceased.

Munday, Aug. 2

Captain John Martin (according to the sumons sent him on Fryday, July 30,) made his personall appearance at the barre, whenas the Speaker having first read unto him the orders of the Assembly that concerned him, he pleaded lardgely for himself to them both and indevoured to answere some other thinges that were objected against his Patente. In fine, being demanded out of the former order whether he would quitte that clause of his Patent which (quite otherwise then Sir William Throckmorton's, Captain Christopher Lawnes and other men's patentes) exempteth himselffe and his people from all services of the Colonie excepte onely in case of warre against a forren or domesticall enemie, His answere was negative, that he would not infringe any parte of his Patente. Whereupon it was resolved by the Assembly that his Burgesses should have no admittance. . . .

It was at the same time further ordered by the Assembly that the Speaker, in their names, should (as he nowe doth) humbly demaunde of the Treasurer, Counsell and Company an exposition of this one clause in Captaine Martin's Patente namely, where it is saide That he is to enjoye his landes in as lardge and ample manner, to all intentes and purposes, as any lord of any manours in England dothe holde his grounde out of which some have collected that he might by the same graunte protecte men from paying their debts and from diverse other dangers of lawe. The least the Assembly can alledge against this clause is, that it is obscure, and that it is a thing impossible for us here to knowe the Prerogatives of all manours in Englande. The Assembly therefore humbly beseeches their lordships and the rest of that Honorable house that in case they shall finde any thing in this or in any other parte of his graunte wherby that clause towards the conclusion of the great charter, (viz., that all grauntes as well of the one sorte as of the other respectively, be made with equall favour, and graunts of like liberties and imunities as neer as may be, to the ende that all complainte of partiality and indifferency may be avoided,) might in any sorte be contradicted or the uniformity and equality of lawes and orders extending over the whole Colony might be impeached, That they would be pleased to remove any such hindrance as may diverte out of the true course the free and publique current of Justice.

Upon the same ground and reason their lordships, together with the rest of the Counsell and Company, are humbly besought by this general assembly that if in that other clause which exempteth the Captaine Martin and his people from all services of the Colony etc., they shall finde any resistance [to] that equality and uniformity of lawes and orders intended nowe by them to be established over the whole Colony, that they would be pleased to reforme it.

In fine, whereas Captaine Martin, for those ten shares allowed him for his personal adventure and for his adventure of £70 besides, doth claim 500 acres a share, that the Treasurer, Counsell and Company woulde vouchsafe to give notice to the Governour here, what kinde of shares they meante he should have when they gave him his Patent.

The premisses about Captaine Martin thus resolved, the Committies appointed to consider what instructions are fitt to be converted into lawes, brought in their opinions, and first of some of the general instructions.

Here begin the lawes drawen out of the Instructions given by his Majesties Counsell of Virginia in England to my Lord de La Warre, Captain Argall and Sir George Yeardley, knight

By this present General Assembly be it enacted that no injury or oppression be wrought by the English against the Indians whereby the present peace might be disturbed and antient quarrells might be revived. And farther be it ordained that the Chicohomini are not to be excepted out of this lawe; untill either that suche order come out of Englande or that they doe provoke us by some newe injury.

Against Idlenes, Gaming, drunkenes and excesse in apparell the Assembly hath enacted as followeth:

First, in detestation of Idlenes be it enacted, that if any man be founde to live as an Idler or renagate, though a freedman, it shal be lawful for that Incorporation or Plantation to which he belongeth to appoint him a Master to serve for wages, till he shewe apparant signes of amendment.

•   •   •

The same morning the lawes abovewritten, drawen out of the instructions, were read, and one by one thoroughly examined, and then passed once again the general consente of the whole Assembly.

This afternoon the comitties brought in a reporte, what they had done as concerning the thirde sorte of lawes, the discussing whereof spente the residue of that daye. Excepte onely the consideration of a pettiton of Mr. John Rolfe's againste Captaine John Martine for writing a letter to him wherein (as Mr. Rolfe alledgeth) he taxeth him both unseemly and amisse of certaine thinges wherein he was never faulty, and besides, casteth some aspersion upon the present government, which is the most temperate and juste that ever was in this country, too milde indeed, for many of this Colony, whom unwoonted liberty hath made insolente and not to know themselves. This Petition of Mr. Rolfe's was thought fitt to be referred to the Counsell of State.

Wednesday, Aug. 4th

This daye (by reason of extream heat, both past and likely to ensue and by that meanes of the alteration of the healthes of diverse of the general Assembly) the Governour, who himself also was not well, resolved should be the last of this first session; so in the morning the Speaker (as he was required by the Assembly) redd over all the lawes and orders that had formerly passed the house, to give the same yett one reviewe more, and to see whether there were any thing to be amended or that might be excepted againste. This being done, the third sorte of lawes which I am nowe coming to sett downe, were read over [and] thoroughly discussed, which, together with the former, did now passe the laste and finall consente of the General Assembly.

A thirde sorte of lawes, suche as may issue out of every man's private conceipte

It shal be free for every man to trade with the Indians, servants onely excepted, upon paine of whipping, unless the Master will redeeme it off with the payment of an Angell [an English gold coin], one-fourth parte whereof to go to the Provost Marshall, one fourth parte to the discoverer, and the other moyty [half] to the publique uses of the Incorporation.

• • •

The last acte of the Generall Assembly was a contribution to gratifie their officers, as followeth:

Aug. 4th, 1619

It is fully agreed at this general Assembly that in regard of the great paines and labour of the Speaker of this Assembly (who not onely first formed the same Assembly and to their great ease and expedition reduced all matters to be treatted of into a ready method, but also his indisposition notwithstanding wrote or dictated all orders and other expedients and is yet to write severall bookes for all the Generall Incorporations and plantations both of the great charter, and of all the lawes) and likewise in respecte of the diligence of the Clerke and sergeant, officers thereto belonging, That every man and manservant of above 16 yeares of age shall pay into the handes and Custody of the Burgesses of every Incorporation and plantation one pound of the best Tobacco, to be distributed to the Speaker and likewise to the Clerke and sergeant of the Assembly, according to their degrees and rankes, the whole bulke whereof to be delivered into the Speaker's handes, to be divided accordingly. And in regarde the Provost Marshall of James citty hath also given some attendance upon the said General Assembly, he is also to have a share out of the same. And this is to begin to be gathered the 24th of February nexte.

In conclusion, the whole Assembly comaunded the Speaker (as nowe he doth) to present their humble excuse to the Treasurer Counsell and Company in England for being constrained by the intemperature of the weather and the falling sick of diverse of the Burgesses to breake up so abruptly—before they had so much as putt their lawes to the ingrossing.

This they wholly comited to the fidelity of their speaker, who therin (his conscience telles him) hath done the parte of an honest man, otherwise he would be easily founde out by the Burgesses themselves, who with all expedition are to have so many bookes of the same lawes as there be both Incorporations and Plantations in the Colony.

In the seconde place, the Assembly doth most humbly crave pardon that in so shorte a space they could bring their matter to no more perfection, being for the present enforced to sende home titles rather than lawes, Propositions rather than resolutions, Attemptes than Acchievements, hoping their courtesy will accepte our poor endevour, and their wisedome wil be ready to supporte the weaknes of this little flocke.

Thirdly, the General Assembly doth humbly beseech the said Treasurer, Counsell and Company, that albeit it belongeth to them onely to allowe or to abrogate any lawes which we shall here make, and that it is their right so to doe, yet that it would please them not to take it in ill parte if these lawes which we have now brought to light, do passe currant and be of force till suche time as we may knowe their farther pleasure out of Englande: for otherwise this people (who nowe at length have gotten the raines of former servitude into their owne swindge [power]) would in shorte time growe so insolent, as they would shake off all government, and there would be no living among them.

Their last humble suite is, that the said Counsell and Company would be pleased, so soon as they shall finde it convenient, to make good their promise sett downe at the conclusion of their commission for establishing the Counsel of Estate and the General Assembly, namely, that they will give us power to allowe or disallowe of their orders of Courte, as his Majesty hath given them power to allowe or to reject our lawes.

In sum Sir George Yeardley, the Governour prorogued the said General Assembly till the firste of Marche, which is to fall out this present yeare of 1619 [1620], and in the mean season dissolved the same.

~§ III §~

Bermuda: *Company Control and Colonial Government*

WE cannot know with absolute certainty who wrote *The Historye of the Bermudaes or Summer Islands,* a long manuscript owned by the British Museum. A good case has been made for Captain John Smith; but the modern attribution is usually to Captain Nathaniel Butler, governor of the little colony from 1619 until 1622. The narrative presents a vivid picture of politics and social conditions during the first decade in Bermuda's history. Butler was an able writer as well as a shrewd politician. In addition to the *Unmasking of Virginia,* he wrote *Six Dialogues About Sea Service*—one of the most important sources of our knowledge of seventeenth-century shipping.

Butler left England for Bermuda late in the summer of 1619, and brought with him instructions to call a general assembly in order to make laws and handle judicial matters. He gave considerable attention to the problem and made some preliminary inquiries, through his more subtle councillors, as to what the "maine pointes wer that would be generally shot at." What he learned discouraged him, for the colonists were determined to enlarge their own liberties as well as restrict those of the adventurers in London. Butler tried to explain the futility of such intentions, since no enactment would be valid until approved by the London court. He pointed out that the adventurers were not obliged to concede any legislative powers at all, for they could continue to govern by decree; nonetheless they magnanimously would allow the colonists to make their own laws once a year.

Butler made his point effectively, and received in turn the assurance that no bill would be proposed until he had approved it. Promptly he called upon the so-called tribes to elect two burgesses each and send them to the new church at St. George's on August 1. Butler's account of the ensuing session (Doc. 9) compares favorably with John Pory's narrative of proceedings in Virginia, and in several important respects is more complete and satisfying. Just as Butler's instructions had included an explicit rationale for representative government, his *Historye* contains detailed comments upon the purposes and political postures representatives should assume. The *Historye* is, of course, only one partisan's perspective upon the origins of representative government in Bermuda. Butler was an able man, however, a man deeply concerned with parliamentary procedures, and his account is invaluable as a unique historical source.

◄§ 9 §►

Governor Nathaniel Butler's Account of the First Assembly in Bermuda, August 1620

About the same time, or not long after, writts wer sent downe to all the baylies, for the summoninge of the generall assembly at St. Georges; and for the choice of burgeoises against the first of August (1620) followeinge, when it was to begin. The Governour . . . was at this time cheifly taken up in fittinge and disposeinge of bussinesse against the meetinge and session of the generall assembly, which nowe drew neere; wherein, at the very first, he mett with many and materiall difficulties; for, haveinge prepared certaine of the ancientest Ilanders, who wer best knowen, and best entrusted by the people (the elder of the ministers being a prime one among the rest), he employed them to gett all the knowledge they could, what the maine pointes wer that would be generally shott at at the assembly; by whom, haveinge for a certainetie bin assured that the cheife aime and

From [Nathaniel Butler], *The Historye of the Bermudaes or Summer Islands*, ed. Sir J. Henry Lefroy (London, 1882), 188–203.

generall scope and drift of most of the bills that wer entended
to be preferred, would beate upon the enlargeing of themselves
and their liberties, and the enfringeing and curbeinge of their
undertakers in England; a course and endeavour which he well
ynough knewe would prove as well effectlesse as sencelesse, and
never be able to worck the entent it was plotted for; and besides,
could not but give great discontentment to the Adventurers. He
'endeavoured, therefore, by all meanes to divert it, and to possesse
the burgeoises with the vanitie of it, and the impossibilitie of
doeing any good that waye; and this he did, as well by the
meanes of those men aforesayd, as by his owne mouthe and person, all conference with many of them; to whom also, to the same
end, he shewed the particuler instruction that he had received
from the Company in England, concerneinge the holdinge of
this assembly, which ranne in this manner:—

> We require you, that as soon as you maye after your arrivall
> in the Ilands, you doe assemble your counsell and as many of the
> ablest and best understandinge men in the Ilands, both of the
> clergie and laitie, as you and your counsell shall thinck fitt, wherein
> we wish you rather to take too many than too fewe, both because
> every man will more willingly obey lawes to which he hath yeilded
> his consent; as likewise because you shall the better discover such
> thinges as have need of redresse by many than by fewe; and that
> in this assembly you deliberately consult and advise of such lawes
> and constitutions as shallbe thought fitt to be made for the good
> of the plantation, and for maintenance of religion, justice, order,
> peace, and unitie among them. As also upon what penalties you
> thinck fitt, the performances of each lawe be enjoyned: wherein
> we advise you to be very moderate, allwayes so proportioninge
> the penaltye to the offence, that the greatnesse of the punishment
> doe not encourage the delinquents to offend out of hope of pardon,
> as it falleth out wher this rule of moderation is not observed. And
> what in assembly shall, by the major or better part, be agreed
> upon, we would have you distinctly to advertize us of by the
> returne of the next shyp, that they may be ratefied and confirmed
> by the authoritie of the Court here, in such manner as by his
> Majesties Letters Patents is limmited and appointed, with such
> alterations, explanations, or amendments as to the sayd Court shall

be thought meet and convenient. And this course of assemblinge of
the gravest and discreetest men in thoes Ilands, to consult and
advise with you and your counsell of such thinges as may conduce
to the generall good of that plantation, and to the well governinge
of the people ther, we advise you to hould at least once in every
yeare, and of your resolutions and determinations from time to time
to advertize us, that they may be established and confirmed by
order of our Courts here as a foresayd: and in the meane time you
shall not need to doubt to putt in execution any such wholsome
Orders or Constitutions as shall by the major part in the sayd
assemblies be agreed upon. Provided that the same be not repugnant to the lawes of England nor contrary to thes your present
instructions, or to the standing lawes already by us established.

Haveing read this instruction, particulerly directed for the
holdinge of the assembly, unto some of the prime ones, who wer
the leadinge speritts of all the rest, he especially and punctually
observed unto them that clause, wherin it was enjoyned that
the Adventurers wer to be distinctly advertized of what so ever
was by the major partye agreed upon, that so it might be ratefied
and confirmed by the authoritie of their Courts in England, in
such manner as by his Majesties letters patents is limited and
appointed: therin "first you maye see (Sirs sayth he) that by
his Majesties letters patents, the undertakers in England have
power and authoritie to give us lawes: as also that howsoever
they have given us licence and libertie to propound here, and
provide some peculier ones for our good and wellfare, by this
our generall assembly, yet they have so restrained us, that whatsoever we enact amongst our selves, it shall not, nor cannot,
stand in force, unlesse it be by them ratefied and confirmed ther;
so that whilst you endeavour and practice thus to advantage
your owne ends only, and to give your selves your full content,
and them noethinge but the contrary; what doe you else, save
only discover your minds and good wills, or rather ill-wills,
towards them, by giveinge them to understande, as it wer, in
plaine tearmes, that you care not how much they be streightened,
so you may be free, and as you would have it: all which they
shall noe sooner heare, but with holdinge up their hands only,

and a dash or two of a penne, shall wholy be annihilated (nay) perhaps be a cause that the quite contrary be concluded; and this is all that you can gett by this course, that you so generally affect. It is mine advise to you therfore, that this affayre be carryed in a better temper and with more moderation and equanimitie: and that the benefitt and commoditie of the Adventurers may be so mixed and enterwoven with our owne, as they may prove impossible to be severed: and this course will certainely be a meanes not only to winne them to a ratefication of what we ennact here; but to joyne with us also (even by our example) to carry and levell all bussinesse and conclusions with an indifferent hand, without which (I doe assure you) such is the reciprocall bond betwixt you and them, ther cannot long continue any hopefull subsistance to either side."

This speache seemed, even at the instant, to gaine well upon them, so that desireinge the Governour to give them leave to impart and make it knowen to the rest of their fellowes, which in a while after they jointly returned this answer, that they had well considered of what he had delivered unto them, and found it so fitt and necessary to be followed, as they wholy resolved to referre the whole conduction of this affayre to his guidance: and that noe bill should be preferred by any of them to the Assembly, but what by him should first be seene and approved, the which resolution gave the Governour good content, as findinge himselfe more than halfe through the waye he was to make by so lucky a settinge out.

Upon the first of August (being the prefixt day) the generall Assembly began, and was held at St. Georges, in the newe framed churche, fitted for that purpose. In which, before I let you knowe what was done, it is meet I should tell you how it was done. The forme and composition thereof was therefore as followeth:—

The persons wer, the governour, the counsell, the baylies [bailiffs] of the tribes, two burgeoises out of every tribe, chosen by plurallitie of voice, a secretary, to whom all the Bills presented, and by him openly reade in the House, and a clearck to recorde the Acts.

The order (appointed and prescribed by the Governour's direction and command) was:—"The first daye (after a sermon in the morneinge) the burgeoises, the secretary, and the clearck tooke their oaths. The secretary was openly sworne by the Governour himselfe, whose oath was that he should receive all Bills presented unto him, or to be presented, and as opportunitie served, distinctly, and word for word, with an audible voice, to reade them publickly in the Assembly: that he should dilligently observe and take especiall care that all Bills wer openly reade three severall dayes before they wer putt to the question, and came to be decided by plurallitie of voices; that he should heedfully and faythfully take account of all such Bills as by most voices should be passed and ennacted for lawes; that he should conceale the secrets of the House, and neither directly nor indirectly reveale or discover them to any person whatsoever not being a member of the Assembly, all which he should duely and truely performe and keepe to his uttermost abilitie, so helpe him God."

The secretary, being sworne himselfe, he gave the oathe to the clearck, which conteyned:—"That he should diligently, exactly, truely, and faythfully, as nere as possible he could, engrosse all such Bills as should be delivered unto him to that entent by the secretary. He should assist and ayde him, the sayd secretary, in all such employements and affayres as (belonginge to the present Assembly) he should have occasion to use his service. He should not reveale any bussinesse or affayre handled or determined by the Assembly, being within his heareinge or knowledge. Thes two being sworne, the secretary gave the oathe to all the burgoisses, which was, that being to be members of that generall Assembly, they should sweare to use and employe their best endeavours as a furtherance therto; that all such propositions as by them or their meanes should be offered unto the consideration and discussinge thereof should especially be entended and levelled at a publick wellfare; that they should not be led by any partiall affection, or respect of private gaine or interest, to oppose or hinder the establisheinge or ennactinge of any lawe aimeinge at the reformation of any disorder and abuse; that in all such

actions as they should practice and contrive dureinge the whole
time of their assistance in that service, they shoulde strive to discharge a good conscience in all equitie and integritie; that they
should by all meanes conceale the secretts of the House, and not
impart nor discover, either by word, writteinge, or any other
meane, directly or indirectly, to any one not being of the present
Assembly, the passage or carriage of any affayre or bussinesse that
should be treated of and disputed dureinge the time of the whole
sittinge and continuance of the sayde Assembly. All this, and
every part therof, they should promise and sweare to keepe and
performe to their uttermost power and abilitie, so help them God."

The whole Assembly being thus sworne, wer called over by
the secretary, and so tooke their places in the House, the counsell
sittinge next the Governour, and the rest as they came. All of
them being seated, and in quiett, the Governour declared the
cause and benefitt of the Assembly, and the duty and due aime
everye particuler member thereof was to carry and bring with
him, together with some instructions and advises to that end, in
thes wordes followeinge:—

Thanckes be to God, that we are thus mett, to so good an end
as the makeinge and ennactinge of good and holsome lawes; and
I hope the blessed effect will manifest that this course was inspired
from heaven into the hearts of the undertakers in England, to
propound and offer it unto us, for the singuler good and wellfare of
this plantation. As for the forme and regularitie to be observed
herein, you have heard it read unto you even nowe by the Secretary: and I hope you are well skilled in it; for to that end I gave
coppies therof unto the baylies at the last Assizes. Concerneinge
the scope and aime that we are to bring with us hether, I shall
(God willinge) briefly deliver somewhat unto you at this time:
and hereof, the principall and maine part is, the Glory of God:
wherein we are to ponder and resolve of all such thinges in generall, as may promote true religion and beate downe the contrary,
which is sinne and prophanenesse. The second aime we ought to have
is the maintenance of our fayth, obedience, and alleigeance to our
Soveraigne the Kinge; and therfore are to provide against all such
courses and actions as may lessen the respect due either unto his

Majesties owne person, or any such as by his authoritie are placed
over us. In particuler, we are to take heed and to scourge, if need
be, that dangerous opinion (which hath too overboldly been wis-
pered and nourished among you) of choseing and electinge your
owne Governour here. Thirdly, it is our dutyes, and will prove our
wisdome, to conclude upon some such courses as may best secure
the undertakers in England from many abuses and wrongs, which
(I must tell you plainely) are by many planters offred unto them.
It is therfore an un-wary and un-wise affection, that some manifest,
while they strive to have all thinges to be carried in this Assembly
to the gripeinge of the adventurers and proffitt (as they fallsly
thinck) of themselves; ther is noe thinge, I can assure you, to be
gotten that waye; it serves only to discover your selves unto them,
to your owne disadvantage: for you must knowe that it is but in
vaine to enact or conclude any thinge here, unlesse it be confirmed
by them ther. We are to be honest, therfore, and discreat, and soe
to mixe our owne good and proffitt, and theirs together, as may
make it inseperable, by being fully received by both sides: and this
you will find to be the true way, for the firmeing of this plantation.
Fourthly, we are to endeavour and aime at the good and benefitt
of our selves in particuler. I meane at the generall good and wellfare of the inhabitants of thes Ilands wherin we live. . . . You
heare by this barke that is newely come in unto us from England,
of the rumours and likelyhoode of great warres in Christian-doome.
If it should so fall out that any soudaine breach happen betweene
England and Spaine (and who knowes how soone this may be),
ther is not any place that it will breake out upon sooner than
upon this. The pyrates, likewise, have a longinge eye after thes
Ilands, and knowe well how behoufefull [advantageous] they would
be for them; let us, therfore, so provide for our selves, that come
an enemye when he will, and be what he will, we may be able to
give him a brave wellcome. And thes are the foure maine pointes
and aimes that we are to respect and looke after in this action we
are nowe to enter upon. Nowe, the waye and meane to be prepared
for them is, by takeing due notice, every one of us, that we come
not hither for our selves only, and to serve our owne turnes, or any
mans els in particular, but to serve and regard the publick. We are,
therfore, to riddle our selves from all base desires of gaine; we are,
to despice all private interests, thus farre at least, as to cause them
to give place to the generall. It may well be that some men chosen

to be burgeoses here may find some bills preferred into this Assembly that may strike at some gettinge and in-come of theirs in particuler. If they doe so, let them yet remember their oathes; let them not shame themselves, and the place they hold here, by doeing the contrary. If, in their owne consciences, they find that hitherto they have done injurye to a common good, let them not augment it by obstinacye. It is vaine to strive against the streame; for in this case, I hope they shall allwayes find the currant to runne against them. I graunt that ther is a freedome of speach and opinion, with modestie, to be held by every man here. It is lawfull and expedient also, that all men should deliver their censures and judgements upon any bill whatsoever, as their discretion shall induce, and their opinion carry them; but yet I hope ther is noe man here amongst us so wedded to his owne conceites as to affect and delight in opposition, much lesse to thinck it a waye and course to obteyne the repute of a wiseman by holdinge straunge and extravagant opinions: to be singuler on this fashion may be a meanes indeed to make him a noted man; but such a noted one, as for my part, I should be full loath to be. It is after that fashion as if one of you should walke through Cheapeside at noone day, all to be bepainted and stuck with feathers like an Americane [Indian] wher he may be sure to be looked at, but laught at; it behouves us therfore to have our judgements rectified in this point as well as in all others, and the meanes therunto are principally three:—

The first is, by comeing hither, without all prejudication. We must bring equall mindes with us; that is to saye, without haveinge our mindes so preoccupied and taken up before, as noe roome is left for justice and right. Secondly, we are to give attention and diligent care to suche reasons as we shall heare delivered, either for or against any bill whatsoever. Thirdly, we must ingenuously and quietly submitt our judgements and suffer our opinions to be ruled, swayed, and ledd by the truth, force, and reason of thoes reasons, and so accordingly give our votes. And certainely thes are the true wayes, this the only clue to conduct us out of the pitt of passion, darcknesse of error, and laberinthe of selfe-love. . . . We ought to knowe that somewhat of worthe and value is expected from this action, and from us the actors in it; and this, bothe by the Company in England and the inhabitants here. Let us make it, therfore, our master peece, and not thincke the time long that we bestowe on this service. . . .

This speech being thus finished, the Assembly rose for that day (for they satt only in the morneinges), the afternoones being bestowed either in consultation with the Governour in his house, or upon some particuler committees to frame bussinesse against the next daye.

At the next meeting of the Assembly, the secretary reade all such Bills as were propounded, the which done, whosoever would rose up and spake either for it or against it, in which action this order was observed. He that entended to speake, stoode up (unlesse it were the Governour), bareheaded, wherby it was discerned that he had a meaneinge to speake. If more stoode up than one at once, he that was judged to arise first, was first heard. Every man was to direct his speach to the secretary, and to be heard without interruption. He that had once spoken to a Bill, though he wer presently answered and confuted, might not replye that day, so that none might speake twise to one and the same Bill in one daye; and this was to avoide over-much and tedeous disputes, and tautologies, and losse of time that waye. In speakeinge against any mans speach the partie spoken against was not personally to be named, to shunne therby heates of contention, and the giveinge of distates one to another. Noe revileinge nor nipinge speaches wer to be used upon any occasion whatsoever. All Bills wer to be reade three severall dayes once, and but once before they came to be consingned and concluded of by voices, that so in the meane time they might be advisedly examined, and every man have space to deliberate, and so to accept or reject them when they came to be put to the question. After a Bill was read three severall dayes, and sufficiently disputed upon, the secretary was to demand whether it should be putt to voices or noe, the which being graunted, the sayd secretary was to hold up the Bill in his hand and to saye, "All you that will have this Bill to passe for a lawe let them saye soe; as many as will not let them saye the contrary"; if the then crye affirmatively yea, wer found apparently greater than the negative noe, the Bill was passed for a lawe, if on the contrary, it was dashed. If it proved doubtfull which crye was the greater, the secretary was to saye thus: "As many as allowe the Bill, stand up on your feete; you that refuse it sitt still"; and then bothe the numbers being counted, the most carried it. And, in this fashion, all the Bills wer decided dureinge the whole session of the Assembly. Upon the last daye, all the Acts that wer passed wer reade, the which being done, the Governour dismissed and brake up the Assembly with a short speach, accordinge as the former passages of bussinesse had given him occasion.

And this order and forme was punctually observed dureing the whole time of the Session, dureing the which fifteene severall Acts wer, with a very great and generall unanimitie, agreed upon and enacted; the titles wherof only with some breife annexed reasons occasioninge them (for brevitie sake), shall be inserted in this history, referringe the reader for a large vewe (if he be so minded) to the bookes of statutes and the publick records, kept in the Ilands for the information of all men that are to live under their subjection.

I. The first whereof was an Act against the unjust sale, and lettinge out of apprentices and other servants, the which especially respected the rightinge of the undertakers in England, it being observed that divers inhabitants here haveinge committed unto their trust, by their undertakers in England, certaine servants and apprentices to be placed and settled upon their shares, the one halfe of whose labours wer to redound to the benefit of the undertaker, the other to the planter . . . and impotent persons. For it being considered that by the unheedefull and carelesse choice of some undertakers in England (who, this waye, caught at all they mett) ther had by some late importations, divers such bin throwne in and forced upon the colonye. . . .

III. The third Act was for the necessary mainteininge of the Kings-Castle. . . .

IV. The fourth provided against the makeinge of rotten and unmerchantable tobacco; triers of tobacco being yearely to be sworne in every tribe for the discovery of all bashawe and unsendible ware, all which by the sayd statute is enjoyned to be burned at the owners dore.

v. The fifth enjoyed the erection and frameinge of certaine publick bridges, and the maintenance of them. . . .

vi. The sixth statute was for a continuall supply of resident corne in the fortes. . . .

vii. The seventh appointed two fixed dayes in every yeare for the holdinge of the generall assize; the which was done by Act of Parliament, upon due and considerate choyce of the most proper and easefull times and seasons, that so, therby, publick notice and answerable preparation might be had of them, and noe mutations moved nor allowed.

viii. The eighth commanded the makeinge of highe wayes, and prohibited the goeing over mens ground. . . .

x. The tenth punished vagabonds, and prohibited the entertaininge of other mens servants.

xi. The eleventh enjoyned the settinge of a due quantitie of corne for every famelie, and a collection and keepeinge of a publick store in every tribe, the which was looked into, upon notice taken of the improvidence generally crept in amongst the inhabitants, both in the provideinge for it, and the keepeing of that litle they had.

xii. The twelfth Act respected the care of the corne being sett, and, therfore, commanded the keepeing in of poultry dureinge certaine weekes, and untill the corne was growen past their damnifieinge. . . .

xiii. The thirteenth was for the maintenance of sufficient fences, and against the fellinge downe of marcked trees appointed for boundes. . . .

xiv. The fourtenth graunted a levye of one thousand pounds of tobacco towards the payments of publick worcks for the yeare 1620.

xv. The fifteenth was bestowed in enjoyneinge an acknowledgement and acception of resident Governours, and for their warrantice, in case it should fall out that the date of their commissions be expired before the arrivall here of a legitimate successor from England, the which was apprehended very necessary and of great importancye, bothe for the avoideinge of the dangerous confusions that an anarchye, by a vacancye of goverment, might bring upon the whole plantation; as also for the cuttinge off of all coulours and pretences of unmeet and presumptious elections among themselues. . . .

And thes wer the contents of the fifteene Acts conferred and ennacted dureinge the Session of this generall Assembly, the which, being digested (as it is sayd by the Governours owne hand) into a convenient methode, wer sent into England by the magazin shyp, the *Joseph,* an. dom. 1620, ther to receive their confirmation and ratification by the Company in their courts ther, in such manner as, by His Majesties letters patents, is limited and appointed; and, in the meane time (as he was warranted by his instruction), the Governour did cause the sayd Acts to be publickly reade in all churches, and so to stand in full force, untill he heard the contrary from England.

❧ IV ❧

Massachusetts Bay: *Social Dispersion and Political Institutions*

THE Massachusetts Bay Company's charter (Doc. 10), granted in 1629, was similar in many respects to that given the Virginia Company in 1612. The Massachusetts Company contained two rival factions, however: a group of London merchants primarily interested in trade, and a group of country gentlemen, led by John Winthrop, who hoped to found an overseas colony that would provide a haven for Puritans. When the second group won control and prepared to emigrate, they decided to take their charter with them. Doing so was neither customary nor legal, and led to many difficulties and constitutional controversies. The political structure of the trading company had the potential for representative, if not democratic, government. The political ideas of the Puritan elite, however, were conservative and authoritarian. Throughout the 1630's, therefore, leaders of the freemen and the respective towns sought to modify the extensive control held by a tight-handed, though usually responsible, minority.

The historian hoping to trace those modifications through the public record of events meets with repeated frustration because the written proceedings of early General Courts were cursory and cryptic (Doc. 11). These proceedings reveal the skeleton of constitutional change, but not the flesh and bones. More helpful in this respect is Governor Winthrop's *History* of events in Massachusetts Bay during the first generation. John Winthrop (1587–1649) came from a Suffolk family of good social rank. He attended Trinity College, Cambridge, studied law at Gray's Inn in London, and established a successful legal practice there. In 1626 he was appointed one of the limited number of attorneys for the court of wards and liveries. Two years later he was admitted to the Inner Temple, and he frequently drafted petitions to be presented in Parliament.

In 1628 he also became involved with a group of Puritans planning to obtain a grant of land in eastern Massachusetts and plant a colony there. In 1630 Winthrop sailed from Southampton to help establish the new settlement on a secure basis. His intelligence, concern, and responsibility were immediately manifest, and in 1631, 1632, and 1633 he was elected governor. In April 1634, at the spring meeting of the General Court, restless freemen requested permission to examine the charter, which they had never seen. Only then did they discover that the General Court alone was entitled to legislate, and they wondered why some of its powers had been assumed by the magistrates.

Winthrop replied that the General Court had become unwieldy in size, and even suggested that it permanently relinquish some of its constitutional powers. The freemen refused to invalidate their charter privileges, and shortly replaced Winthrop as governor with Thomas Dudley. Winthrop records the political events of the next five years in his historical journal (Doc. 12), a source notable for its clear, earnest prose. It is the fullest single source for the first generation in Massachusetts history, but did not receive its initial publication until 1790. Like Governor Butler's *Historye of the Bermudaes,* it is the account of a partisan —a partisan of deep conviction, integrity, and candor. Winthrop was correct in noting (in 1639) what a flexible instrument the charter was, and that the freemen could be loose or strict constructionists as it suited their purpose.

Winthrop's journal is perhaps more useful for the 1630's than for the 1640's. Fortunately, the records of the General Court are fuller in the 1640's, and in them we can trace a variety of structural and procedural changes: bicameralism in 1644; an order concerning the election of magistrates and a proposition to reduce the number of deputies in 1644; and some orders affecting personnel in the General Court, 1648 (Doc. 13).

◦§ 10 §◦

The Charter of the Massachusetts Bay Company, 1629

. . . Thomas Adams, John Browne, Samuell Browne, Thomas Hutchins, William Vassall, William Pinchion, and George Fox-crofte, and all such others as shall hereafter be admitted and made free of the Company and Society hereafter mentioned, shall from tyme to tyme, and att all tymes forever hereafter be, by Vertue of theis presents, one Body corporate and politique in Fact and Name, by the Name of the Governor and Company of the Mattachusetts Bay in Newe-England, and them by the Name of the Governour and Company of the Mattachusetts Bay in Newe-England, one Bodie politique and corporate, in Deede, Fact, and Name; Wee doe for us, our Heires and Successors, make, ordeyne, constitute, and confirme by theis Presents, and that by that name they shall have perpetuall Succession, and that by the same Name they and their Successors shall and maie be capeable and enabled as well to implead, and to be impleaded, and to prosecute, demaund, and aunswere, and be aunsweared unto, in all and singuler Suites, Causes, Quarrells, and Accons, of what kinde or nature soever. And also to have, take, possesse, acquire, and purchase any Landes, Tenements, or Hereditaments, or any Goodes or Chattells, and the same to lease, graunte, demise, alien, bargaine, sell, and dispose of, as other our liege People of this our Realme of England, or any other corporation or Body politique of the same may lawfully doe.

AND FURTHER, That the said Governour and Companye, and their Successors, maie have forever one comon Seale, to be used in all Causes and Occasions of the said Company, and the same Seale may alter, chaunge, breake, and newe make, from tyme to

From Thorpe, ed., *The Federal and State Constitutions, Colonial Charters, and Other Organic Laws* . . . , III, pp. 1852-7.

tyme, at their pleasures. And our Will and Pleasure is, and Wee
doe hereby for Us, our Heires and Successors, ordeyne and
graunte, That from henceforth for ever, there shal be one Governor, one Deputy Governor, and eighteene Assistants of the same
Company, to be from tyme to tyme constituted, elected and
chosen out of the Freemen of the saide Company, for the tyme
being, in such Manner and Forme as hereafter in theis Presents
is expressed, which said Officers shall applie themselves to take
Care for the best disposeing and ordering of the generall buysines
and Affaires of, for, and concerning the said Landes and Premisses hereby mentioned, to be graunted, and the Plantation
thereof, and the Government of the People there. . . .

AND FURTHER, Wee will, and by theis Presents, for Us, our
Heires and Successors, doe ordeyne and graunte, That the Governor of the saide Company for the tyme being, or in his Absence
by Occasion of Sicknes or otherwise, the Deputie Governor for
the tyme being, shall have Authoritie from tyme to tyme upon
all Occasions, to give order for the assembling of the saide Company, and calling them together to consult and advise of the
Bussinesses and Affaires of the saide Company, and that the said
Governor, Deputie Governor, and Assistants of the saide Company, for the tyme being, shall or maie once every Moneth, or
oftener at their Pleasures, assemble and houlde and keepe a
Courte or Assemblie of themselves, for the better ordering and
directing of their Affaires, and that any seaven or more persons
of the Assistants, togither with the Governor, or Deputie Governor soe assembled, shal be saide, taken, held, and reputed to
be, and shal be a full and sufficient Courte or Assemblie of the
said Company, for the handling, ordering, and dispatching of
all such Buysinesses and Occurrents as shall from tyme to tyme
happen, touching or concerning the said Company or Plantation;
and that there shall or maie be held and kept by the Governor,
or Deputie Governor of the said Company, and seaven or more
of the said Assistants for the tyme being, upon every last Wednesday in Hillary, Easter, Trinity, and Michaelmas Termes respectivelie forever, one greate generall and solem assemblie,
which foure generall assemblies shal be stiled and called the

foure greate and generall Courts of the saide Company; IN all and every, or any of which saide greate and generall Courts soe assembled, WEE DOE for Us, our Heires and Successors, give and graunte to the said Governor and Company, and their Successors, That the Governor, or in his absence, the Deputie Governor of the saide Company for the tyme being, and such of the Assistants and Freemen of the saide Company as shal be present, or the greater number of them so assembled, whereof the Governor or Deputie Governor and six of the Assistants at the least to be seaven, shall have full Power and authoritie to choose, nominate, and appointe, such and soe many others as they shall thinke fitt, and that shall be willing to accept the same, to be free of the said Company and Body, and them into the same to admitt; and to elect and constitute such Officers as they shall thinke fitt and requisite, for the ordering, mannaging, and dispatching of the Affaires of the saide Governor and Company, and their Successors; And to make Lawes and Ordinances for the Good and Welfare of the saide Company, and for the Government and ordering of the saide Landes and Plantation, and the People inhabiting and to inhabite the same, as to them from tyme to tyme shal be thought meete, soe as such Lawes and Ordinances be not contrarie or repugnant to the Lawes and Statuts of this our Realme of England.

AND, our Will and Pleasure is, and Wee doe hereby for Us, our Heires and Successors, establish and ordeyne, That yearely once in the yeare, for ever hereafter, namely, the last Wednesday in Easter Tearme, yearely, the Governor, Deputy-Governor, and Assistants of the saide Company and all other officers of the saide Company shal be in the Generall Court or Assembly to be held for that Day or Tyme, newly chosen for the Yeare ensueing by such greater parte of the said Company, for the Tyme being, then and there present, as is aforesaide. AND, if it shall happen the present governor, Deputy Governor, and assistants, by theis presents appointed, or such as shall hereafter be newly chosen into their Roomes, or any of them, or any other of the officers to be appointed for the said Company, to dye, or to be removed from his or their severall Offices or Places before the

saide generall Day of Election (whome Wee doe hereby declare
for any Misdemeanor or Defect to be removeable by the Governor, Deputie Governor, Assistants, and Company, or such
greater Parte of them in any of the publique Courts to be assembled as is aforesaid). That then, and in every such Case, it shall
and maie be lawfull, to and for the Governor, Deputie Governor,
Assistants, and Company aforesaide, or such greater Parte of them
soe to be assembled as is aforesaide, in any of their Assemblies, to
proceade to a new Election of one or more others of their Company in the Roome or Place, Roomes or Places of such Officer or
Officers soe dyeing or removed according to their Discretions,
And, immediately upon and after such Election and Elections
made of such Governor, Deputie Governor, Assistant or Assistants, or any other officer of the saide Company, in Manner and
Forme aforesaid, the Authoritie, Office, and Power, before given
to the former Governor, Deputie Governor, or other Officer and
Officers soe removed, in whose Steade and Place newe shal be
soe chosen, shall as to him and them, and everie of them, cease
and determine. . . .

AND, further our Will and Pleasure is, and Wee doe hereby
for Us, our Heires and Successors, ordeyne and declare, and
graunte to the saide Governor and Company, and their Successors, That all and every the Subjects of Us, our Heires or Successors, which shall goe to and inhabite within the saide Landes
and Premisses hereby mentioned to be graunted, and every of
their Children which shall happen to be borne there, or on the
Seas in goeing thither, or retorning from thence, shall have and
enjoy all liberties and Immunities of free and naturall Subjects
within any of the Domynions of Us, our Heires or Successors, to
all Intents, Constructions, and Purposes whatsoever, as if they
and everie of them were borne within the Realme of England.
And that the Governor and Deputie Governor of the said Company for the Tyme being, or either of them, and any two or
more of such of the saide Assistants as shal be thereunto appointed by the saide Governor and Company at any of their
Courts or Assemblies to be held as aforesaide, shall and maie at
all Tymes, and from tyme to tyme hereafter, have full Power

and Authoritie to minister and give the Oathe and Oathes of
Supremacie and Allegiance, or either of them, to all and everie
Person and Persons, which shall at any Tyme or Tymes hereafter
goe or passe to the Landes and Premises hereby mentioned to
be graunted to inhabite in the same. AND, Wee doe of our further
Grace, certen Knowledg and meere Motion, give and graunte to
the saide Governor and Company, and their Successors, That it
shall and maie be lawfull, to and for the Governor or Deputie
Governor, and such of the Assistants and Freemen of the said
Company for the Tyme being as shal be assembled in any of
their generall Courts aforesaide, or in any other Courtes to be
specially sumoned and assembled for that Purpose, or the greater
Parte of them (whereof the Governor or Deputie Governor, and
six of the Assistants to be alwaies seaven) from tyme to tyme,
to make, ordeine, and establishe all Manner of wholesome and
reasonable Orders, Lawes, Statutes, and Ordinances, Directions,
and Instructions, not contrairie to the Lawes of this our Realme
of England, as well for setling of the Formes and Ceremonies
of Government and Magistracy, fitt and necessary for the said
Plantation, and the Inhabitants there, and for nameing and setting of all sorts of Officers, both superior and inferior, which
they shall finde needefull for that Governement and Plantation,
and the distinguishing and setting forth of the severall duties,
Powers, and Lymytts of every such Office and Place, and the
Formes of such Oathes warrantable by the Lawes and Statutes
of this our Realme of England, as shal be respectivelie ministred
unto them for the Execution of the said severall Offices and
Places; as also, for the disposing and ordering of the Elections
of such of the said Officers as shal be annuall, and of such others
as shal be to succeede in Case of Death or Removeall, and
ministring the said Oathes to the newe elected Officers, and for
Impositions of lawfull Fynes, Mulcts, Imprisonment, or other
lawfull Correction, according to the Course of other Corporations
in this our Realme of England, and for the directing, ruling, and
disposeing of all other Matters and Thinges, whereby our said
People, Inhabitants there, may be soe religiously, peaceablie,
and civilly governed, as their good Life and orderlie Conver-

sation, maie wynn and incite the Natives of Country, to the Knowledg and Obedience of the onlie true God and Savior of Mankinde, and the Christian Fayth, which in our Royall Intention, and the Adventurers free Profession, is the principall Ende of this Plantation.

⋖❦ 11 ❧⋗

The Proceedings of Two General Courts Held in Boston, 1632 and 1634

A Generall Court, holden att Boston, May 9th, 1632.
Present, The Governor,   Mr. Nowell,
         Deputy Governor,   Mr. Pinchon,
         Mr. Ludlowe,   S. Bradstreete

It was generally agreed upon, by erection of hands, that the Governor, Deputy Governor, & Assistants should be chosen by the whole Court of Governor, Deputy Governor, Assistants, & freemen, and that the Governor shall alwaies be chosen out of the Assistants.

John Winthrop, Esq, was chosen to the place of Governor (by the generall consent of the whole Court, manefested by erection of hands) for this yeare nexte ensueing, & till a newe be chosen, & did, in presence of the Court, take an oath to his said place belonging. . . .

It was ordered, that there should be two of every plantation appointed to conferre with the Court about raiseing of a publique stocke. . . .

It was ordered, that the towne of Waterton shall have that priviledge and interest in the [fish] weir they have built upp [the] Charles Ryver, according as the Court hereafter shall thinke meete to confirme unto them.

From Nathaniel B. Shurtleff, ed., *Records of the Governor and Company of the Massachusetts Bay in New England* (5 vols., Boston, 1853–4), I, 95–6 and 116–20.

Att a Generall Courte, holden at Boston, May 14th, 1634

. . . it is agreed, that none but the Generall Court hath power to chuse and admitt freemen.

That none but the Generall Court hath power to make and establishe lawes, nor to elect and appoynt officers, as Governor, Deputy Governor, Assistants, Tresurer, Secretary, Captain, Leiuetenants, Ensignes, or any of like moment, or to remove such upon misdemeanor, as also to sett out the dutyes and powers of the said officers.

That none but the Generall Court hath power to rayse moneyes & taxes, & to dispose of lands, viz, to give & confirme proprietyes. . . .

It was further ordered, that the constable of every plantation shall, upon proces receaved from the Secretary, give tymely notice to the freemen of the plantation where hee dwells to send soe many of their said members as the proces shall direct, to attend upon publique service; & it is agreed, that noe tryall shall passe upon any, for life or banishment, but by a jury soe summoned, or by the Generall Courte.

It is likewise ordered, that there shal be foure Generall Courts held yearely, to be summoned by the Governor, for the tyme being, & not to be dissolved without the consent of the major parte of the Court.

It was further ordered, that it shal be lawfull for the freemen of every plantation to chuse two or three of each towne before every Generall Court, to conferre of & prepare such publique busines as by them shal be thought fitt to consider of at the nexte Generall Court, & that such persons as shal be hereafter soe deputed by the freemen of [the] severall plantations, to deale in their behalfe, in the publique affayres of the commonwealth, shall have the full power and voyces of all the said freemen, deryved to them for the makeing & establishing of lawes, graunting of lands, etc., & to deale in all other affaires of the commonwealth wherein the freemen have to doe, the matter of election of magistrates & other officers onely excepted, wherein every freeman is to gyve his owne voyce. . . .

There is leave graunted to the inhabitants of Newe Towne to seeke out some convenient place for them, with promise that it shal be confirmed unto them, to which they may remove their habitations, or have as an addition to that which already they have, provided they doe not take it in any place to prejudice a plantation already setled. . . .

It was further ordered, that if any Assistant, or any man deputed by the freemen to deale in publique occasions of the commonwealthe, doe absent himselfe without leave in tyme of publique business, hee shal be fined att the discretion of the Court.

It is further ordered, that in all rates & publique charges, the townes shall have respect to levy every man according to his estate, & with consideration of all other his abilityes, whatsoever, & not according to the number of his persons.

⋙ 12 ⋘

Governor John Winthrop's Account
of Proceedings in 1632, 1634, and 1639

[February 17, 1632] The governor and assistants called before them, at Boston, divers [men] of Watertown; the pastor and elder by letter, and the others by warrant. The occasion was, for that a warrant being sent to Watertown for levying of £8, part of a rate of £60, ordered for the fortifying of the new town [Cambridge], the pastor and elder, etc., assembled the people and delivered their opinions, that it was not safe to pay moneys after that sort, for fear of bringing themselves and posterity into bondage. Being come before the governor and council, after much debate, they acknowledged their fault, confessing freely, that they were in an error, and made a retractation and submission under their hands, and were enjoined to read it in the assembly the next Lord's day. The ground of their error was,

From James K. Hosmer, ed., *Winthrop's Journal. "History of New England" 1630–1649* (New York, 1908), I, 75–9, 122–5, 302–5.

for that they took this government to be no other but as of a mayor and aldermen, who have not power to make laws or raise taxations without the people; but understanding that this government was rather in the nature of a parliament, and that no assistant could be chosen but by the freemen, who had power likewise to remove the assistants and put in others, and therefore at every general court (which was to be held once every year) they had free liberty to consider and propound anything concerning the same, and to declare their grievances, without being subject to question, or, etc., they were fully satisfied; and so their submission was accepted, and their offence pardoned.

[March 5, 1632] The first court after winter. It was ordered, that the courts (which before were every three weeks) should now be held the first Tuesday in every month.

. . .

[May 1, 1632] The governor and assistants met at Boston to consider of the deputy [Thomas Dudley] deserting his place. The points discussed were two. The 1st, upon what grounds he did it: 2d, whether it were good or void. For the 1st, his main reason was for public peace; because he must needs discharge his conscience in speaking freely; and he saw that bred disturbance, etc. For the 2d, it was maintained by all, that he could not leave his place, except by the same power which put him in; yet he would not be put from his contrary opinion, nor would be persuaded to continue till the general court, which was to be the 9th of this month. . . .

After dinner, the governor told them, that he had heard, that the people intended, at the next general court, to desire, that the assistants might be chosen anew every year, and that the governor might be chosen by the whole court, and not by the assistants only. Upon this, Mr. Ludlow grew into passion, and said, that then we should have no government, but there would be an interim, wherein every man might do what he pleased, etc. This was answered and cleared in the judgment of the rest of the assistants, but he continued stiff in his opinion, and protested he would then return back into England. . . .

[May 8, 1632] A general court at Boston. Whereas it was (at our first coming) agreed, that the freemen should choose the assistants, and they the governor, the whole court agreed now, that the governor and assistants should all be new chosen every year by the general court, (the governor to be always chosen out of the assistants;) and accordingly the old governor, John Winthrop, was chosen; accordingly all the rest as before, and Mr. Humfrey and Mr. Coddington also, because they were daily expected.

The deputy governor, Thomas Dudley, Esq., having submitted the validity of his resignation to the vote of the court, it was adjudged a nullity, and he accepted of his place again, and the governor and he being reconciled the day before, all things were carried very lovingly amongst all, etc., and the people carried themselves with much silence and modesty.

John Winthrop, the governor's son, was chosen an assistant.

A proposition was made by the people, that every company of trained men might choose their own captain and officers; but the governor giving them reasons to the contrary, they were satisfied without it.

Every town chose two men to be at the next court, to advise with the governor and assistants about the raising of a public stock, so as what they should agree upon should bind all, etc.

• • •

[April 1, 1634] Order was taken for ministering an oath to all house keepers and sojourners, being twenty years of age and not freemen, and for making a survey of the houses and lands of all freemen.

Notice being sent out of the general court to be held the 14th day of the third month, called May, the freemen deputed two of each town to meet and consider of such matters as they were to take order in at the same general court; who, having met, desired a sight of the patent, and, conceiving thereby that all their laws should be made at the general court, repaired to the governor to advise with him about it, and about the abrogating of some orders formerly made, as for killing of swine in corn, etc. He told them, that, when the patent was granted, the number of freemen was supposed to be (as in like corporations) so few, as they might well join in making laws; but now they were grown to so great a body, as it was not possible for them to make or execute laws, but they must choose others for that purpose: and that howsoever it would be necessary hereafter to have a select company to intend that work, yet for the present they were not furnished with a sufficient number of men qualified for such a business, neither could the commonwealth bear the loss of time of so many as must intend it. Yet this they might do at present, viz., they might, at the general court, make an order, that, once in the year, a certain number should be appointed (upon summons from the governor) to revise all laws, etc., and to reform what they found amiss therein; but not to make any new laws, but prefer their grievances to the court of assistants; and that no assessment should be laid upon the country without the consent of such a committee, nor any lands disposed of. . . .

[May 14, 1634] At the general court, Mr. Cotton preached, and delivered this doctrine, that a magistrate ought not to be turned into the condition of a private man without just cause, and to be publicly convict, no more than the magistrates may not turn a private man out of his freehold, etc., without like public trial, etc. This falling in question in the court, and the opinion of the rest of the ministers being asked, it was referred to further consideration.

The court chose a new governor, viz., Thomas Dudley, Esq., the former deputy; and Mr. Ludlow was chosen deputy; and John Haines, Esq., an assistant, and all the rest of the assistants chosen again.

At this court it was ordered, that four general courts should be kept every year, and that the whole body of the freemen should be present only at the court of election of magistrates, etc., and that, at the other three, every town should send their deputies, who should assist in making laws, disposing lands, etc. Many good orders were made this court. It held three days, and all things were carried very peaceably, notwithstanding that some of the assistants were questioned by the freemen for some errors in their government, and some fines imposed, but remitted again before the court brake up. The court was kept in the meeting-house at Boston, and the new governor and the assistants were together entertained at the house of the old governor, as before.

• • •

[May 22, 1639] The court of elections was; at which time there was a small eclipse of the sun. Mr. Winthrop was chosen governor again, though some laboring had been, by some of the elders and others to have changed, not out of any dislike of him, (for they all loved and esteemed him,) but out of their fear lest it might make way for having a governor for life, which some had propounded as most agreeable to God's institution and the practice of all well ordered states. But neither the governor nor any other attempted the thing; though some jealousies arose which were increased by two occasions. The first was, there being want of assistants, the governor and other magistrates thought fit (in the warrant for the court) to propound three, amongst which Mr. Downing, the governor's brother-in-law, was one, which they conceived to be done to strengthen his party, and therefore, though he were known to be a very able man, etc., and one who had done many good offices for the country, for these ten years, yet the people would not choose him. Another occasion of their jealousy was, the court, finding the number of deputies to be much increased by the addition of new plantations, thought fit, for the ease both of the country and the court, to reduce all towns to two deputies. This occasioned some to fear, that the magistrates intended to make themselves stronger, and the deputies weaker, and so, in time, to bring all power into the hands of the magistrates; so as the people in some towns were much displeased with their deputies for yielding to such an order. Whereupon, at the next session, it was propounded to have the number of deputies restored; and allegations were made, that it was an infringement of their liberty; so as, after much debate, and such reasons given for diminishing the number of deputies, and clearly proved that their liberty consisted not in the number, but in the thing, divers of the deputies, who came with intent to reverse the last order, were, by force of reason, brought to uphold it; so that, when it was put to the vote, the last order for two deputies only was confirmed. Yet, the next day, a petition was brought to the court from the freemen of Roxbury, to have the third deputy restored. Whereupon the reasons of the court's proceedings were set down in writing, and all objections answered, and sent to such towns as were unsatisfied with the advice, that, if any could take away those reasons, or bring us better for what they did desire, we should be ready, at the next court, to repeal the said order.

The hands of some of the elders (learned and godly men) were to this petition, though suddenly drawn in, and without due consideration, for the lawfulness of it may well be questioned: for when the people have chosen men to be their rulers, and to make their laws, and bound themselves by oath to submit thereto, now to combine together (a lesser part of them) in a public petition to have any order repealed, which is not repugnant to the law of God, savors of resisting an ordinance of God; for the people, having deputed others, have no power to make or alter laws, but are to be subject; and if any such order seem unlawful or inconvenient, they were better prefer some reasons, etc., to the court, with manifestation of their desire to move them to a review, than peremptorily to petition to have it repealed, which amounts to a plain reproof of those whom God hath set over them, and putting dishonor upon them, against the tenor of the fifth commandment. *love thy father + mother*

There fell out at this court another occasion of increasing the people's jealousy of their magistrates, viz.: One of the elders, being present with those of his church, when they were to prepare their votes for the election, declared his judgment, that a governor ought to be for his life, alleging for his authority the practice of all the best commonwealths in Europe, and especially that of Israel by God's own ordinance. But this was opposed by some other of the elders with much zeal, and so notice was taken of it by the people, not as a matter of dispute, but as

if there had been some plot to put it in practice, which did occasion the deputies, at the next session of this court, to deliver in
an order drawn to this effect: That, whereas our sovereign lord,
King Charles, etc., had, by his patent, established a governor,
deputy and assistants, that therefore no person, chosen a coun-
sellor for life, should have any authority as a magistrate, except
he were chosen in the annual elections to one of the said places of
magistracy established by the patent. This being thus bluntly
tendered, (no mention being made thereof before,) the governor
took time to consider of it, before he would put it to vote. So,
when the court was risen, the magistrates advised of it, and
drew up another order to this effect: That whereas, at the
court in [*blank*,] it was ordered, that a certain number of magistrates should be chosen to be a standing council for life, etc.,
whereupon some had gathered that we had erected a new order of magistrates not warranted by our patent, this court
doth therefore declare, that the intent of the order was, that
the standing council should always be chosen out of the magistrates, etc.; and therefore it is now ordered, that no such coun-
sellor shall have any power as a magistrate, nor shall do any
act as a magistrate, etc., except he be annually chosen, etc.,
according to the patent; and this order was after passed by
vote. That which led those of the council to yield to this
desire of the deputies was, because it concerned themselves,
and they did more study to remove these jealousies out of the
people's heads, than to preserve any power or dignity to themselves above others; for till this court those of the council, viz.,
Mr. Endecott, had stood and executed as a magistrate, without
any annual election, and so they had been reputed by the elders
and all the people till this present. But the order was drawn
up in this form, that it might be of less observation and freer
from any note of injury to make this alteration rather by way
of explanation of the fundamental order, than without any
cause shown to repeal that which had been established by
serious advice of the elders, and had been in practice two or
three years without any inconvenience. And here may be
observed, how strictly the people would seem to stick to their

patent, where they think it makes for their advantage, but are content to decline it, where it will not warrant such liberties as they have taken up without warrant from thence, as appears in their strife for three deputies, etc., when as the patent allows them none at all, but only by inference, etc., voting by proxies, etc.

◄§ 13 §►

Structural and Procedural Changes in the General Court, 1644–1648

A. Bicameralism: The Magistrates and Deputies Decide to Sit Apart, March 7, 1644

Forasmuch as, after long experience, wee find divers inconveniences in the manner of our proceeding in Courts by magistrates & deputies siting together, & accounting it wisdome to follow the laudable practice of other states who have layd groundworks for government & order in the issuing of busines of greatest & highest consequence,—

It is therefore ordered, first, that the magistrates may sit & act busines by themselves, by drawing up bills & orders which they shall see good in their wisdome, which haveing agreed upon, they may present them to the deputies to bee considered of, how good & wholesome such orders are for the country, & accordingly to give their assent or dissent, the deputies in like manner siting apart by themselves, & consulting about such orders & lawes as they in their discretion & experience shall find meete for common good, which agreed upon by them, they may present to the magistrates, who, according to their wisdome, haveing seriously considered of them, may consent unto them or disalow them; & when any orders have passed the approbation of both magistrates & deputies, then such orders to bee ingrossed, & in the last day of the Court to bee read deliberately, & full assent to bee given; provided, also, that all

From Shurtleff, ed., *Records of the Governor and Company of the Massachusetts Bay* . . . , II, 58–9, 87–9, 259–60.

matters of judicature which this Court shall take cognisance of
shal bee issued in like manner.

B. An Order Concerning the Election of Magistrates, and
A Proposition to Reduce the Number of Deputies
and Change the Manner of Electing Them,
November 13, 1644

It is ordered, that the freemen of this jurisdiction shall meete
in their severall townes within two months after the date
hereof, to consider of whom they would nominate to be put
to vote upon the day of election for newe magistrates, to the
number of seaven, at which meeting every freeman shall have
liberty to put in his vote for whom hee thinketh fit, all which
votes shal be sealed up at that meeting, & sent by some one
or two (whom they shall choose) to the sheire townes in each
sheire, upon the last 5th day of the last month, at which meeting
the said selectmen of every towne (by whom the votes being
brought) shall not have power to open them, being sealed up,
as before, but shall choose one or two from amongst themselves,
by whom they shall send the aforesaid votes, being all sealed
up in one paper, unto Boston, on the last third day of the first
month, at which meeting there shal be two magistrates, before
whom the proxies shal be opened & sorted; & those persons
nominated for magistrates that have most votes, to the number
of seaven, shal be they that shal be put to vote at the day of
election; & that such as have most votes to be first nominated
& put to election, that the freemen may know for whom to
send in their proxies. The select men of every sheire, being at
this meeting, shall take care to send to the aforesaid selectmen
of every towne whom they be that are to be put to vote, which
select men of every towne shall call a meeting of their townes,
& acquaint them whom they are, that so the freemen may have
time to consider of them, & send in their proxies accordingly; &
no other shal be put to vote but such as are agreed upon, as
before.

Whereas wee haveing found by experience that the charge of this Generall Court groweth very great & burthensome, in regard of the continuall increase of deputies sent unto the same, & further forseeing that as townes increase the number wil be still augmented, to the unsupportable burthen of this common wealth; as also it being thought a matter worthy the triall, dureing the standing of this order, to have the use of the negative vote forborne, both by magistrates & deputies, the premisses considered, it is declared by this Court, (if the freemen shall accept thereof,) that a tryall shal be made for one yeare ensuing the day of election next, by choyce of twenty deputies out of the severall sheires to equall the number of magistrates chosen upon the day of election, the choyce of them to be thus divided: Suffolke shall choose sixe, Middlesex sixe, & Essex & Norfolk, being joyned in one, shall choose eight; and further, to the end the ablest gifted men may be made use of in so weighty a worke, it shal be at the liberty of the freemen to choose them, in their own sheires, or elsewhere, as they shall see best, the choyce to be after this manner: the freemen of each shire, meeting in their owne severall townes together within two months next following, shall there give in their severall votes for so many deputies as belong unto their sheire to choose, which votes shal be forthwith sealed up, & one or two chosen to carry them sealed to their sheire towne the last 5th day of the last month following, where, in the presence of one magistrate, they shal be opened & conferd togeather, & so many as shall have the major vote of the sheire are chosen, not exceeding the number aforesaid; & such as are so chosen shall assemble themselves at the next Court of Election, presented under the hands of those which were sent from the townes to the sheire meetings aforesaid, the names & severall number of votes they there had, from which assembly those onely that had the greatest number of votes, to equall the number of magistrates then chosen, shal be confirmed, & the rest dismissed from the present service, from every sheire alike number, so neare as may be; the magistrates & deputies thus chosen shall sit togeather as a full

& sufficient Generall Court, to act in all things by the major
vote of the whole Court; & further, it is declared, that every
towne shall fourthwith, namely, by the last of the next month,
send in under the hands of their late deputies their vote, assent-
ing or dissenting to this proposition, to the house of Mr. Nowell,
who, together with one of the late deputies of Charlestowne,
one of Cambridge, & one of Boston, shall have power to peruse
the said votes, & if they shall find that the greater number of
the townes shall agree that this may be propounded to them
shall proceed, they shall thereupon fourthwith certify the Governor thereof, who shall thereupon give speedy notice to every
towne that they may proceed according to this declaration; &
whereas it may fall out that two or more sheires may make
choyce of one & the same men, it is therefore provided, that
Suffolk shall begin makeing knowne to Middlesex whom they
have chosen, who the next 4th day following shall make their
choyce, & send word to Essex & Norfolke whom Suffolk & themselves have chosen; then the next 4th day shall Essex & Norfolke
make their choyce.

C. Some Orders Concerning Procedures and
Personnel in the General Court, October 18, 1648

For the better carrying on the occasions of the Generall Court,
& to the end that the records of the same, together with what
shall be presented by way of petition, etc, or passes by way of
vote, either amongst the magistrates or deputies, may hereafter
be more exactly recorded, & kept for publike use,—

It is hereby ordered, that as there is a secretary amongst
the magistrates, (who is the generall officer of the common
wealth, for the keeping the publike records of the same,) so
there shall be a clarke amongst the deputies, to be chosen by
them, from time to time; that (by the Courte of Elections, and
then the officers to begin their entryes, their recompence accordingly) there be provided, by the auditor, four large paper books,
in folio, bound up with velum & pastboard, two whereof to be

delivered to the secretary, & two to the clarke of the House of Deputies, one to be a journall to each of them, the other for the faire entry of all lawes, acts, & orders, etc, that shall passe the magistrates & deputies, that of the secretaries to be the publike record of the country, that of the clarkes to be a booke onely of coppies.

That the secretary & clarke for the deputies shall briefly enter into their journals, respectively, the titles of all bills, orders, lawes, petitions, etc, which shal be presented & read amongst them, what are referd to committees, & what are voted negatively or affirmatively, & so for any addition or alteration.

That all bills, lawes, petitions, etc, which shal be last concluded amongst the magistrates, shall remaine with the Governor till the latter end of that sessions, & such as are last assented to be the deputies shall remaine with the speaker till the said time, when the whole Courte shall meete together, or a committee of magistrates & deputies, to consider what hath passed that sessions, where the secretary & clarke shall be present, & by their journals call for such bils, etc, as hath passed either house, & such as shall appeare to have passed the magistrates & deputies shall be delivered to the secretary to record, who shall record the same within one month after every sessions, which being done, the clarke of the deputies shall have liberty, for one month after, to transcribe the same into his booke; & such bills, orders, etc, that hath onely passed the magistrates, shall be delivered to the secretary to keepe upon file, & such as have onely passed the deputies shal be delivered to their clarke to be kept upon file, in like manner, or otherwise disposed of, as the whole Court shall appoint; that all lawes, orders, & acts of Courte, contained in the ould bookes, that are of force, & not ordered to be printed, be transcribed in some alphabeticall or methodicall way, by direction of some committee that this Courte shall please to appoint, & delivered to the secretary to record in the first place, in the said booke of records, & then the acts of the other sessions in order accordingly, & a coppy of all to be transcribed by the clarke of the deputies, as aforesaid.

That the secretary be alowed, for his paines, twenty marke per annum, & the clarke of the deputies ten pound per annum, to be paid out of the treasury, till the Court shall appoint their recompence by fees, or otherwise.

❧ V ❧

The Carolinas:
Constitutional Designs and Political Realities

ON March 24, 1663, Charles II approved a charter granting a huge area of land south of Virginia, called
Carolina, to eight of his political supporters. The grantees were
designated "the true and absolute Lords and Proprietaries" of the
province, and their charter (Doc. 14) provided the basis for
the beginnings of representative government in both Carolinas.
It also gave the proprietors feudal powers equal to those possessed centuries earlier by the bishop of the county palatine of
Durham. By 1663 a few settlers from Virginia had begun to
move into the area adjoining Albemarle Sound. Proprietors and
settlers alike assumed that this area had been included in the
charter grant. In fact it had not. Not until June 1665 were the
proprietors given legal authority over the Albemarle area (and
other territory) by issuance of a second charter.

For most of its first two years, government in Carolina
was based upon the proprietors' temporary authorizations and
instructions. In January 1665 they adopted a more formal and
permanent plan of government, which they incorporated in an
agreement made with a group of colonists from Barbados who
proposed to settle in the Cape Fear region. These Concessions
and Agreement of 1665 (Doc. 15) constituted the first over-all
plan of government put into effect in Carolina. Although designed primarily for new settlements, it applied also to the
existing colony in Albemarle. One of the most significant features
of the Concessions and Agreement was the considerable power

given to the popular assembly—far more than was required by
the proprietors' charter. In consequence, the assembly became
a major institution of government during the early years of the
Albemarle colony. Later, under the Fundamental Constitutions
of 1669 (Doc. 16), the assembly lost much of its power; and
many years passed before it regained its former status.

In 1669, the proprietors adopted this new plan of government, known officially as the "Fundamental Constitutions of
Carolina." Its primary purpose was to promote the interests of
the proprietors and to "avoid erecting a numerous Democracy."
Presumably the Fundamental Constitutions could provide a constitutional structure that would enable the proprietors to exercise
the feudal powers granted by their charters. Thus the supreme
agency of government provided for Carolina was the palatine's
court, composed of the eight proprietors, the eldest of whom
would hold the office of palatine.

The eight proprietors (or their deputies) and the 42 councillors who sat with them would constitute a grand council
meeting on the first Tuesday in each month. Among its other
duties, this grand council would prepare all matters to be put
before parliament, a body that was to meet automatically every
two years, as was the case in most of the experimental constitutions put forward by the Levellers and others after the Civil
War in England. The parliament envisioned for Carolina would
differ from them, however, by including in the same chamber
a hereditary body (proprietors, landgraves, and caciques) and
an elected group of four freemen from each county. Equilibrium
was the prime concern.

Although the proprietors expected eventually to make the
Fundamental Constitutions fully operative, they never succeeded.
The various written instructions sent to governors were, in effect,
modifications; and from time to time the proprietors issued formal revisions. On March 1, 1670, for example, they adopted a new
version which supplanted its original predecessor.

But since *de facto* government in the Carolinas occurred
through modifications of the Constitutions contained in pro-

prietary instructions, alterations in the formal, official version
had little effect. Hence the importance of instructions sent to
the governor and council of the Ashley River settlement (South
Carolina) on May 1, 1671 (Doc. 17). More than that, a letter
from Governor Joseph West and the council at Albemarle in
March 1671 (Doc. 18) reveals just how far removed were political realities from constitutional designs. West and his colleagues
firmly believed that there were too few people in Carolina to elect
a parliament, that despite the presence of good parliamentarians,
a parliament was less urgently needed than the planting of
corn. By the close of this letter the council had made clear its
determination to control the convening of an assembly, if one
had to exist at all.

◄§ 14 §►

Charter to the Lords Proprietors
of Carolina, March 1663

KNOW YE, that We, of our further grace, certain knowledge, and
mere motion, HAVE thought fit to Erect the same Tract of Ground,
Country, and Island into a Province, and, out of the fullness of
our Royal power and Prerogative, WE DO, for us, our heirs and
Successors, Erect, Incorporate, and Ordain the same into a province, and do call it the Province of CAROLINA, and so from henceforth will have it called.

AND FORASMUCH AS we have hereby made and Ordained the
aforesaid Edward, Earl of Clarendon; George, Duke of Albemarle; William, Lord Craven; John, Lord Berkley; Anthony,
Lord Ashley; Sir George Carterett; Sir William Berkley; and Sir
John Colleton, their heirs and Assigns, the true Lords and Proprietors of all the Province aforesaid:

KNOW YE, therefore, moreover, that We, reposing especial
Trust and Confidence in their fidelity, Wisdom, Justice, and
provident circumspection, for us, our heirs and Successors, Do

From Mattie E. E. Parker, ed., *North Carolina Charters and Constitutions, 1578–1698* (Raleigh, N.C., 1963), 78–9.

Grant full and absolute power, by virtue of these presents, to them, the said Edward, Earl of Clarendon; George, Duke of Albemarle; William, Lord Craven; John, Lord Berkley; Anthony, Lord Ashley; Sir George Carterett; Sir William Berkley; and Sir John Colleton, and their heirs, for the good and happy Government of the said Province:

To ORDAIN, make, Enact, and under their Seals to publish any Laws whatsoever, either appertaining to the public State of the said Province or to the private utility of particular Persons, according to their best discretion, of and with the advice, assent, and approbation of the Freemen of the said Province, or of the greater part of them, or of their Delegates or Deputies; whom, for enacting of the said Laws, when and as often as need shall require, WE WILL that the said Edward, Earl of Clarendon; George, Duke of Albemarle; William, Lord Craven; John, Lord Berkley; Anthony, Lord Ashley; Sir George Carterett; Sir William Berkley; and Sir John Colleton, and their heirs, shall, from time to time, assemble, in such manner and form as to them shall seem best;

AND the same Laws duly to execute upon all people within the said Province and Limits thereof for the time being, or which shall be Constituted under the power and Government of them, or any of them, either Sailing towards the said Province of CAROLINA or returning from thence towards England, or any other of our foreign Dominions; by Imposition of penalties, Imprisonment, or any other punishment, YEA, if it shall be needful and the quality of the Offence require it, by taking away member and life, either by them, the said Edward, Earl of Clarindon; George, Duke of Albemarle; William, Lord Craven; John, Lord Berkley; Anthony, Lord Ashley; Sir George Carterett; Sir William Berkley; and Sir John Colleton, and their heirs, or by them or their Deputies, Lieutenants, Judges, Justices, Magistrates, Officers, and Ministers, to be Ordained or appointed according to the tenor and true intention of these presents.

❧ 15 ❧

The Concessions and Agreement Between the Lords Proprietors and Major William Yeamans and Others, January 1665

10. ITEM, That the Inhabitants being freemen, or Chief agents to others, of the Counties aforesaid do, as soon as this our Commission shall arrive, by Virtue of a writ in our Names, by the Governor to be, for the present, Until our seal comes, Sealed and signed, make Choice of twelve Deputies or representatives from amongst themselves, who, being Chosen, are to Join with him, the said Governor, and Council, for the making of such Laws, Ordinances, and Constitutions as shall be necessary for the present good and welfare of the Several Counties aforesaid; but as soon as Parishes, divisions, tribes, or districts of the said Counties are made, that then, the Inhabitants or Freeholders of the Several and respective Parishes, Tribes, divisions, or districts of the Counties aforesaid do, by our writs, under our Seal, which we Engage shall be in due time issued, Annually meet on the first day of January and Choose freeholders for each respective division, Tribe, or parish, to be the deputies or representatives of the same; which body of Representatives, or the Major part of them, shall, with the Governor and Council aforesaid, be the General Assembly of the County for which they shall be Chosen, the Governor, or his Deputy, being present, Unless they shall wilfully refuse; in which Case, they may appoint themselves a president during the absence of the Governor, or his Deputy Governor.

WHICH ASSEMBLIES ARE TO HAVE POWER:

1. ITEM, To appoint their own times of meeting and to adjourn their Sessions from time to time to such times and places as they shall think Convenient; as also, to ascertain the Number of their Quorum; Provided, that such numbers be not less than

From Parker, ed., *North Carolina Charters and Constitutions, 1578– 1698*, 115–18.

the third part of the whole, in whom or more shall be the full power of the General Assembly, Viz.:

2. ITEM, To Enact and make all such Laws, Acts, and constitutions as shall be necessary for the well Government of the County for which they shall be Chosen, and them to repeal; Provided, that the same be consonant to reason and, as near as may be Conveniently, agreeable to the Laws and Customs of his Majesty's Kingdom of England; Provided also, that they be not against the Interest of Us, the Lords Proprietors, our heirs or assigns, nor any of these our present Concessions, Especially that they be not against the Article for Liberty of Conscience above mentioned; which Laws, etc., so made, shall receive publication from the Governor and Council, but as the Laws of Us and our General Assembly, and be in force for the space of one year and a half, and no more, Unless Contradicted by the Lords Proprietors, within which time they are to be presented to Us, our heirs, etc., for our Ratification; and being confirmed by Us, they shall be in Continual force till expired by their own Limitation, or by Act of Repeal, in like manner, as aforesaid, to be passed and Confirmed.

3. ITEM, By act, as aforesaid, to Constitute all Courts for their respective Counties, together with the Limits, powers, and Jurisdictions of the said Courts; as also, the Several Offices and Number of officers belonging to each of the said respective Courts, Together with their Several and respective Salaries, fees, and perquisites, Their appellations and dignities, with the penalties that shall be due to them for breach of their Several and respective duties and Trusts.

4. ITEM, By act, as aforesaid, to lay equal taxes and Assessments, equally to raise monies or goods, Upon all Lands (excepting the Lands of Us, the Lords Proprietors, before Settling) or persons within the Several precincts, Hundreds, Parishes, Manors, or whatsoever other divisions shall hereafter be made and Established in the said Counties, as oft as necessity shall require, and in such manner as to them shall seem most equal and easy for the said Inhabitants, in order to the better supporting

of the public Charge of the said Government, and for the mutual
safety, defence, and Security of the said Counties. . . .

10. ITEM, The General Assembly, by Act, as aforesaid, shall
make provision for the Maintenance and Support of the Governor
and for the defraying of all Necessary Charges of the Government; As also, that the Constables of the respective Counties
shall Collect the half penny per acre payable to the Lords in their
Counties, and pay the same to the receiver that the Lords shall
appoint to receive the same, unless the said General Assembly
shall prescribe some other way whereby the Lords may have
their rents duly Collected without Charge or trouble to them.

11. LASTLY, To enact, constitute, and Ordain all such other
Laws, acts, and constitutions as shall or may be necessary for
the good prosperity and Settlement of the said Counties, excepting what by these presents are excepted, and Conforming to
Limitations herein expressed.

◦§ 16 §◦

The Fundamental Constitutions
of Carolina, July 21, 1669

65. There shall be a Parliament, consisting of the Proprietors,
or their deputies, the Landgraves and Caciques, and one Freeholder out of every Precinct, to be Chosen by the Freeholders
of the said Precinct respectively. They shall sit all together in
one Room, and have every member one Vote.

66. No man shall be Chosen a member of Parliament who
has less than five hundred Acres of Freehold within the Precinct

From Parker, ed., *North Carolina Charters and Constitutions, 1578–
1698*, 145–7. At least 4 different Ms. versions of the Fundamental Constitutions (July 21, 1669) have been found, and historians cannot be sure
which was the first actually put into use. The version used here, called the
Locke Manuscript, has been chosen because of its association with the
famous political philosopher and because its full text is readily available for
consultation by students. The version of March 1670 was most likely the
one formally adopted by the proprietors and held by them to be official.

for which he is Chosen; nor shall any have a vote in choosing the said member that has less than fifty acres of Freehold within the said precinct.

67. A new Parliament shall be assembled the first Monday of the Month of November every second year, and shall meet and Sit in the Town they last Sat in, without any Summons, unless by the Palatine, or his Deputy, together with any three of the Proprietors, or their Deputies, they be Summoned to meet at any other place; and if there shall be any occasion of a Parliament in these Intervals, it shall be in the power of the Palatine, with any three of the Proprietors, to assemble them on forty days' notice, at such time and place as they shall think fit; and the Palatine, or his Deputy, with the advice and consent of any three of the Proprietors, or their Deputies, shall have power to dissolve the Said Parliament when they shall think fit.

68. At the opening of every Parliament, the first thing that shall be done shall be the reading of these fundamental constitutions, which the Palatine, and Proprietors, and the rest of the members then present shall Subscribe. Nor shall any Person whatsoever Sit or Vote in the Parliament till he has, that Sessions, Subscribed these fundamental constitutions in a book kept for that purpose by the Clerk of the Parliament.

69. And in order to the due Election of members for this Biennial Parliament, it shall be lawful for the Freeholders of the respective precincts to meet the first Tuesday in September every two years, in the Same Town or place that they last met in, to choose Parliament men, and there choose those members that are to Sit the next November following, unless the Steward of the Precinct shall, by Sufficient notice Thirty days before, appoint some other place for their meeting in order to the Election.

70. No act or Order of Parliament shall be of any force unless it be Ratified in open Parliament, during the same Session, by the Palatine, or his Deputy, and three more of the Proprietors, or their deputies; and then not to continue longer in force but until the End of the next Biennial Parliament, unless in the mean time it be Ratified under the hand and seal of the Palatine

him self and three more of the Proprietors them selves, and, by their Order, published at the next Biennial Parliament.

71. Any Proprietor, or his Deputy, may enter his Protestation against any act of the Parliament, before the Palatine or his deputy's consent be given as aforesaid, if he shall conceive the said act to be contrary to this Establishment or any of these Fundamental Constitutions of the Government; and in Such case, after a full and free debate, the several Estates shall retire into four several Chambers, the Palatine and Proprietors into one, the Landgraves into another, and the Caciques into another, and those Chosen by the Precincts into a fourth; and if the major part of any four of these Estates shall Vote that the law is not agreeable to this Establishment and fundamental constitution of the Government, then it shall pass no further, but be as if it had never been proposed.

72. To avoid multiplicity of laws, which by degrees always change the Right foundations of the Original Government, all acts of Parliament whatsoever, in what form soever passed or enacted, shall, at the end of Sixty years after their enacting, respectively Cease and determine of them selves, and, without any repeal, become Null and void, as if no such acts or laws had ever been made.

◄§ 17 §►

The Lords Proprietors' Instructions to the Governor
and Council of Ashley River
[South Carolina], May 1, 1671

1. You are within thirty days after receit hereof to summon the Freeholders of the Plantation, & require them in our names to elect 20 persons who, togeather with our Deputys as our Representatives, for the present are to be your Parliament, by and with whose consent, or the major part of them, you are to make such Laws as you shall finde necessary which Acts shall

From *The Shaftesbury Papers*, in *Collections of the South Carolina Historical Society* (Charleston, S.C., 1897*)*, V, 322–3.

be in force as in that case is provided in our Fundamentall Constitutions & Temporary Laws.

2. After the same maner till our Fundamentall Constitution can be put in practice you are to call a Parliament the first Monday in November every two years, and as often besides as the state of our affaires in our Plantation shall require.

3. You are to require the Parliament to choose five men whom they thinke fittest to be joyned with our five Deputys, who with the five eldest men of the Nobility are to be your Grand Councell.

◄§ 18 §►

A Letter from Governor Joseph West and the Council at Albemarle Point to the Lords Proprietors of Carolina, March 21, 1671

May itt please your Honours

Itt is nott a little trouble to us, that wee should have occasion, to presente before your Honours, those unsavory accounts in this Collony, which wee have indeavored, soe much to suppress . . . thus from tyme to tyme since our Arrivall in this place, have wee found the like intrusions, which hitherto wee have smothered, butt of late, those sparks meeting with more fuell, have binn indeavored to bee blown upp into a flame, by Mr. William Owen chiefly & Mr Wiliam Scrivener, Deputy to our very good Lord, the Lord Berkly, which wee are as unwilling to take notice of, or remember, as to give your Honours the trouble, were itt Nott to purge the aire from such infeccons. . . .

When wee Safely arrived att Port Royall . . . the said Late Governor Pursuant to your Honours directions Summoned all the freemen, & there to Ellect & choose five men to bee of the Councill, as your Honours have directed; The freemen proceeding to Ellection, having by that tyme thoroughly discovered the said william Owen, wholely rejected him: & chose Mr Paule Smith, Mr Roberte Donne, Mr Ralphe Marshall, Mr Samuell

From *The Shaftesbury Papers*, in *Collections of the South Carolina Historical Society*, V, 290–5.

West, & Mr Joseph Dalton, to bee their representitives, which accordingly was recorded; butt the said william Owen finding his desiers (alwaies itching to bee in Authority) frustrated, could nott butt Censure the legality of the Election, whereupon the said freeholders or the major parte of them, mett a second tyme, & confirmed their former Election, by subscribing of their severall names: This instead of a reformacon in the said william Owen, (which wee could well have wished) prooved one sparke more to his fire, as hereafter will appeare.

About the 4th of July last, the said late Governor & Councell, having binn informed how much the Sabboth Day was Prophanely violated, & of divers other grand abuses, practised by the people, to the greate dishonor of God Almighty, & the destruction of good Neighbourhood; the said Governor & Councell did seriously consider, by which way or means, the same might bee redrest, & finding, that the Number of freehoulders in the Collony nott neere sufficient to Electe a Parliament; the said late Governor by & with the advice, & consent of us his Councell, did make such orders, as wee did think convenient to suppress the same, upon which the said Governor did Summons all the People to heare the said Orders, all the said freemen consenting thereunto the said Governor & Councell caused the said orders to bee published; whereupon the said william Owen, willing to doe anything, though ever soe ill in itt selfe, rather than not to apeare to bee a man of action, indeavored to possesse the people, that without a Parliament noe such orders ought, or could passe; the rather, being seconded by the said Mr william Scrivener, and while the said Governor & Councell were discursing That, & other matters, the said william Owen perswaded the people, to Elect a Parliament among themselves, which they did, & reterned to the said Governor; The Originall, being the writing of the said william Owen, wee have sent heere inclosed to your Honours, two of which Parliament men were then in dispute, whether they were Servants or freemen . . . butt how the said william Owen Did proceed in the Election, wee doe nott yett understand, All the rest of the freemen being moved, by the said william Owen, in another

Spheere than their owne, After that the said william Owen had taken their Names, without any farther notice takinge of the said william Owen, or their Election into dignity, (as the said Owen perswaded them itt would bee) lefte the said Owen, & his Paper, & followed their other Labours, which indeed neerely concerned them & us too. And the said Owen having noe inclination to bee alone, went home for Company. . . . Butt the said william Owen finding himselfe swalloed up in a generall consent; invents a New Stratagem, & Singles out the Cheife of the people, Especially the New Comers, & Possess them, that hee had discovered, that the great seale of the Province nott beinge in the Collony, whatever land they had or should take up, & their Improvements therein, would nott bee assured to them, butt might bee taken away att pleasure, unlesse a parliament bee forthwith chosen to prevent the same; this takes with the people (most men being Naturally inclined, sooner to receive the beleife of a seeming injury, than a reall truth) That they should venture soe far for land, the tytle whereof was uncertaine, & thereupon the people might well bee incited to an Incredulity of the performance of your Honours other Declarations; Now the said Owen hath hit the marke, hee is what hee would bee, the leader of a company of people upon any tearmes; he is now the peoples prolocutor, & therefore must have roome in the Councell, to show himselfe & the peoples grievances; thus before the said Governor & Councell, & att the fronte of the people Champion-like, hee would undertake to reveale, what hee long had Studdied, the true Interpretation of your Honours Instructions, & the peoples rights, & Priviledges involved therein, with various argumentations . . . The said Governor having patiently heard, what the said Owen had to say, & finding, that the said Owen had ill advised the people, directed his Speech to the said people, & gave them to understand, that by vertue of Authority, derived from your Honours Instructions, Dated the 26th July, 1669: with the Consent of his Councell, hee did Conceive, he had Sufficient Power to Convey, & assuer to them, All such lands, for such Estates, & with such provisoes, & limitations, as your Honours by your Instructions, & consessions, on that behalfe had directed, & would carefully doe the same, untill hee had received the said seale of the Province, from your Honours; And when the said seale shall come, All their Grants should for the better Confirmation of their tytles Pass under the said seale: And as for the Election of the Parliament, which the said Owen had soe long Studied Rhetorically to Demande, the said Governor declared, that That tyme was some what unseasonable, & that hee did intend to summons the people for the Election of a parliament when opportunity did serve or necessity of makinge lawes did requier, upon which, All or most of the said freemen, being fully satisfied of the truth thereof, (& upon the said Governors command) were about to withdraw themselves; as that all doubts were removed from them. . . . Thus having given your Honours a relation of what wee have done, wee shall now, give an Account of what wee intend to doe; having hitherto endeavored as much as in us lyes, to have all our Actions well represented abroad, that soe the merritt of this place, & the manadgment thereof keeping tyme, the harmony might bee approved of, by all Judicious Eares, and having (blessed bee god) binn successfull in our reports of this place, & confirmed by those, that thereupon are now becom eye wittnesses, wee should be very sorry, that anything should be Acted here, that might proove distastefull abroad; being very sencible, that the name of a Parliament is strangly represented abroad; that the quality of our Parliament men, might not give an occasion of Disputing in other parts, & noe great necessity att present of a Parliament, our tyme being well imployed, if wee cann imploy it well, in Planting & other necessary works that lyeth upon us, knowing how treacherous reports are, wee have therefore deferred the summoning of a Parliament till the shipps be gone, att which tyme the heat of Planting being over, we shall, (now some more people are come), proceed to the prosecution of your Honours Instructions, by and with the Consent of the Parliament or the major parte of them, to make such lawes, as wee shall finde necessary in this Place; in the meane tyme wee humbly desier your Honours, farther to Inlardge your Instructions, (vizt) how long this Parliament is to continue; as we humbly Conceive itt wil bee moste convenient, for 2 or 3 yeares yett to com, that they bee dissolved upon pleasure of the Governor & Councill for the tyme being, & a summons for a new Election, may bee issued out att any tyme; by means whereof many people arriving here, from tyme, to tyme, some of worth, such as a Parliament may bee found ere Long, whose wisedome, & experience, may nott onely consent, butt assist, your Honours Governor, & Councell, for the tyme being, in the making of all such Acts, & Lawes, as may bee to the best avail of your Honours Interests, & the peoples good in this Cuntrey, which are the only desiers, & the thing aymed att, by

Your Honours most obedient humble Servants.

ᦂᦉ VI ᦆᦉ

New York: *Proprietary Prerogatives versus the Rights of Englishmen*

SHORTLY after the English conquest of New Netherland in 1664, royal commissioners issued a proclamation promising the people protection "and all other privileges with his Majesty's subjects." Early the next year, Governor Nicolls addressed a circular to the inhabitants of Long Island calling for deputies to meet with him at Hempstead on March 1, 1665 (Doc. 19). They remained in session for only two or three days, however, exercised no legislative functions, represented only Long Island and Westchester, and were given no expectation that they would be convened again. A code known as "The Duke's Laws" was prepared and promulgated at this meeting, by executive authority, but the people were allowed no role in legislation. Thereafter, the inhabitants grew restive and frustrated, and voiced their discontents publicly. Nicolls was adroit enough to placate these people; but his departure in 1669 led to new agitation.

When war between Holland and England resumed in 1673, New Netherland fell back to the Dutch and was not restored to the English until 1674. Major Edmund Andros, the new governor, was then instructed to execute the laws established earlier by Governors Nicolls and Lovelace, and to govern by executive fiat with the advice of his council. When Andros attempted in 1675 to warn the Duke of York about popular resentments, the responses he received (Doc. 20) were authoritarian and unsuited to the needs of provincial politics. By 1681 the situation had

totally deteriorated. Lieutenant Anthony Brockholls, in charge
of the New York government, reported that his constituents refused to pay import duties. With the customs declared illegal,
suits were promptly initiated against the collector of the port of
New York for detaining goods on which duties had not been
paid. Brockholls informed London that the government as then
established was "much disliked by the People who generally cry
out for an ASSEMBLY, and to that end a Petition was ordered to
be drawn up and sent to his Royal Highnesse."

The council of the Duke of York now, for the first time,
began to doubt his power to impose customs legitimately; so
Sir John Werden "hinted" to Brockholls in 1682 that a change
might be forthcoming. Almost a year later the new governor,
Thomas Dongan, was given instructions providing at last for a
general representative assembly in New York (Doc. 21). He
reached the colony in August 1683, and began immediately to
implement the new provincial polity. As soon as the assembly
met, it drafted a Charter of Libertyes and Priviledges (Doc. 22)
to which the governor gave his approval, sending it on to the
Duke of York. At first the Duke apparently accepted it; but
before final assent could be given, he became King James II.
The Privy Council soon after vetoed the charter and declared
that New York should have the same form of government as the
Dominion of New England. The legislature was thereby abolished, and was not re-established until 1691.

It is important to realize that throughout their agitation
for an assembly before 1683, the citizens of New York insisted
that they were only seeking the same privileges possessed by
all other colonies. In passing the Charter of Libertyes in 1683,
the assembly hoped to perpetuate itself, and intentionally mis-
used the word "charter." It could not and had not legislated a
charter, but it *had* created a frame of government; and the new
assembly in 1691 very promptly agreed upon another charter of
liberties almost identical with that of 1683.

◄§ 19 §►

A Letter from Governor Richard Nicolls
to the Inhabitants of Long Island, February 1665

Whereas the Inhabitants of *Long Island,* have for a Long time groaned under many grievous inconveniences, and discouragements occasioned partly from their subjection, partly from their opposition to a forraigne Power, in which distracted condition, few or no Lawes could bee putt in due Execution, Bounds and Titles to Lands disputed, Civill Libertyes interrupted, and from this Generall Confusion, private dissentions and animosityes, have too much prevailed against Neighborly Love, and Christian Charity; To the preventing of the future growth of like Evils, his Majesty as a signall grace and honor to his subjects upon *Long Island,* hath at his owne charge reduc't the forraigne Power to his obedience and by Pattent hath invested his Royall Highness the Duke of *York* with full and absolute Power, in and over all and every the Particular Tracts of Land therein mentioned, which said Powers by Commission from his Royall Highnesse the Duke of *York,* I am deputed to put in execution. In discharge therefore of my Trust and Duty, to Settle good and knowne Laws within this government for the future, and receive your best advice and Information in a General Meeting, I have thought fitt to Publish unto you, That upon the last day of this present February, at *Hempsteed* upon *Long Island,* shall be held a Generall Meeting, which is to consist of Deuptyes chosen by the major part of the freemen only, which is to be understood, of all Persons rated according to their Estates, whether *English,* or *Dutch,* within your severall Towns and precincts, whereof you are to make Publication to the Inhabitants, foure dayes before you proceed to an Election appointing a certain day to that purpose; You are further to impart to the Inhabitants from mee, that I do heartily recommend to them the choice of the most sober, able and discreet persons, without partiality or faction,

From E. B. O'Callaghan, ed., *Documents Relating to the Colonial History of the State of New York* (15 vols., Albany, N.Y., 1883), XIV, 564–5.

the fruite & benefitt whereof will return to themselves in a full and perfect settlement and composure of all controversyes, and the propagation of true Religion amongst us. They are also required to bring with them a Draught of each Towne Limits, or such writings as are necessary to evidence the Bounds and Limitts, as well as the right by which they challenge such Bounds and Limits, by Grant or Purchase, or both, as also to give notice of this meeting to Sachems of the Indyans, whose presence may in some cases bee accessary. Lastly I do require you to Assemble your Inhabitants and read this Letter to them, and then and there to nominate a day for the Election of two Deputyes from your Towne, who are to bring a certificate of their due election, (with full power to conclude any cause or matter relating to their several Townes) to mee at *Hempsteed* upon the last day of February, where (God willing) I shall expect them.

◅§ 20 §▻

Two Letters from the Duke of York to Governor Edmund Andros, April 6, 1675, and January 28, 1676

First then, touching Generall Assemblyes which the people there seeme desirous of in imitation of their neighbour Colonies, I thinke you have done well to discourage any motion of that kind, both as being not at all comprehended in your Instructions nor indeed consistent with the forme of government already established, nor necessary for the ease or redresse of any greivance that may happen, since that may be as easily obtained, by any petition or other addresse to you at their Generall Assizes (which is once a yeare) where the same persons (as Justices) are usually present, who in all probability would be theire Representatives if another constitution were allowed.

I have formerly writt to you touching Assemblyes in those countreys and have since observed what severall of your lattest

From O'Callaghan, ed., *Documents Relating to the Colonial History of the State of New York,* III, 230 and 235.

letters hint about that matter. But unless you had offered what qualifications are usuall and proper to such Assemblyes, I cannot but suspect they would be of dangerous consequence, nothing being more knowne then the aptness of such bodyes to assume to themselves many priviledges which prove destructive to, or very oft disturbe, the peace of the government wherein they are allowed. Neither doe I see any use of them which is not as well provided for, whilest you and your Councell governe according to the laws established (thereby preserving every man's property inviolate) and whilest all things that need redresse may be sure of finding it, either at the Quarter Sessions or by other legall and ordinary wayes, or lastly by appeale to myselfe. But howsoever if you continue of the same opinion, I shall be ready to consider of any proposalls you shall send to that purpose.

◆§ 21 §◆

The Duke of York's Instructions to Governor Thomas Dongan, January 27, 1683

With these Instructions you will receive a Commission under my hand and seale constituteing you my Lieutenant and Governor of New Yorke & its Dependencyes in America.

And you are thereupon to fitt your selfe with all convenient speed and to repaire thither to New Yorke, and being arrived there you are to take upon you the execution of the place and trust I have reposed in you, and forthwith to call together Fredericke Phillipps, Stephen Courtland and soe many more of the most eminent inhabitants of New Yorke, not exceeding tenn, to be of my Councill, and with due and usuall solemnity to cause my said comission constituteing you my present Lieutenant and Governor as aforesaid, to be then and there read and published; which being done, you are to administer to each of the members of the said Councill as well the Oaths of Allegiance to the King and Fealty to me as Lord and Proprietor of the place, & an Oath for the due execution of their places and trusts, and forthwith

From O'Callaghan, ed., *Documents Relating to the Colonial History of the State of New York*, III, 331–4.

to communicate such and soe many of these my instructions to the said Councill wherein their advice and consent are mentioned to be requisite, as likewise all such others from time to time as you shall find convenient for my service to be imparted unto them and the Members of the said Councill respectively shall and may have and enjoy freedome of debates and vote in all affaires of publique concerne. And in case any of the persons who are or shal be of my Councill shall misbehave themselves to that degree that you shall judge him unfitt to continue any longer of the Council, I doe hereby authorize and empower you to suspend him from assisting or attending the said Councill, and to transmitt to me the grounds and reasons of such suspension & such evidence as you have against him, that I may be able to judge whether he be fitt to be restored or absolutely excluded & discharged from the Councill.

You are also with advice of my Councill with all convenient speed after your arrivall there, in my name to issue out Writts or warrants of Sumons to the severall Sheriffes or other proper Officers in every part of your said governement wherein you shall expresse that I have thought fitt that there shall be a Generall Assembly of all the Freeholders, by the persons who they shall choose to represent them in order to consulting with yourselfe and the said Councill what laws are fitt and necessary to be made and established for the good weale and governement of the said Colony and its Dependencyes, and of all the inhabitants thereof, & you shall issue out the said Writt or Sumons at least thirty dayes before the time appointed for the meeting of the said Assembly, which time and alsoe the place of their meeting (which I intend shal be in New Yorke) shall alsoe be menconed & expressed in the said Writt or Sumons, and you with advice of my said Councill are to take care to issue out soe many writts or sumons and to such officers, in every part, not exceeding eighteene, soe that the planters or Inhabitants of every part of the said government may have convenient notice thereof and attend at such ellection, if they shall thinke fitt. And when the said Assembly soe elected shal be mett at the time and place directed, you shall lett them know that for the future it is my resolucon that the said Generall Assembly shall have free liberty to consult and debate among themselves all matters as shall be apprehended proper to be established for laws for the good governement of the said Colony of New Yorke and its Dependencyes, and that if such laws shal be propounded as shall appeare to mee to be for the manifest good of the Country in generall and not prejudiciall to me, I will assent unto and confirme them In the passing and enacting of all such laws as shal be agreed unto by the said Assembly, which I will have called by the name of the Generall Assembly of my Colony of New Yorke and its Dependencyes wherein the same shal be (as I doe hereby ordaine they shal be) presented to you for your assent thereunto.

You are to consider whether the same be for the generall good and not prejudiciall to me; and if you find them soe to be, then you are to give your assent thereunto. But if you shall judge them inconvenient or prejudiciall, you are to refuse your assent thereunto, and in all cases you are to have a negative voice to refuse all Laws that are presented to you; and when you shall have given your consent to such laws as shal be soe agreed, you shall by the first opportunity transmitt the same to me under the hands of your selfe and Councill, and under the seale of the Colony, (which you are to use in passing of grants) to the end that I may ratifye and confirme the same, if I shall approve or reject them if I doe not thinke them reasonable. But the said laws soe assented unto by you, shal be good and binding untill such time as I shall cause my dislike of & refusall to passe them to be signifyed unto you, and from thenceforth the same shall cease and be null and voyd to all intents. And I doe alsoe give you power from time to time to cause the said Generall Assembly to be summoned which I also authorize you to adjourne or dissolve as you shall see reason and cause. And I doe further direct you not to passe any law upon any occasion whatsoever for rayseing any publique revenue, unlesse expresse mencon be made therein that the same is levyed and granted unto me, or unto me for the support of the Governement or to such uses as the said law shall appoint. And you are as much as in you lyeth to take effectuall care that there may be a constant Establishment for raiseing of money sufficient to support and maintaine the charge of the government of those parts both Civil & Military; and alsoe that there may be money raised for paying and dischargeing the arreares now due to the Officers & Soldiers and other expenses of the government, And are not to suffer any publique money whatsoever to be issued or disposed of otherwise then by a warrant under your hand.

And it is my expresse will and pleasure that all laws whatsoever for the good governement and support of my said Colony of New Yorke with its Dependencyes be made indefinite and without limitacon of time, except the same be for a temporary end, & which shall expire and have its full effect within a certaine time. And you are not to passe any laws or doe any act by Graunt, Settlement or otherwise whereby my revenue may be remitted, lessened or impaired, without my especiall leave or commands therein. You shall not displace any of the Judges Justices Sheriffes or other Officers or Ministers within New Yorke or its Dependencyes under your governement without good cause, nor execute your selfe or by a Deputy any of the said offices nor suffer any person to execute more offices than one by a Deputy.

And I doe hereby require and command you that noe mans life, member, freehold, or goods, be taken away or harmed in any of the places under your governement but by established and knowne laws not repugnant to but as nigh as may be agreeable to the laws of the kingdome of England.

Given under my hand at St. James's the 27th day of January 1682–3

❧ 22 ❧

The Charter of Libertyes and Priviledges
Passed by the First General Assembly
of New York, October 30, 1683

The Charter of Libertyes and priviledges granted by his
Royall Highnesse to the Inhabitants of New Yorke
and its Dependencyes.

For The better Establishing the Government of this province of
New Yorke and that Justice and Right may be Equally done to
all persons within the same

BEE It Enacted by the Governour Councell and Representatives
now in Generall Assembly mett and assembled and by the authority of the same.

THAT The Supreme Legislative Authority under his Majesty and
Royall Highnesse James Duke of Yorke, Albany, &c Lord proprietor of the said province shall forever be and reside in a Governour, Councell, and the people mett in Generall Assembly.

THAT The Exercise of the Cheife Magistracy and Administracon
of the Government over the said province shall bee in the said
Governour assisted by a Councell with whose advice and Consent
or with at least four of them he is to rule and Governe the same
according to the Lawes thereof. . . .

THAT According to the usage Custome and practice of the
Realme of England a sessions of a Generall Assembly be held in
this province once in three yeares at least.

THAT Every freeholder within this province and freeman in
any Corporacon Shall have his free Choise and Vote in the Electing of the Representatives without any manner of constraint or
Imposicon. And that in all Eleccons the Majority of Voices shall
carry itt and by freeholders is understood every one who is Soe
understood according to the Lawes of England.

THAT the persons to be Elected to sitt as representatives in the

From *The Colonial Laws of New York from the Year 1664 to the
Revolution* (5 vols., Albany, N.Y., 1894), I, 111–13.

Generall Assembly from time to time for the severall Cittyes,
townes, Countyes, Shires, or Divisions of this province and all
places within the same shall be according to the proporcon and
number hereafter Expressed that is to say for the Citty and
County of New Yorke four, for the County of Suffolke two, for
Queens County two, for Kings County two, for the County of
Richmond two, for the County of West Chester two. For the
County of Ulster two, for the County of Albany two, and for
Schenectade within the said County one, for Dukes County two,
for the County of Cornwall two and as many more as his Royall
Highnesse shall think fitt to Establish.

THAT All persons Chosen and Assembled in manner aforesaid
or the Major part of them shall be deemed and accounted the
Representatives of this province which said Representatives together with the Governour and his Councell Shall forever be the
Supreame and only Legislative power under his Royall Highnesse of the said province.

THAT The said Representatives may appoint their owne Times
of meeting dureing their sessions and may adjourne their house
from time to time to such time as to them shall seeme meet and
convenient.

THAT The said Representatives are the sole Judges of the Qual-
ificacons of their owne members, and likewise of all undue Eleccons and may from time to time purge their house as they shall
see occasion dureing the said sessions.

THAT noe member of the general Assembly or their servants
dureing the time of their Sessions and whilest they shall be goeing to and returning from the said Assembly shall be arrested
sued imprisoned or any wayes molested or troubled nor be
compelled to make answere to any suite, Bill, plaint, Declaracon
or otherwise, (Cases of High Treason and felony only Excepted)
provided the number of the said servants shall not Exceed three.

THAT All bills agreed upon by the said Representatives or the
Major part of them shall be presented unto the Governour and
his Councell for their Approbacon and Consent All and Every
which Said Bills soe approved of Consented to by the Governour
and his Councell shall be Esteemed and accounted the Lawes of

the province, Which said Lawes shall continue and remaine of force untill they shall be repealed by the authority aforesaid that is to say the Governour Councell and Representatives in General Assembly by and with the Approbacon of his Royal Highnesse or Expire by their owne Limittacons.

THAT In all Cases of death or removall of any of the said Representatives The Governour shall issue out Sumons by Writt to the Respective Townes, Cittyes, Shires, Countyes, or Divisions for which he or they soe removed or deceased were Chosen, willing and requireing the freeholders of the Same to Elect others in their place and stead. . . .

THAT Noe aid, Tax, Tallage, Assessment, Custome, Loane, Benevolence or Imposicon whatsoever shall be layed assessed imposed or levyed on any of his Majestyes Subjects within this province or their Estates upon any manner of Colour or pretence but by the act and Consent of the Governour Councell and Representatives of the people in Generall Assembly mett and Assembled.

Pennsylvania: *Quaker Deliberations and Structural Change*

I N 1681, William Penn received the last great proprietary grant of the seventeenth century. Because a new colonial policy of closer political and economic supervision was then being considered in London, Penn's charter (Doc. 23) contained many limitations not found in earlier charters, either trading company or proprietary. Inhabitants of the province were explicitly given the right of appeal to the Crown. All acts of the provincial legislature were required to be submitted to the Crown for approval within five years. The proprietor was obliged to keep an agent in England to represent his interests and those of the colony. And Parliament's right to tax the new colony was clearly understood.

In April 1682, after considering many drafts, Penn made public a Frame of Government and Charter of Liberties for his colony. Compared with either the West New Jersey Concessions and Agreements of 1677 or the New York Charter of Libertyes of 1683, Penn's Frame of 1682 offered a conservative and restrictive system of government. In both neighboring colonies, unlike Penn's plan, the lower house stood as a separate legislative body, possessing the initiative and right to decide upon its own adjournment. Even in East New Jersey, the cumbersome Constitution of 1683 conferred greater power on the elected assembly than was permitted in Pennsylvania. In the very first provincial assembly—held late in 1682, essentially as a ratifying body—the deputies rejected Penn's Frame, flatly denied 19 of the 90 laws proposed by him, and moved to allow any member of the assembly to propose a bill "except in Case of levying Taxes."

Thereafter, the principal task of the assembly became that of modeling a new frame of government to replace the rejected one. The central issue under debate was the proper distribution of power among the proprietor, council, and assembly. All agreed upon the need for a smaller legislature than Penn had projected, and the elected assemblymen reluctantly accepted a new innovation—the governor's veto power. At a session of the general assembly in October 1683, the members pressed again for the right to initiate legislation. Penn made a small concession by agreeing that after the assembly was adjourned, members might consult informally with the governor and council. Otherwise the power balance remained unchanged, and Penn obtained passage of the Frame of 1683 (Doc. 24).

Throughout the proceedings of the first two assemblies in Pennsylvania (Doc. 25), one finds rigorous concern with ground rules. The members sought to establish clear precedents which would guide them and their successors in future times. Readers will note the speaker's critical importance in this process, as again and again he showed the members just how the House of Commons in England functioned and behaved. With so much at stake, and with parliamentary experience so precious, the assembly's obsessive insistence upon good attendance is not surprising.

After two decades of unstable settlement, Penn and his assembly finally negotiated a constitution that would endure for 75 years. The Charter of Privileges (Doc. 26), as the Frame of 1701 was called, at last conferred on the assembly many of the parliamentary prerogatives which Penn had denied that body for years: the right to prepare legislative bills, elect its own officers, appoint committees, decide upon its own adjournment, judge the qualifications of its own members, and impeach government officials. In short, privileges that the assembly had accumulated in random fashion over more than a decade were rendered legitimate in 1701. Even so, Penn did not intend to concede political autonomy to the colony, and after his departure the politics of constitutionalism continued between the popular and proprietary parties.

◆§ 23 §◆

The Charter for the Province
of Pennsylvania, 1681

Charles the Second, by the Grace of God, King of *England, Scotland, France,* and *Ireland,* Defender of the Faith, &c. To all whom these presents shall come, *Greeting.* . . . We have thought fitt to erect, and We doe hereby erect the aforesaid Countrey and Islands into a Province and Seigniorie, and doe call itt PENSILVANIA, and soe from henceforth we will have itt called.

AND forasmuch as Wee have hereby made and ordained the aforesaid *William Penn,* his heires and assignes, the true and absolute Proprietaries of all the Lands and Dominions aforesaid, KNOW YE THEREFORE, That We reposing speciall trust and Confidence in the fidelitie, wisedom, Justice, and provident circumspection of the said *William Penn* for us, our heires and Successors, Doe grant free, full, and absolute power by vertue of these presents to him and his heires, and to his and their Deputies, and Lieutenants, for the good and happy government of the said countrey, to ordeyne, make, and enact, and under his and their Seales to publish any Lawes whatsoever, for the raising of money for the publick use of the said Province, or for any other End, apperteyning either unto the publick state, peace, or safety of the said Countrey, or unto the private utility of perticular persons, according unto their best discretions, by and with the advice, assent, and approbation of the Freemen of the said Countrey, or the greater parte of them, or of their Delegates or Deputies, whom for the Enacting of the said Lawes, when, and as often as need shall require, Wee will that the said *William Penn* and his heires, shall assemble in such sort and forme, as to him and them shall seeme best, and the same Lawes duly to

From Thorpe, ed., *The Federal and State Constitutions, Colonial Charters, and Other Organic Laws* . . . , V, 3036–9.

execute, unto and upon all People within the said Countrey and the Limitts thereof. . . .

AND forasmuch as in the Government of soe great a Countrey, sudden Accidents doe often happen, whereunto itt will bee necessarie to apply remedie before the Freeholders of the said Province, or their Delegates or Deputies, can bee assembled to the making of Lawes; neither will itt bee convenient that instantly upon every such emergent occasion, soe greate a multitude should be called together: Therefore for the better Government of the said Countrey Wee will, and ordaine, and by these presents, for us, our Heires and successors, Doe Grant unto the said *William Penn* and his heires, by themselves or by their Magistrates and Officers, in that behalfe duely to bee ordeyned as aforesaid, to make and constitute fitt and wholesome Ordinances, from time to time, within the said Countrey to bee kept and observed, as well for the preservation of the peace, as for the better government of the People there inhabiting; and publickly to notifie the same to all persons, whome the same doeth or anyway may concerne. Which ordinances, Our Will and Pleasure is, shall bee observed inviolably within the said Province, under Paines therein to be expressed, soe as the said Ordinances bee consonant to reason, and bee not repugnant nor contrary, but soe farre as conveniently may bee agreeable with the Lawes of our Kingdome of *England,* and soe as the said Ordinances be not extended in any Sort to bind, charge, or take away the right or Interest of any person or persons, for or in their Life, members, Freehold, goods, or Chattles. And our further will and pleasure is, that the Lawes for regulateing and governing of Propertie within the said Province, as well for the descent and enjoyment of lands, as likewise for the enjoyment and succession of goods and Chattles, and likewise as to Felonies, shall bee and continue the same, as they shall bee for the time being by the generall course of the Law in our Kingdome of *England,* untill the said Lawes shall bee altered by the said *William Penn,* his heires or assignes, and by the Freemen of the said Province, their Delegates or Deputies, or the greater Part of them.

AND to the End the said *William Penn,* or his heires, or other the Planters, Owners, or Inhabitants of the said Province, may not att any time hereafter by misconstruction of the powers aforesaid through inadvertencie or designe depart from that Faith and due allegiance, which by the lawes of this our Kingdom of *England,* they and all our subjects, in our Dominions and Territories, always owe unto us, Our heires and Successors, by colour of any Extent or largnesse of powers hereby given, or pretended to bee given, or by force or colour of any lawes hereafter to bee made in the said Province, by vertue of any such Powers; OUR further will and Pleasure is, that a transcript or Duplicate of all Lawes, which shall bee soe as aforesaid made and published within the said Province, shall within five yeares after the makeing thereof, be transmitted and delivered to the Privy Councell, for the time being, of us, our heires and successors: And if any of the said Lawes, within the space of six moneths after that they shall be soe transmitted and delivered, bee declared by us, Our heires or Successors, in Our or their Privy Councell, inconsistent with the Sovereigntey or lawful Prerogative of us, our heires or Successors, or contrary to the Faith and Allegiance due by the legall government of this Realme, from the said *William Penn,* or his heires, or of the Planters and Inhabitants of the said Province, and that thereupon any of the said Lawes shall bee adjudged and declared to bee void by us, our heires or Successors, under our or their Privy Seale, that then and from thenceforth, such Lawes, concerning which such Judgement and declaration shall bee made, shall become voyd: Otherwise the said Lawes soe transmitted, shall remaine, and stand in full force, according to the true intent and meaneing thereof.

◄§ 24 §►

The Frame of Government
of Pennsylvania, 1683

The Frame of the Government of the Province of Pennsylvania *and Territories thereunto annexed, in* America

. . . *Imprimis,* That the government of this province and

From Thorpe, ed., *The Federal and State Constitutions, Colonial Charters, and Other Organic Laws* . . . , V, 3064–7.

territories thereof, shall, from time to time, according to the powers of the patent and deeds of feoffment aforesaid, consist of the Proprietary and Governor, and freemen of the said province and territories thereof, in form of provincial Council and General Assembly; which provincial Council shall consist of eighteen persons, being three out of each county, and which Assembly shall consist of thirty-six persons, being six out of each county, men of most note for their virtue, wisdom and ability; by whom all laws shall be made, officers chosen, and public affairs transacted, as is hereafter limited and declared.

II. There being three persons already chosen for every respective county of this province and territories thereof, to serve in the provincial Council, one of them for three years; one for two years, and one for one year; and one of them to go off yearly, in every county; that on the tenth day of the first month yearly, for ever after, the freemen of the said province and territories thereof, shall meet together, in the most convenient place, in every county of this province and territories thereof, then and there to chuse one person, qualified as aforesaid, in every county, being one-third of the number to serve in provincial Council, for three years; it being intended, that one-third of the whole provincial Council, consisting and to consist of eighteen persons, falling off yearly, it shall be yearly supplied with such yearly elections, as aforesaid; and that one person shall not continue in longer than three years; and in case any member shall decease before the last election, during his time, that then, at the next election ensuing his decease, another shall be chosen to supply his place for the remaining time he was to have served, and no longer.

III. That, after the first seven years, every one of the said third parts, that goeth yearly off, shall be incapable of being chosen again for one whole year following, that so all that are capable and qualified, as aforesaid, may be fitted for government, and have a share of the care and burden of it.

IV. That the provincial Council in all cases and matters of moment, as their arguing upon bills to be passed into laws, or proceedings about erecting of courts of justice, sitting in judgment upon criminals impeached, and choice of officers, in such manner as is herein after expressed, not less than two-thirds of the whole shall make a *quorum;* and that the consent and approbation of two-thirds of that quorum shall be had in all such cases, or matters, of moment: and that, in all cases and matters of lesser moment, one-third of the whole shall make a *quorum,* the majority of which shall and may always determine in such cases and causes of lesser moment.

V. That the Governor and provincial Council shall have the power of preparing and proposing to the Assembly, hereafter mentioned, all bills, which they shall see needful, and that shall, at any time, be past into laws, within the said province and territories thereof, which bills shall be published and affixed to the most noted places, in every county of this province and territories thereof, twenty days before the meeting of the Assembly, in order to passing them into laws.

VI. That the Governor and provincial Council shall take care that all laws, statutes and ordinances, which shall, at any time, be made within the said province and territories, be duly and diligently executed.

VII. That the Governor and provincial Council shall, at all times, have the care of the peace and safety of this province and territories thereof; and that nothing be, by any person, attempted, to the subversion of this frame of government.

VIII. That the Governor and provincial Council shall, at all times, settle and order the situation of all cities, and market towns, in every county, modelling therein all public buildings, streets and market places; and shall appoint all necessary roads and highways, in this province and territories thereof.

IX. That the Governor and provincial Council shall, at all times, have power to inspect the management of the public treasury, and punish those who shall convert any part thereof to any other use, than what hath been agreed upon by the Governor, provincial Council and Assembly. . . .

XI. That one-third part of the provincial Council, residing with the Governor, from time to time, shall with the Governor have the care of the management of public affairs, relating to the peace, justice, treasury and improvement of the province and territories, and to the good education of youth, and sobriety of the manners of the inhabitants therein, as aforesaid.

XII. That the Governor, or his Deputy, shall always preside in the provincial Council, and that he shall, at no time, therein perform any public act of state whatsoever, that shall, or may, relate unto the justice, trade, treasury, or safety of the province and territories as aforesaid, but by and with the advice and consent of the provincial Council thereof.

XIII. And to the end that all bills prepared and agreed by the Governor and provincial Council, as aforesaid, may yet have the more full concurrence of the freemen of the province and territories thereof, it is declared, granted and confirmed, that, at the time and place in every county for the choice of one person to serve in provincial Council, as aforesaid, the respective Members thereof, at their said meeting, shall yearly chuse out of themselves six persons of most note, for virtue, wisdom and ability, to serve in Assembly, as their representatives, who shall yearly meet on the tenth day of the third month, in the capital town or city of the said Province, unless the Governor and provincial Council shall think fit to appoint another place to meet in, where, during eight days, the several Members may confer freely with one another; and if any of them see meet, with a committee of the provincial Council, which shall be, at that time, purposely appointed, to receive from any of them proposals for the alterations, or amendments, of any of the said proposed and promulgated bills; and on the ninth day from their so meeting, the said Assembly, after their reading over the proposed bills, by the Clerk of the provincial Council, and the occasions and motives for them being opened by the Governor or his Deputy, shall, upon the question by him put, give their affirmative or negative, which to them seemeth best, in such manner as is hereafter expressed: but not less than two-thirds shall make a *quorum* in the passing of all bills into laws, and choice of such officers as are by them to be chosen.

XIV. That the laws so prepared and proposed, as aforesaid, that are assented to by the Assembly, shall be enrolled as laws of this province and territories thereof, with this stile: *By the*

Governor, with the assent and approbation of the freemen in provincial Council and Assembly met, and from henceforth the meetings, sessions, acts, and proceedings of the Governor, provincial Council and Assembly, shall be stiled and called, *The meeting, sessions and proceedings of the General Assembly of the province of Pennsylvania, and the territories thereunto belonging.*

XV. And that the representatives of the people in provincial Council and Assembly, may, in after ages, bear some proportion with the increase and multiplying of the people, the number of such representatives of the people may be, from time to time, increased and enlarged, so as at no time, the number exceeds seventy-two for the provincial Council, and two hundred for the Assembly; the appointment and proportion of which number, as also the laying and methodizing of the choice of such representatives in future time, most equally to the division of the country, or number of the inhabitants, is left to the Governor and provincial Council to propose, and the Assembly to resolve, so that the order of proportion be strictly observed, both in the choice of the Council and the respective committees thereof, *viz.:* one third to go off, and come in yearly.

XVI. That from and after the death of this present Governor, the provincial Council shall, together with the succeeding Governor, erect, from time to time, standing courts of justice, in such places and number as they shall judge convenient for the good government of the said province and territories thereof; and that the provincial Council shall, on the thirteenth day of the second month then next ensuing, elect and present to the Governor, or his Deputy, a double number of persons, to serve for Judges, Treasurers, and Masters of the Rolls, within the said province and territories, to continue so long as they shall well behave themselves, in those capacities respectively; and the freemen of the said province, in an Assembly met on the thirteenth day of the third month, yearly, shall elect and then present to the Governor, or his Deputy, a double number of persons to serve for Sheriffs, Justices of the Peace, and Coroners, for the year next ensuing; out of which respective elections and presentments, the

Governor, or his Deputy, shall nominate and commissionate the proper number for each office, the third day after the said respective presentments; or else the first named in such presentment, for each office, as aforesaid, shall stand and serve in that office, the time before respectively limited; and in case of death or default, such vacancy shall be supplied by the Governor and provincial Council in manner aforesaid.

XVII. That the Assembly shall continue so long as may be needful to impeach criminals, fit to be there impeached, to pass such bills into laws as are proposed to them, which they shall think fit to pass into laws, and till such time as the Governor and provincial Council shall declare, that they have nothing further to propose unto them, for their assent and approbation, and that declaration shall be a dismiss to the assembly, for that time; which Assembly shall be, notwithstanding, capable of assembling together, upon the summons of the Governor and provincial Council, at any time, during that year, if the Governor and provincial Council shall see occasion for their so assembling.

XVIII. That all the elections of members, of representatives of the people to serve in provincial Council and Assembly, and all questions to be determined by both or either of them, that relate to choice of officers, and all, or any other personal matters, shall be resolved or determined by the *ballot*, and all things relating to the preparing and passing of bills into laws, shall be openly declared and resolved by the vote.

◄§ 25 §►

Proceedings of the First and Second Assemblies
in Pennsylvania, November 1682 and March 1683

At An Assembly held At Chester, the Fourth Day of the Tenth Month [December], 1682.

CHRISTOPHER TAYLOR, for the county of *Bucks.* President *MOORE,* for *Philadelphia. John Simcock* for *Chester.* Wil-

From Gertrude MacKinney, ed., *Votes and Proceedings of the House of Representatives of the Province of Pennsylvania, 1682–1776* in *Pennsylvania Archives,* 8th series (Philadelphia, Pa., 1931–5), I, 1–43.

liam Clark, for *Deal, Francis Whitewell,* for *Jones,* To be a Committee for Elections and Privileges.

Question being put, Whether the Persons above named should be a Committee as aforesaid. *Resolved in the affirmative.* N. C. D. [no one disagreeing]

The Said Committee to meet at Eight a Clock in the Morning, at this House, and sit till Ten, being the Time the House sits. . . .

The Committee of Privileges and Elections, being assembled at the Time appointed, they proceeded to choose a Chairman, whereupon it was determined, that Doctor *Moore,* President of the Society [of Friends] in *Philadelphia, etc.* Should be preferred as Chairman. . . .

The Speaker having taken the Chair, the Chairman of Committee of Privileges and Elections, reports to the House, that *Abraham Man* and his Party, had made some illegal Procedure the Day of Election, at *Newcastle,* that he might be elected a Member of the House; several Witnesses having been heard and examined on both Sides, the Committee adjudged *John Moll,* to be duly elected. Reasons having been given to the House for the same, it was put to the Vote, Whether *Abraham Man,* or *John Moll,* was duly elected; it was *carried in the Affirmative* for *John Moll,* N. C. D.

A member of the House moved, that a Committee be elected out of the two Committees now in being, to manage and bring in all Bills relating to the Province, etc. The Question being put, it was *carried in the Affirmative,* N. C. D.

Then the House proceeds to elect Members of Committee of Foresight, for the Preparation of Provincial Bills. . . .

Proposed by the Speaker, Whether any Member of this House, offending, &c. should for the first Offence be reproved only, for the second, reproved, with a Fine of *Twelve-pence,* and so gradually for every Offence, not exceeding *Ten Shillings;* put to the Vote, and *carried in the Affirmative,* N. C. D.

It was moved again by the Speaker, Whether the aforementioned Delinquent or Delinquents, should for their Offence or Offences be brought to the Bar or not, which, by Consent of the Whole House, was *carried in the Affirmation.*

Proposed to the Vote by the Speaker, Whether the whole House might resolve itself into a grand Committee [of the whole] or not; carried in the Affirmative, N. C. D.

Proposed, That no Member of Assembly, during the Sessions, should go a Journey, without the Speaker's Leave. ————— *carried in the Affirmative.*

Voted, That no Proposal be put to the Question, before seconded or thirded, and if so, that then the House resolving itself into a grand Committee, may debate or discourse upon the Matter propounded, which was generally agreed unto, and *carried in the Affirmative.*

Voted, That any Member of the House may have Privilege to make an Addition to any Proposal, excepting against any Part, as at the present stated; *carried in the Affirmative.*

Voted, That for the regular Proceeding of the House, all Questions are to pass, either in the Negative, or Affirmative; carried in the Affirmative by general Votes.

Proposed to the House, That if any Member of the House shall presume to pervert the Sense of a Question agreed unto by the House, that then and in such Case, the said Member shall be put out of the House. ————— *Carried in the Affirmative.* . . .

Voted, That two Members be elected to inspect which Party carried it by the major Votes, on Diversity of Votes arising in the House; *Carried in the Affirmative.*

Proposed, That when the Votes of the House are equal upon Debate, the Speaker should have the casting Vote, to decide the Matter in Controversy, which by general Consent was *carried in the Affirmative.*

Proposed, If a Matter be in Debate, and the Question arise, Whether the House shall proceed therein this Time or not, upon Division, the *No's* go out; if for Adjournment, the *Yea's;* put to the Vote, and *carried in the Affirmative.*

Proposed, That none speak above once before the Question

is put nor after, but once: No Member, in any Discourse, to mention the Name of another Member; but as, That Member that last or lately spoke; only a Member may be us'd by his Office, or Sitting in a certain Place; as, Near the Chair, etc. None to fall from the Matter to the Person; and superfluous and tedious Speeches may be stopt by the Speaker. . . .

Proposed, That whenever the House is resolv'd into a grand Committee, the Speaker leaving the Chair, they shall immediately proceed to the Election of a Chairman, which shall be for that Time promoted to the Chair by the Committee, to whom every one shall direct his Speech, as unto the Speaker; and as soon as the Matter in Debate is agreed on, the Chairman shall return to his Place, and the Speaker reassume the Chair; then the Chairman of the grand Committee shall make report to the House, and leave it in Writing with the Clerk; the grand Committee never to adjourn without Consent of the House; and that no other Committee shall determine the Right or Property of the Subject without Leave from the House; put to the Vote, and *carried in the Affirmative*.

Proposed, That no private Committee can alter a Question agreed amongst themselves, without Consent of the Whole House, and that Committee always name in their Report, what Committee they came from. *Voted, and carried in the Affirmative*.

Proposed, That any Member of the House may have Access into any Committee, except Committees of Secrecy. *Voted, and Carried in the Affirmative*. . . .

Proposed, That an orderly Proceeding be made in presenting of Bills, according to the Contents of the Charter of Order *etc. viz.* That Bills at Committees be considered by Parts, the Preamble last considered; the Bills not to be blotted, but mended in other Papers, and the Amendments to be put to the Question and voted singly. Bills to be without Razures or Interlineations, and the Clerk to read the Bill, then deliver it to the Speaker, who standing up with the Bill in his Hand, reads the Title, and declares it to be the first Reading of that Bill, and no Member to speak to it till a second Reading, unless to cast it out. If Exceptions to a Bill be not mendable at the Table, then committed; but no Bill without Exceptions; if not committed or rejected, then engrossed. He that is against the Body of a Bill, shall not be of a Committee about that Bill; no private or personable Bills to be brought in without Leave; publick Bills, the Matter to be opened before brought into the House.

No Bill to be brought in to repeal a Law, without Leave.

Bills amended to be engrossed, but first in a full House, the Title to be indorsed on the Back of the Bill. These considerations relating to Bills, were put to the Vote, and *carried in the Affirmative.*

Proposed, That any Member may offer any Bill, publick or private, tending to the publick Good, except in Case of levying Taxes, *Voted in the Affirmative.*

Proposed, That any Law, Statute, or Ordinance, constituted by a Committee, shall not be of Force, except established by the whole House. *Voted in the Affirmative.*

Proposed, That any Member of the House directing his Discourse to the Speaker, shall stand up, that the Speaker and Members may see him. *Voted in the Affirmative.*

Proposed, That the Speaker may have Liberty in his Speech, without an Interruption from any Member. *Voted in the Affirmative.*

The House adjourn'd till Nine a Clock the Next Morning.

The House met again the sixth of the *10th Month,* 1682, about Ten in the Morning; the Speaker having taken his Chair.

Proposed by the Speaker and President, Whether any absolute Note of Distinction, betwixt one Officer and another, should be concluded on by Vote; as the Carrying a white Rod or Reed, etc. *Left in Suspence. . . .*

A Member moves, That the Members of the Lower Counties were in a great Strait, by reason of their being to assemble again about 21 Days hence, and desire the Governor may be acquainted therewith. Two members are appointed for that Undertaking.

The Members employed, bring Intelligence, That the Governor is willing that the Assembly be adjourn'd for 21 Days, which was accordingly done, by Order of the Speaker. . . .

At an Assembly held at Philadelphia, the Twelfth Day of the First Month, 1682–3 [March 12, 1683. A list of elected members follows]

By the King's Authority, and special Command of *William Penn,* Proprietary and Governor of the Province of *Pennsylvania,* and Territories thereunto belonging, by his Writs issued forth to the Sheriffs of each respective County, for the Election of the Members of Assembly of Parliment, being the Deputies of the Freemen of the Province, *etc.* met at *Philadelphia,* at the Time aforesaid; and the Names of the several Members of each County were read over, then proceed to choose their Speaker; and by the Assent of the Whole House, *Thomas Winn* (one of the elected Members) having presented to the Governor, as Speaker, the Governor being very well satisfied therewith, approved of their Choice.

They return again, and the Speaker being seated in the Chair, adjourns the House to the fourth Hour in the Afternoon.

About the fifth Hour in the Afternoon, the House sat, the Speaker assumes the Chair, and puts the House in Mind of the Intent of their Coming, gives them Advise suitable to their present Undertakings, and bids them be mindful of their Duties towards one another.

The Speaker then reads the Orders and Decorum of the House, both towards him, as Speaker, and one towards another; he reads their Method to be observed in Debates, and that every Matter ought to be debated in the House, before it can be put to Vote.

It was moved by the Speaker, Whether the Charter of the Province should be read over. *Voted for, and carried in the Affirmative.*

The Charter was accordingly read, and then by the Clerk delivered into the Speaker's Hand.

A Debate arose touching the select Numbers mentioned in

the Charter, for Members of Provincial Council, and General Assembly, but immediately ceased. . . .

A very good Proposal was made by a Member of the House, That it might be requisite, by way of Petition or otherwise, to move the Governor and Provincial Council, that the House might be allowed the Privilege of proposing to them such Things as might tend to the Benefit of the Province, *etc.* which possibly the Governor and Council might not think of, nor of very long Time remember, which might, in the Interim, tend to the great Detriment of the Province, *etc.*

The Speaker calling it to Remembrance, reproves several Members of the House, for neglecting to convene at the Time appointed, when the House last adjourn'd. . . .

By Consent, the Speaker adjourns the House to the ninth Hour the next Morning.

About the tenth Hour the House sat. The Speaker assumes the chair. The Names of the Members were called over, and several being wanting in the Assembly, occasioned the Speaker to reprove them as they came, for neglect of Attendance.

Then the Speaker declares the Governor's Answer, touching their Request for Conference with him and the Council, *which answer was condescential to their Request.*

A Debate arose in the House, concerning sundry needful Things as might require the aforesaid Privilege of Conference with the Governor, *etc.* concerning them.

Moved by a Member of the House, touching that Power, which the Member said the Assembly was invested with, to debate concerning Bills to be sent into the House by the Governor and Provincial Council. And it was debated, and further argued, that the House presuming to take that Power aforesaid, seemed too much to infringe upon the Governor's Privileges, and Royalties, and to render him Ingratitude for his Goodness towards the People. Several of the Members agree, That (the Governor's Good-will, and Demeanour towards the People, being considered) they are all in Duty bound, rather to restore that Privilege in his too great Bounty he hath conferred upon them, *viz.* Of Having the Power of giving a negative Voice, *etc.* to the

Bills proposed unto them by himself, and Provincial Council, than to endeavour to diminish his Power.

The Governor, *etc.* sends to the Assembly for Conference with them. Put to the Vote, Whether the Assembly should resort to the Governor *etc.* according to his Desire or not; the Number of Votes was decided by Beans, put into the Balloting-box; and by the major Votes, it was *carried in the Affirmative.*

The Assembly removes to the Governor and Council, and confer with them. Afterwards return, and the Speaker reassumes the Chair. He advises the Assembly to take into serious Consideration, the good Council of the Governor, as touching that weighty Matter of their establishing a Government for future Ages, *etc.*

A Test requiring Fidelity, and lawful Obedience, from the Members of Assembly to the Governor, was twice read, and after reading it was concluded by general Vote of the House, that *Griffith Jones,* and *John Cann,* two Members, should be employ'd to demand of the Governor, *etc.* whether that Test had been sign'd by the Provincial Council.

They return, and bring Answer, That it was sign'd by the Provincial Council; therefore the whole Assembly subscribed their Names to the aforesaid Test.

The Speaker adjourns the House till the fourth Hour in the Afternoon precisely.

About the Time appointed, the House met again.

The Speaker having assum'd the Chair, orders the Members Names to be called over; some of them being wanting, the Speaker sends the Door-keeper for them.

The House waits in Expectation of Bills from the Governor, and Provincial Council. In the Interim, one of the Members of the House moves, That a Way might be considered of by the House, how every Member might defray his particular Charges, during his attendance in the House for the Country's Service; which Motion, the Speaker putting to Vote, it was *carried in the Affirmative, viz.* That the Governor and Provincial Council, should be addressed unto by the House, touching that Matter.

A Debate arose in the House, concerning the Absence of some Members, where their Neglect of due Attendance is generally observed, and they therefor concluded by the present Members of the House, to merit some severe Penalty for the same.

The Governor sends for one of the Members of the House, to come and speak with him; whereupon the Speaker orders *William Yardly*, one of the Members, to wait upon him. He returns, and signifies, that the Governor by him informed the House, That what Matters of Moment himself and the Provincial Council, did intend to present to the House, were at present unprepared; and therefore desires the House to adjourn themselves until the next Day; whereupon,

The Speaker adjourns the House till the ninth Hour the next Morning.

About the Time appointed the House sat, the Speaker assumes the Chair, and orders the Clerk to call over the Burgesses Names, which was accordingly done. And the Speaker orders the Clerk to set down the Names of such Members as were absent Yesterday, and are now absent without Leave of the House; which was done accordingly, and delivered to the Speaker. . . .

The Speaker proposes to the House, to debate amongst themselves, whether or no it be requisite that any of the Members of the House shall be tolerated to absent themselves from the House, without Licence from the Speaker, and all the other Members of the House; whereupon a Debate arose in the House concerning That Matter; the Result whereof was, That all Members absenting themselves from the House without Licence, shall, for the future, be very considerably fined, according to the Discretion of the present Members. This was voted throughout the whole House.

The Speaker reads to the House the orderly Method of Parliaments, and the Demeanour of the Members, thereof observed in *England,* which he recommended to them, as civil and good: As also the Method observed by the *English* in Committees. . . .

Proposed by the Speaker, That the House should be adjourn'd till the fourth Hour in the Afternoon, which was generally agreed unto.

The Speaker adjourn'd the House till the fourth Hour in the
Afternoon.

About the Time appointed the House sat. . . .

Proposed, That two Members be sent to the Governor and
Council, to be informed whether they had any present for the
Assembly, or not; put to the Vote, and *carried in the Affirmative.* Whereupon *Griffith Jones,* and *John Songhurst,* two Members, were elected for that Purpose————They return, and
signify to the House, That some Business would immediately be
sent them from the Governor and Provincial Council, a Debate
arose in the House touching the Number of Members of the
Provincial Council intimating their Number to be too great; as
also the same, touching the Number of Members of Assembly;
but nothing relating thereto determined.

The Governor sends for two Members of the House, and
ordered by the House, that *John Cann* and *William Yardly* be
sent unto him.————They return, and signify, That the
Governor and Provincial Council desire the Attendance of the
Whole House.

Whereupon the House withdraws to attend the Governor,
etc. as was desired.————The House, after some Time, returns; the Speaker reassumes the Chair, and refers to the House's
Consideration, the good Disposition and Wisdom of the Governor, the Excellency of his Speech unto them before the Provincial Council.

Another Member hints at the undeserving Reflections and
Aspersions cast upon the Governor, which the Governor, himself, and all good Members and Subjects, do, not without cause,
resent as evil, from any Subject, but especially proceeding from
any of the Members of Assembly. . . .

The Governor sends for a Bill, tendered to the House in
the Forenoon, but not read in the House, deeming it then im-
proper to be expos'd to the View of the House.————The
Speaker, with two other Members, return the Bill into the Hands

of the Governor and Council, then return and report it to the House.

A Member proposes, That the Governor and Council might be moved, that some Means may be by them prescribed, for the Recording of the Minutes and Transactions of the Court, *viz.* some Order for the providing of Books, *etc.* for that Purpose. This was put to Vote, and *resolved in the Affirmative,* viz. that such Motion should be made.

The Clerk of the Provincial Council brought a Bill into the House, touching a Method to be observed in Proceedings of the Provincial Council, and General Assembly————The Time of their Sitting, the Manner of their Establishing of Laws, with the Title to be prefixed unto such Laws as are by them enacted, *etc.* This Bill, by Order of the Speaker, was read by the Clerk: After some Debate on the said Bill, the Clerk was ordered to read over again some part of it, which was accordingly done, and finding in the said Bill some Variations from the printed Charter, it was put to Vote, Whether the fourteenth Article of the printed Charter should stand firm, together with those Variations thereof in the Bill, and it was *resolved in the Affirmative.*————The Clerk, by Command of the Speaker, reads the latter Part of the Bill; then it was put to Vote, Whether the whole Bill, together with the printed Charter (the Explanation of the said Charter mentioned in the Bill, being also admitted) should stand firm or not, and it was *resolved in the Affirmative.*

The Clerk by Order of the Speaker, adjourns the House to the third Hour in the Afternoon, the next Day.

About the Time appointed the House sat. The Speaker having assum'd the Chair, orders the Clerk to call over the names of the Members; which done, he proposes to the House, That the Bill read Yesterday, might be read over a second Time, which the House assented to. The Bill, by Order of the Speaker, was read in the House, whereupon a Debate arose, touching the Number of Members of Assembly thought meet for Election; this being a while debated, it was put to Vote, Whether six Members in each County were by the House thought a competent Number for the Assembly the next Year. The Question being put, it was *resolved in the Affirmative.*

The Bill having been read a second Time, the Question was put to the House. Whether the said Bill (the Alteration of it at the second Reading being admitted) should stand firm or not, and it was *resolved in the Affirmative.* . . .

Whereas the Speaker, with great Labour and kind Respect to the House, after signifying to the House, those Customs practiced in Parliaments, concerning the Duty which each Member owes to each other, and so to this House; several Members having shewed themselves disrespectful, having made Contumacies by absenting themselves, and breaking other good Customs agreed upon by this House: It is therefore, by the major Vote of this House, concluded, and by the Speaker ordered, that whosoever shall hereafter be guilty of the like Offences, unless in case of Sickness, or some very urgent and extraordinary Case, which the House shall judge to be so, every such Person shall pay *twelve-pence, Sterling,* forthwith, or the Value of it.

Signed in the Behalf of the Members, by
THOMAS WINN, Speaker

The Governor and Members being present, it pleased the Governor, to give Liberty to the House of making Proposals of such Things, and Matters, as they thought might prevent such Evils and Aggrievances, as were likely otherwise to fall upon the People of this Province; that so such Matters as aforesaid, might be pass'd into Laws, for the Good of its Inhabitants. Whereupon a Debate arose, touching the Value and Weight of Coin *Spanish, etc.* but in the End, was suspended. . . .

A Committee was chosen of six Members of the House, out of each of the six Counties; one, *viz.* to conclude and determine a Fine to be levied upon the Members that had absented themselves during the whole Sessions of the Assembly, *etc.*

An article was read, touching several Laws already resolved on by the House, *viz.* That they should stand firm and irrepealable, except six Parts of Seven of Provincial Council and Assembly should consent thereto; *resolved* (N.C.D.) *in the Affirmative.*

◄§ 26 §►

The Frame of Government of Pennsylvania, October 28, 1701

Charter of Privileges Granted by William Penn, Esq. to the Inhabitants of Pennsylvania and Territories, 1701

I. Because no People can be truly happy, though under the greatest Enjoyment of Civil Liberties, if abridged of the Freedom of their Consciences, as to their Religious Profession and Worship: . . .

I do hereby grant and declare, That no Person or Persons, inhabiting in this Province or Territories, who shall confess and acknowledge *One* almighty God, the Creator, Upholder and Ruler of the World; and profess him or themselves obliged to live quietly under the Civil Government, shall be in any Case molested or prejudiced, in his or their Person or Estate, because of his or their conscientious Persuasion or Practice, nor be compelled to frequent or maintain any religious Worship, Place or Ministry, contrary to his or their Mind, or to do or suffer any other Act or Thing, contrary to their religious Persuasion. . . .

II. FOR the well governing of this Province and Territories, there shall be an Assembly yearly chosen, by the Freemen thereof, to consist of *Four* Persons out of each County, of most Note for Virtue, Wisdom and Ability, (or of a greater number at any Time, as the Governor and Assembly shall agree) upon the *First* Day of *October* for ever; and shall sit on the *Fourteenth* Day of the same Month, at *Philadelphia,* unless the Governor and Council for the Time being, shall see Cause to appoint another Place within the said Province or Territories: Which Assembly shall have Power to chuse a Speaker and other their Officers; and shall be Judges of the Qualifications and Elections of their own

From Thorpe, ed., *The Federal and State Constitutions, Colonial Charters, and Other Organic Laws* . . . , V, 3076–81.

Members; sit upon their own Adjournments; appoint Committees; prepare Bills in order to pass into Laws; impeach Criminals, and redress Grievances; and shall have all other Powers and Privileges of an Assembly, according to the Rights of the free-born Subjects of *England,* and as is usual in any of the King's Plantations in *America.*

AND if any County or Counties, shall refuse or neglect to chuse their respective Representatives as aforesaid, or if chosen, do not meet to serve in Assembly, those who are so chosen and met, shall have the full Power of an Assembly, in as ample Manner as if all the Representatives had been chosen and met, provided they are not less than *Two Thirds* of the whole Number that ought to meet.

AND that the Qualifications of Electors and Elected, and all other Matters and Things relating to Elections of Representatives to serve in Assemblies, though not herein particularly expressed, shall be and remain as by a Law of this Government, made at *New-Castle* in the Year *One Thousand Seven Hundred,* entitled, *An Act to ascertain the Number of Members of Assembly, and to regulate the Elections.*

III. THAT the Freemen in each respective County, at the Time and Place of Meeting for Electing their Representatives to serve in Assembly, may as often as there shall be Occasion, chuse a double Number of Persons to present to the Governor for Sheriffs and Coroners to serve for *Three* Years, if so long they behave themselves well; out of which respective Elections and Presentments, the Governor shall nominate and commissionate one for each of the said Offices, the *Third* Day after such Presentment, or else the *First* named in such Presentment, for each Office as aforesaid, shall stand and serve in that Office for the Time before respectively limited; and in Case of Death or Default, such Vacancies shall be supplied by the Governor, to serve to the End of the said Term.

PROVIDED ALWAYS, That if the said Freemen shall at any Time neglect or decline to chuse a Person or Persons for either or both the aforesaid Offices, then and in such Case, the Persons that are or shall be in the respective Offices of Sheriffs or Coroners, at the Time of Election, shall remain therein, until they shall be removed by another Election as aforesaid.

AND that the Justices of the respective Counties shall or may nominate and present to the Governor *Three* Persons, to serve for Clerk of the Peace for the said County, when there is a Vacancy, one of which the Governor shall commissionate within *Ten* Days after such Presentment, or else the *First* nominated shall serve in the said Office during good Behavior.

IV. THAT the Laws of this Government shall be in this Stile, viz. *By the Governor, with the Consent and Approbation of the Freemen in General Assembly met;* and shall be, after Confirmation by the Governor, forthwith recorded in the Rolls Office, and kept at *Philadelphia,* unless the Governor and Assembly shall agree to appoint another Place. . . .

AND NOTWITHSTANDING the Closure and Test of this present Charter as aforesaid, I think fit to add this following Proviso thereunto, as Part of the same, *That is to say,* That notwithstanding any Clause or Clauses in the above-mentioned Charter, obliging the Province and Territories to join together in Legislation, I am content, and do hereby declare, that if the Representatives of the Province and Territories shall not hereafter agree to join together in Legislation, and that the same shall be signified unto me, or my Deputy, in open Assembly, or otherwise from under the Hands and Seals of the Representatives, for the Time being, of the Province and Territories, or the major Part of either of them, at any Time within *Three* Years from the Date hereof, that in such Case, the Inhabitants of each of the *Three* Counties of this Province, shall not have less than *Eight* Persons to represent them in Assembly, for the Province; and the Inhabitants of the Town of *Philadelphia* (when the said Town is incorporated) *Two* Persons to represent them in Assembly; and the Inhabitants of each County in the Territories, shall have as many Persons to represent them in a distinct Assembly for the Territories, as shall be by them requested as aforesaid.

◆§ VIII §◆

The Eighteenth-Century Inheritance

THE assertiveness of representative bodies in the eighteenth-century colonies is described again and again by provincial governors in memorials and letters to the authorities in London. Especially was this true of Massachusetts Bay, where the assembly had a long, honorable, and largely autonomous history. Following a military career in the Duke of Marlborough's armies, Samuel Shute (1662–1742) became governor of Massachusetts and New Hampshire in 1716. Seven years later he returned to England to present the Crown with a lengthy memorial concerning the politics and financial condition of the Bay colony (Doc. 27). His memorial was given over to the Board of Trade, which confirmed its accuracy and declared that the people of Massachusetts "are daily endeavouring to wrest the small remains of power out of the hands of the Crown, and to become independent of their Mother Kingdom."

Two years after Shute presented his memorial, David Lloyd published a *Vindication of the Legislative Power* in Pennsylvania (Doc. 28). Lloyd (c.1656–1731) was a Welsh-born lawyer and politician who emigrated to Pennsylvania in 1686 after the proprietor had commissioned him to be attorney general of the province. Within a very short time Lloyd was also appointed clerk of the county court, clerk of the provincial court, and deputy master of the rolls. In 1693 he was elected to the assembly as a representative from Chester County; the next year he began his long (and intermittent) career as speaker of that body. In 1700 a political and personal dispute caused Lloyd to become a lifelong enemy of William Penn and James Logan, provincial secretary and chief representative of the proprietary interest in Pennsylvania. Throughout these years Lloyd insisted upon constitutional reform, upon the right of the assembly to meet and adjourn at its own pleasure, and upon popular control of the judiciary. From 1717 until his death in 1731, Lloyd served as chief justice of the province. During his long career as speaker and justice, Lloyd steadily resisted efforts by the governor and council to control the judiciary and encroach upon the functions and privileges of the assembly. Lloyd was undoubtedly the finest lawyer in colonial Pennsylvania, and perhaps exerted the greatest single influence on the character of its early legislation. His *Vindication of the Legislative Power* sums up his concerns and reflections after a lifetime in assembly affairs.

The career of John Randolph (c.1693–1737) resembled Lloyd's in some respects. His high intelligence and native shrewdness would make him the lawyer most distinguished for ability and learning in the first half of the eighteenth century in Virginia. He held as many different provincial offices as Lloyd; but unlike the Pennsylvanian, Randolph was a member of the establishment. He became clerk of the House of Burgesses in 1718, and held that profitable and influential office until 1734. In that year, when it became clear that the speakership of the House of Burgesses would fall vacant, Randolph gave up his clerkship, was elected by the faculty of the College of William and Mary as their representative, was seated and elected speaker within the record span of three days. Later in the same session he was also made treasurer of the colony. The burgesses re-elected Randolph their speaker in 1736, though with some opposition, and he chose that occasion to deliver two splendid speeches on his conception of the assembly in the colonial constitution (Doc. 29).

Like Lloyd and Randolph, John Adams (1735–1826) was also trained in the law. He was admitted to the Boston bar in 1758, and soon after began writing on public affairs for newspapers. In opposition to the Stamp Act, he wrote for Braintree some resolutions of protest which were subsequently followed throughout Massachusetts. In 1770–1 he served briefly as a representative of Boston in the General Court; and in 1774 he was chosen as one of the delegates from Massachusetts to the first Continental Congress. There he served as a member of the committee to prepare a petition to George III, and on another committee to draft a declaration of rights, for which he wrote a section on taxation, representation, and consent to the regulation of external commerce.

In January 1776 Thomas Paine published *Common Sense,* advocating a plan of government which Adams hoped to counteract by his *Thoughts on Government* . . . (Doc. 30). Adams's pamphlet was originally prepared for the delegates of North Carolina, but was published (at first anonymously) to meet a wider demand. Paine's plan had annoyed Adams because it "was so democratical, without any restraint or even an attempt at equilibrium." Instead, Adams hoped it would be possible to devise republican governments with inner balances as effective as those of a mixed monarchy, that is, a government embracing monarchy, aristocracy, and democracy. Foremost in Adams's scheme was the need for a representative national assembly. His urgent recommendation was widely endorsed, and amplified in the polemical literature of the constitution-making generation.

◄§ 27 §►

A Memorial to King George I from Governor Samuel Shute in Massachusetts, 1723

[Upon arrival in the Massachusetts Bay in October 1716] I soon called the General Assembly together. I found the House of Representatives, who are chosen annually, possessed of all the same powers of the House of Commons, and of much greater, they having the power of nominating once a year the persons that constitute your Majesty's Council, etc., and giving the salary of the governor and lieutenant-governor but from six months to six months; and likewise giving such only as is no way suitable to the rank of your Majesty's governor and lieutenant-governor, or

From Cecil Headlam, *et al.,* eds., *Calendar of State Papers, Colonial Series, America and West Indies, 1722–23* (London, 1934), 324–30.

to the known abilities of the province, and this notwithstanding your Majesty's instructions, directing them to settle a salary suitable to their stations and for such time as they shall continue in [them?]. The said House likewise appoint the salary of the treasurer every year whereby they have in effect the sole authority over that important office, which they often use in order to intimidate the treasurer from obeying the proper orders for issuing money, if such orders are not agreeable to their views and inclinations. By all which means the House of Representatives are in a manner the whole legislative, and in a good measure the executive power of the province. This House consists of about one hundred, who by an act of Assembly must be persons residing in the respective towns which they represent, whereby it happens that the greatest part of them are of small fortunes and mean education; men of the best sense and circumstances generally residing in or near Boston; so that by the artifice of a few designing members, together with the insinuations of some people in the town of Boston, the country representatives are easily made to believe that the House is barely supporting the privileges of the people, whilst they are invading the undoubted prerogatives of the Crown. Were it not for this act, the Assembly would certainly consist of men of much better sense, temper, and fortune than they do at present. The Assembly usually sit at Boston, the capital of this province, a large and populous town supposed to contain about 18,000 inhabitants, under no magistracy, by the want of which many of the inhabitants become too much disposed to a levelling spirit, too apt to be mutinous and disorderly, and to support the House of Representatives in any steps they take towards encroaching on the prerogative of the Crown. That this is too much the prevailing temper in the majority of the inhabitants of this town is plain from hence, that if I have at any time, according to the known power vested in your Majesty's governor of that province, with the strongest reasons, given my negative to any person nominated to be of your Majesty's Council there, the said town have hardly ever failed to choose him their representative. Three negatived councillors are the present representatives of the town of Boston. This practice is so notoriously known and justified that it is a common maxim that a negatived councillor makes a good representative. The House of Representatives thus constituted and abetted, notwithstanding the many uncommon privileges they enjoy by virtue of their charter, far from being contented therewith, have for some years last past been making attempts upon the few prerogatives that have been reserved to the Crown; which for that reason, as well as from the obligation of my oath and the trust reposed in me by your Majesty, I have endeavoured to my utmost to maintain against all invasions whatsoever.

◅§ 28 §►

Justice David Lloyd's *Vindication of the Legislative Power* in Pennsylvania, 1725

May it please this Honourable House,

Having perused *James Logan's* Memorial and other Papers lately published by your Authority, I find the Governour hath vindicated the Powers of our Legislature and the method you are now in, with such convincing Arguments, urged with so much clearness and good reasoning, that it seems needless to say any more; yet, I hope it will be no offence to offer some legal Authorities to prove what has been so Excellently advanced in favour of the Rights and Liberties of the Subject, as well as the regular Powers and Franchises of Government in the Points now under Consideration.

It is Evident to me, that the Royal Charter granted to our late Proprietary *William Penn,* under the great Seal of *England,* may safely be deemed the Fundamental Constitution of our Legislative Authority, by which Charter the late King CHARLES the second, in a very gracious and bountiful Manner, was pleased to signify his Royal Will and Pleasure in these Words, *to wit,* "*That we,* reposing special Trust and Confidence in the Fidelity,

From David Lloyd, A *Vindication of the Legislative Power, Submitted to the Representatives of all the Free-men of the Province of Pennsylvania, now sitting in Assembly* (Philadelphia, Pa., 1725), 1–3. Reproduced by courtesy of the Historical Society of Pennsylvania.

Wisdom, Justice and provident Circumspection of the said *William Penn*, for Us, Our Heirs and Successors, *Do Grant* free, full and absolute Power, by Virtue of these presents, to him and his Heirs, to his and their Deputies and Lieutenants, for the good and happy Government of the said Country, to Ordain, Make and Enact, and, under his and their Seals, to publish any Laws whatsoever, for the raising of Money for the Publick uses of the said Province, or for any other End, appertaining either unto the publick State, Peace or Safety of the said Country, or unto the private Utility of particular Persons, according unto their best Direction, *By and with* the Advice, Assent and Approbation of the Free-men of the said Country, or the greater part of them, or of their Delegates or Deputies, *Whom*, for the Enacting of the said Laws, when and as often as need shall require, We will, That the said *William Penn* and his Heirs shall Assemble in such sort and form as to him and them shall seem best."

By Virtue of this Clause the Proprietor had Power to make Deputies and Lieutenants, in which Case (as it is in all other Cases where a Deputy may be appointed) the Law says, he has full Power to do any act or thing which his Principal may do: And that is so essentially incident to a Deputy, that a Man cannot be a Deputy to do any single act or thing, nor can a Deputy have less Power than his Principal, and if his Principal make him Covenant, *That he will not do any particular thing which the Principal may do,* the Covenant is void and repugnant.

The next thing observable in the above recited Clause of the Royal Charter, is the Right and Power of Legislation, granted to the Proprietor and his Heirs and to his and their Deputies and Lieutenants, by and with the Assent of the Free-men of this Province; which being expressed as amply as any Liberty or Privilege of that kind can be granted, I am induced to conclude, that, by the Virtue of this Grant, there was such a Right originally vested and become inherent in every Free-man of this Province as wanted not the help of any Grant or Charter from the Proprietary to confirm it.

But the Proprietor, pursuant to the said recited Clause, made

Charters which prescribed the form of Assembling the Free-men
to act in Legislation after the Modes mentioned in the Memorial;
and it may be the People were regardless of a new Charter after
the Resignation of the first, not out of any liking they had to be
convened by Writs, but as the Right of Meeting together to make
Laws was virtually in them by the said Royal Grant, so the form
of their Elections and Assembling might be settled by Law,
which was effected afterwards by an Act to Ascertain the number of Members of Assembly and to regulate Elections, which
passed in the fourth Year of Queen *Anne's* Reign, and settled
yearly Elections of Representatives in Assembly without Writs,
and appointed the Time when and by whom those Elections
should be made, as also the Time of the Assembly's Meeting, and
how they should qualify themselves to act, choose their Speaker,
and be Judges of the Qualifications and Elections of their own
Members, sit upon their own Adjournments, appoint Committees,
prepare Bills in order to pass into Laws, *Impeach Criminals* and
redress Grievances, & etc.

By this Law and last Charter (wherein the Proprietary, according to his Right made one side of the agreement, which he
could not alter or avoid without the Concurrence of the parties
concerned on the other side) it is evident, That the whole Legislative Authority here is lodged in the Governour and Representatives of the People; and I have met none so senseless as to say,
that the Governour is thereby concluded of having a Council to
advise and assist in Legislation and other matter relating to the
State, and I have known divers of the Members of that Board
very serviceable in that Station, and, I doubt not may be so still,
therefore I desire they may not withdraw from their Service
nor insist upon a Negative to the Acts of those that Represent
them, which, by a reasonable Construction of the said Law and
Charter, is lodged with the Governour, and is so vested in him
by his Commission stamped with the Royal Allowance and Authority of the King's Letters Patent, That the Proprietary could
by no Instruction or other Act whatsoever, without the Governour's Consent, divest him of his Right to Govern, unless by
resuming the Government or Deputing another in his stead. And

if the Governour has given any Bond or Covenant to observe Instructions that abridge or restrain the Authority granted him by Commission to Exercise the Powers of Government in this Province, the same is void, as appears by the above cited Resolutions, from whence it may be observed how careful the Law is to keep Powers entire, as the best means to preserve good Order in States and Governments, where no such absurdity can be admitted, as to allow the Persons Represented to controul the Acts of their Representatives, especially in those Matters which the other Branch of the Legislature may think to be reasonably Proposed.

And altho' the Law declares, that Bonds and Covenants (given to Guard the Principal, when he would diminish or abridge the Power of his Deputy) are Repugnant to his Office, and therefore void and against Law, having a tendency to deny or delay Justice (as in our Case) yet, if the Governour came under any Security to observe the Directions of the King's Grant, which forbids to depart from the Faith and Allegeance due to the King, or to maintain Correspondence with his Enemies, or to commit Hostility against such as are in League with him, or Transgress against the Laws of Trade and Navigation, or for discharging of his Trust and Duty in the Administration of the Government according to the purport of the said Royal Grant and the Laws and Constitutions of this Province; I conceive that in those Cases such Security is binding upon the Governour and will be most effectual and available in Law, unless some illegal or repugnant Condition be annexed thereunto.

As to the Power of making Ordinances with the assistance of other Persons than the People's Delegates, it appears by the Patent, that those Ordinances cannot be Extended, in any sort, to bind, change or take away the Right or Interest of any Person or Persons for or in their Life, Members, Free-hold, Goods or Chattels, nor are they directed to be made except sudden Accidents happen, whereto it may be necessary to apply Remedy, before the Free-holders or their Delegates can be assembled to make Laws,—Besides our Lawmakers (who ought to have Notice of such Occasions) may be convened as soon as the Magis-

trates, and Officers of the respective Counties, who are to assist
in making Ordinances: But if the Ordinance-makers should happen to get the start; yet when the Delegates of the People come
together and acquaint the Governour of their readiness to assist
him in the publick Service of the Government, and to answer
the Exigences thereof, I think the Power of making Ordinances
should then be waved, and the Legislative Authority applyed
to, because their Acts are deemed more Extensive and Binding,
as appears by the express Words of the said Patent.

But if the Governour could be prevailed with not to Summon
the Assembly upon such Emergency, or when Assembled would
not Concurr with them in what may be for the Publick Good, as
the Case was, when former Governours, being under an ill direction, withstood the Representatives' proposals and cordial Advice,
and (contrary to Law and Charter) set up Ordinances instead
of Laws, to the great dissatisfaction of the Assembly then attending, who declared themselves ready and willing to Concurr in a
regular Establishment, according to the Laws and Practice of
England, instead of what was Imposed by Ordinance, which
highly concerned the Lives, Liberties and Estates of the Subjects;
There are divers Worthy Members of this House have been well
acquainted with these Proceedings, and if it were not so, yet the
Journal of that Time will manifest what I hint.

It may do well for the Secretary [James Logan] to Consider,
with what views he acted his part in that Tragedy, and whether it
was not designed to render the People's Power in Legislation useless? whereby this Country, from a State of Freedom, should be
changed into an Arbitrary Government, subjected to the Power
of one Person, as the Secretary in another Case matterially ob-
serves. I am apt to think by what I gather from this Memorial
and some more of these Printed Papers, that the ready way to
bring us under this Change must be by enjoyning a Negative
upon the Governour and Assembly, and checking the Freedom
of Communication between them by Speeches and Messages, and
then get a new Council, (for the present Members of that Honourable Board will not give in to this Arbitrary Scheme) who
must be such as will assent to all the Secretary proposes, and

when a Council Board is thus furnished, any Body (without much Penetration) may guess who that *one Person* must be.

⌐§ 29 §⌐

John Randolph's Speeches to the Virginia House
of Burgesses, Governor and Council,
Upon Being Chosen Speaker, August 5 and 6, 1736

A. To the House of Burgesses, August 5

Gentlemen,

The Testimony you give, to the Probity and Integrity of the Person, whom you think fit to chuse for your Speaker, must be a considerable Addition to any Man's Character; and to make Excuses for refusing it, which we hope may not be accepted, were only to make a false Shew of Modesty, that can be of no more Worth than Ostentation.

IN me it would be an absurd Hypocrisy, since my Willingness to continue in the Service of this House has been well known among you, tho' I have not endeavoured to anticipate any Man's Judgment, by soliciting his Vote: Therefore I shall not hesitate in owning the Satisfaction with which I accept the Honour you now bestow upon me; and I do it with the greater Pleasure, seeing many worthy Gentlemen, experienced Members of the House of Burgesses, who have been long Witnesses of my Behaviour, still retain a good Opinion of it. I am very sensible of your Favour, and that the Obligations you lay me under, are too great to be satisfied with the ordinary Returns of Thanks and Compliments; which would be paying a vast Debt with a small Matter: But it will require a great Degree of Circumspection and Prudence, Labour and Diligence, Steadiness and Impartiality to acquit me. And when so many Qualities must concur in the right Execution of an Office, the Difficulties which must attend it, cannot but be very obvious. And if all this shall not be sufficient; if every Action shall be construed with the utmost Rigour

From H. R. McIlwaine, ed., *Journals of the House of Burgesses of Virginia, 1727–1734* (Richmond, Va., 1910), 239–40, 241–2.

and Severity; no allowances made for common Mistakes; and That which upon due Examination may appear to be just, shall be equally censured, with what is apparently not so; who can withstand so great Discouragements.

BUT I rely upon your Candour, not doubting but your Animadversions upon me will always be just, and my Conduct interpreted with some Indulgence.

Gentlemen,

WE must consider ourselves chosen by all the People; sent hither to represent them, to give their Consent in the weightiest of their Concerns; and to bind them by Laws which may advance their Common Good. Herein they trust you with all that they have, place the greatest Confidence in your Wisdoms and Discretions, and testify the highest Opinion of your Virtue. And surely, a Desire of pleasing some, and the Fear of offending others; Views to little Advantages and Interests; adhering too fondly to ill-grounded Conceits; the Prejudices of Opinions too hastily taken up; and Affectation to Popularity; Private Animosities or Personal Resentments; which have often too much to do in Popular Assemblies, and sometimes put a Bias upon Mens Judgments, can upon no Occasion, turn us aside in the Prosecution of this important Duty, from what shall appear to be the true Interest of the People: Tho' it may be often impossible to conform to their Sentiments, since, when we come to consider and compare them, we shall find them so various and irreconcileable.

THE Honour of the House of Burgesses hath of late been raised higher than can be observed in former Times; and I am persuaded you will not suffer it to be lessened under your Management.

IN every Thing that depends upon me, I shall never fail to be zealous for what may redound most to your Honour. And tho' I must not pretend to sway your Debates, I will endeavour to preserve Rule and Order in them.

I WILL be watchful of your Privileges, without which we should be no more than a dead Body; and advertise you of every Incident that may have the least Tendency to destroy or diminish them. And lastly, I will labour to give all proper Dispatch to your Proceedings, and to bring them to a good Issue; which are the only Means, whereby I may be able to pay the Duty I owe you, to deserve the great Favour you have shewn me, or any Applause from the Public.

B. To the Governor and Council, August 6

I humbly thank you for this your favourable Opinion; which I don't pretend to deserve, but will use it as a proper Admonition, whereby I ought to regulate my Conduct in the Exercise of the Office you are now pleas'd to confirm me in; which I do not intend to magnify to the Degree some have done, feeling we are no more than the Representative Body of a Colony, naturally and justly dependent upon the Mother Kingdom, whose Power is circumscribed by very narrow Bounds; and whose Influence is of small Extent. All we pretend to, is to be of some Importance to Those who send us hither, and to have some Share in their Protection, and the Security of their Lives, Liberties, and Properties.

The Planters, who sustain'd the Heat and Burthen of the first Settlment of this Plantation, were miserably harrassed by the Government, in the Form it was then established, which had an unnatural Power of Ruling by Martial Law, and Constitutions passed by a Council in *England*, without the Consent of the People, which were no better: This made the Name of *Virginia* so infamous, that we see the Impressions of those Times, hardly yet worn out in other Countries, especially among the Vulgar: And such have been in all Ages, and for ever must continue to be, the Effects of an Arbitrary Despotic Power; of which the Company in *London*, in whom all Dominion and Property was then lodged, were so sensible, that they resolved to establish another Form of Government more agreeable and suitable to the Temper and Genius of the *English* Nation. And accordingly, in July, 1621, pass'd a Charter under their Common Seal, which was founded upon Powers before granted by Charters under the Great Seal of *England;* whereby they ordered and declared, That for preventing Injustice and Oppression for the Future; and for

advancing the Strength and Prosperity of the Colony, there
should be Two Supreme Councils; One to be called, *The Council
of State,* consisting of the Governor, and certain Councillors, particularly named, to serve as a Council of Advice to the Governor;
the other to be called by the Governor, Yearly, consisting of
the Council of State, and Two Burgesses to be chosen by the
Inhabitants of every Town, Hundred, or other Plantation; to be
called, *The General Assembly:* And to have free Power to treat,
consult, and conclude, of all Things concerning the Public Weal;
and to enact such Laws for the Behoof of the Colony, and the
good Government thereof, as from Time to Time should appear
necessary or requisite: Commanding them to imitate and follow
the Policy, Form of Government, Laws, Customs, Manner of
Trial, and other Administration of Justice used in *England*; and
providing that no Orders of their General Court should bind
the Colony, unless ratified in the General Assemblies, This is the
Original of our Constitution, confirmed by King *James* the First,
by King *Charles* the First, upon his Accession to the Throne, and
by all the Crown'd Heads of *England,* and *Great-Britain,* suc-
cessively, upon the Appointment of every new Governor, with
very little Alteration. Under it, we are grown to whatever we
now have to boast of. And from hence, the House of Burgesses
do derive diverse Privileges, which they have long enjoy'd, and
claim as their undoubted Right. Freedom of Speech is the very
Essence of their Being, because, without it, nothing could be
thoroly debated, nor could they be look'd upon as a Council;
an Exemption from Arrests, confirm'd by a Positive Law, otherwise their Counsels and Debates might be frequently interrupted, and their Body diminished by the Loss of its Members;
a Protection for their Estates, to prevent all Occasions to withdraw them from the necessary Duty of their Attendance; a
Power over their own Members, that they may be answerable to
no other Jurisdiction for any Thing done in the House; and a
sole Right of determining all Questions concerning their own
Elections, lest contrary Judgments, in the Courts of Law, might
thwart or destroy Theirs.

All these, I say, besides others which spring out of them,

are incident to the Nature and Constitution of our Body; and I am commanded by the House, to offer a Petition in their Behalf, that You will be pleas'd to discountenance all Attempts that may be offer'd against them, and assist us with Your Authority in supporting and maintaining them against all Insults whatsoever: And Lastly, I must beg Your Favour to my self, that You will not construe my Actions with too much Severity, nor impute my particular Errors and Failings to the House.

◄§ 30 §►

John Adams's Thoughts on Representative Government in 1776

We ought to consider what is the end of government, before we determine which is the best form. Upon this point all speculative politicians will agree, that the happiness of society is the end of government, as all divines and moral philosophers will agree that the happiness of the individual is the end of man. From this principle it will follow, that the form of government which communicates ease, comfort, security, or, in one word, happiness, to the greatest number of persons, and in the greatest degree, is the best. . . .

The foundation of every government is some principle or passion in the minds of the people. The noblest principles and most generous affections in our nature, then, have the fairest chance to support the noblest and most generous models of government.

A man must be indifferent to the sneers of modern Englishmen, to mention in their company the names of Sidney, Harrington, Locke, Milton, Nedham, Neville, Burnet, and Hoadly. No small fortitude is necessary to confess that one has read them. The wretched condition of this country, however, for ten or fifteen years past, has frequently reminded me of their princi-

From [John Adams], *Thoughts on Government: Applicable to the Present State of the American Colonies. In a Letter from a Gentleman to His Friend* (Philadelphia, Pa., 1776) in Charles Francis Adams, ed., *The Works of John Adams* (10 vols., Boston, 1851), IV, 193–7.

ples and reasonings. They will convince any candid mind, that
there is no good government but what is republican. That the
only valuable part of the British constitution is so; because the
very definition of a republic is "an empire of laws, and not of
men." That, as a republic is the best of governments, so that
particular arrangement of the powers of society, or, in other
words, that form of government which is best contrived to secure
an impartial and exact execution of the laws, is the best of republics.

Of republics there is an inexhaustible variety, because the
possible combinations of the powers of society are capable of
innumerable variations.

As good government is an empire of laws, how shall your
laws be made? In a large society, inhabiting an extensive country, it is impossible that the whole should assemble to make
laws. The first necessary step, then, is to depute power from
the many to a few of the most wise and good. But by what
rules shall you choose your representatives? Agree upon the
number and qualifications of persons who shall have the benefit
of choosing, or annex this privilege to the inhabitants of a certain
extent of ground.

The principal difficulty lies, and the greatest care should be
employed, in constituting this representative assembly. It should
be in miniature an exact portrait of the people at large. It
should think, feel, reason, and act like them. That it may be
the interest of this assembly to do strict justice at all times, it
should be an equal representation, or, in other words, equal interests among the people should have equal interests in it. Great
care should be taken to effect this, and to prevent unfair, partial, and corrupt elections. Such regulations, however, may be
better made in times of greater tranquillity than the present; and
they will spring up themselves naturally, when all the powers
of government come to be in the hands of the people's friends.
At present, it will be safest to proceed in all established modes,
to which the people have been familiarized by habit.

A representation of the people in one assembly being obtained, a question arises, whether all the powers of government,

legislative, executive, and judicial, shall be left in this body? I
think a people cannot be long free, nor ever happy, whose
government is in one assembly. My reasons for this opinion are
as follow:—

1. A single assembly is liable to all the vices, follies, and
frailties of an individual; subject to fits of humor, starts of passion,
flights of enthusiasm, partialities, or prejudice, and consequently
productive of hasty results and absurd judgments. And all these
errors ought to be corrected and defects supplied by some controlling power.

2. A single assembly is apt to be avaricious, and in time will
not scruple to exempt itself from burdens, which it will lay,
without compunction, on its constituents.

3. A single assembly is apt to grow ambitious, and after a
time will not hesitate to vote itself perpetual. This was one fault
of the Long Parliament; but more remarkably of Holland, whose
assembly first voted themselves from annual to septennial, then
for life, and after a course of years, that all vacancies happening
by death or otherwise, should be filled by themselves, without
any application to constituents at all.

4. A representative assembly, although extremely well qualified, and absolutely necessary, as a branch of the legislative, is
unfit to exercise the executive power, for want of two essential
properties, secrecy and despatch.

5. A representative assembly is still less qualified for the
judicial power, because it is too numerous, too slow, and too little
skilled in the laws.

6. Because a single assembly, possessed of all the powers of
government, would make arbitrary laws for their own interest,
execute all laws arbitrarily for their own interest, and adjudge
all controversies in their own favor.

But shall the whole power of legislation rest in one assembly?
Most of the foregoing reasons apply equally to prove that the
legislative power ought to be more complex; to which we may
add, that if the legislative power is wholly in one assembly, and
the executive in another, or in a single person, these two powers
will oppose and encroach upon each other, until the contest shall

end in war, and the whole power, legislative and executive, be usurped by the strongest.

The judicial power, in such case, could not mediate, or hold the balance between the two contending powers, because the legislative would undermine it. And this shows the necessity, too, of giving the executive power a negative upon the legislative, otherwise this will be continually encroaching upon that.

To avoid these dangers, let a distinct assembly be constituted, as a mediator between the two extreme branches of the legislature, that which represents the people, and that which is vested with the executive power.

Let the representative assembly then elect by ballot, from among themselves or their constituents, or both, a distinct assembly, which, for the sake of perspicuity, we will call a council. It may consist of any number you please, say twenty or thirty, and should have a free and independent exercise of its judgment, and consequently a negative voice in the legislature.

These two bodies, thus constituted, and made integral parts of the legislature, let them unite, and by joint ballot choose a governor, who, after being stripped of most of those badges of domination, called prerogatives, should have a free and independent exercise of his judgment, and be made also an integral part of the legislature. This, I know, is liable to objections; and, if you please, you may make him only president of the council, as in Connecticut. But as the governor is to be invested with the executive power, with consent of council, I think he ought to have a negative upon the legislative. If he is annually elective, as he ought to be, he will always have so much reverence and affection for the people, their representatives and counsellors, that, although you give him an independent exercise of his judgment, he will seldom use it in opposition to the two houses, except in cases the public utility of which would be conspicuous; and some such cases would happen.

In the present exigency of American affairs, when, by an act of Parliament, we are put out of the royal protection, and consequently discharged from our allegiance, and it has become necessary to assume government for our immediate security, the governor, lieutenant-governor, secretary, treasurer, commissary, attorney-general, should be chosen by joint ballot of both houses. And these and all other elections, especially of representatives and counsellors, should be annual, there not being in the whole circle of the sciences a maxim more infallible than this, "where annual elections end, there slavery begins."

BIBLIOGRAPHY & INDEX

✑ Bibliography ✑

The documentation to the "Prolegomenon: An Interpretive Inquiry" cites many of the basic printed sources, primary and secondary, for the study of colonial assemblies in the seventeenth century. In this brief note I shall not (with a very few exceptions) recapitulate that bibliography, but rather suggest additional materials and, hopefully, some profitable lines of inquiry.

The best bibliographical introduction of a general nature is by Helen M. Cam, A. Marongiu, and G. Stökl, "Recent Work and Present Views on the Origins and Development of Representative Assemblies," *Relazione Del X Congresso Internazionale Di Scienze Storiche*, vol. 1: *Metodologia Problemi Generali* (Florence, Italy, 1955), 1–101. Robert S. Hoyt surveyed "Recent Publications in the United States and Canada on the History of Representative Institutions Before the French Revolution," in *Speculum*, XXIX (1954), 356–77. Gordon Griffiths has put together an extraordinarily comprehensive collection of sources with lengthy editorial notes: *Representative Government in Western Europe in the Sixteenth Century* (Oxford, 1968). Griffiths, Lesley B. Simpson, and Woodrow Borah collaborated on three related essays published under the title "Representative Institutions in the Spanish Empire in the Sixteenth Century," in *The Americas*, XII (1955–6), 223–57.

Wallace Notestein's classic essay, "The Winning of the Initiative by the House of Commons," *Proceedings of the British Academy*, XI (1924), 125–75, emphasizes the importance of procedural tactics, and may still be read as a model of narrative analysis. R. W. K. Hinton examines the very same period and argues for "The Decline of Parliamentary Government Under Elizabeth I and the Early Stuarts" in the *Cambridge Historical Journal*, XIII (1957), 116–32. Louise F. Brown describes "Ideas of Representation from Elizabeth to Charles II," in the *Journal of Modern History*, XI (1939), 23–40. Margaret A. Judson has written perhaps the best study of constitutional controversy during the reigns of James I and Charles I, *The Crisis of the Constitution: An Essay in Constitutional and Political Thought in England, 1603–1645* (New Brunswick, N.J., 1949). Between Hooker and Hobbes, although very few comprehensive or original political treatises were written, the most critical debates in all of English history were under way.

There are many valuable sources for parliamentary history during the era of James I. The best beginning might be made with Elizabeth Read Foster, ed., *Proceedings in Parliament, 1610* (2 vols., New Haven, Conn., 1966), and Wallace Notestein, ed., *Commons Debates, 1621* (7 vols., New Haven, Conn., 1935), which contains 14 parliamentary accounts, a book of orders, and a volume of documents. Four monographs are especially relevant: D. H. Willson, "Summoning and Dissolving Parliament, 1603–25," *American Historical Review*, XLV (1940), 279–300; Thomas L. Moir, *The Addled Parliament of 1614* (Oxford, 1958), which analyzes elections and the composition of both houses; Robert M. Zaller, "The Parliament of 1621: A Study in Constitutional Conflict" (unpubl. Ph.D. dissertation [Washington University, St. Louis, 1968]), which contends that the monarchy and Parliament had become fundamentally incompatible by 1621; and Robert E. Ruigh, "The Parliament of 1624: Foreign Policy, Prerogative and Politics" (unpubl. Ph.D. dissertation [Harvard University, 1966]).

For the middle and later seventeenth century, students should consult Vernon F. Snow, "Parliamentary Re-apportionment Proposals in the Puritan Revolution," *English Historical Review*, LXXIV (1959), 409–42, and Philip A. Gibbons, *Ideas of Political Representation in Parliament, 1660–1832* (Oxford, 1914). The two most useful source collections are J. R. Tanner, ed., *Constitutional Documents of the Reign of James I, A.D. 1603–1625* (2nd ed., Cambridge, 1930), and J. P. Kenyon, ed., *The Stuart Constitution, 1603–1688* (Cambridge, 1966). Don M. Wolfe has edited *Leveller Manifestoes of the Puritan Revolution* (New York, 1944), which includes Richard Overton's *Appeale from the Degenerate Representative Body the Commons of England Assembled at Westminster: to the Body Represented, the Free People in Generall* (London, 1647). The Putney Debates of October 1647, so deeply concerned with theories of representation and consent, appear in A. S. P. Woodhouse, ed., *Puritanism and Liberty. Being the Army Debates (1647–9) from the Clarke Manuscripts* (Chicago, 1951), 1–124.

Fruitful insights may well emerge from comparisons between the early colonial assemblies and those of England's other dependencies, Ireland and Scotland. The deliberative and legislative methods of the Scottish Parliament, for example, differed rather widely from English custom. The most notable feature of Scottish parliamentary procedure involved the delegation of authority to the famous Committee of the Articles. The practice lasted until 1690 and originated as a device for expediting the conduct of business in an assembly not altogether capable of government and a country not altogether ready for parliamentary rule. See A. A. M. Duncan, "The Early Parliaments of Scotland," *The Scottish Historical Review*, XLV (1966), 36–58; Robert S. Rait, *The Scottish Parliament* (London, 1925); C. S. Terry, *The Scottish Parliament, Its Constitution and Procedure, 1603–1707* (Glasgow, 1905); and H. G. Richardson and G. O. Sayles, *The Irish Parliament in the Middle Ages* (Philadelphia, Pa., 1952), which treats the years 1264 to 1495.

The best study of colonial legislative origins in relation to changes in English political thought is J. R. Pole's *The Seventeenth Century: The Sources of Legislative Power* (Charlottesville, Va., 1969). I am deeply grateful to Dr. Pole for an early opportunity to read his essay when it was in typescript. Wesley Frank Craven discusses some of the historiography of representative government (especially in Virginia), unsolved problems, and opportunities for future scholarship in ". . . And so the Form of Government Became Perfect," *Virginia Magazine of History and Biography*, LXXVII (1969), 131–45. The second chapter of A. C. McLaughlin, *Foundations of American Constitutionalism* (New York, 1932), despite some dubious details and questionable generalizations, remains the best brief study of institutional origins. In *Public and Republic: Political Representation in America* (New York, 1951), Alfred de Grazia concentrated upon theories of representation. Chapter 3 skips over origins and describes the developed colonial system. *Parliamentary Privilege in the American Colonies* (New Haven, Conn., 1943), by Mary P. Clarke, is a very useful book focusing largely upon the eighteenth century. The famous protests by John Wise of Ipswich against taxation without representation, 1687–9, are discussed and quoted at length in George A. Cook, *John Wise. Early American Democrat* (New York, 1952), Chapter 4.

Journals of the colonial assemblies form an indispensable source. Those still in manuscript are surveyed by Miss Clarke in *Parliamentary Privilege*, 275–9. Among printed collections not cited above are

"Minutes of the [Virginia] Council and General Court, 1622–1629," in *The Virginia Magazine of History and Biography*, XXII (1914), 1–5, 131–9, and XXIII (1915), 1–23, 124–38, 269–79, 404–6 (these are sketchy records published from originals in the Library of Congress); William Hand Browne, ed., *Archives of Maryland* (Baltimore, Md., 1883–   ), Vol. I, *Proceedings and Acts of the General Assembly of Maryland, January 1637/38—September 1664;* J. Hammond Trumbull, ed., *The Public Records of the Colony of Connecticut* (Hartford, Conn., 1850–90), Vol. I, especially 9–46; John Russell Bartlett, ed., *Records of the Colony of Rhode Island* (Providence, R.I., 1856–65), Vol. I, especially 143–208; *Journals of the Assembly of Jamaica* (Jamaica, 1811–29), Vol. I (1664–1709). William S. Powell, ed., *Ye Countie of Albemarle in Carolina: A Collection of Documents, 1664–1675* (Raleigh, N.C., 1958), provides previously unavailable sources to confirm the existence of Albemarle assemblies in 1665, 1667, 1668, and 1669. A selection of writs and returns for early assemblies in various colonies appears in Cortlandt F. Bishop, *History of Elections in the American Colonies* (New York, 1893), Appendix A.

Legislation passed by the first assemblies reveals a great deal about their impulses and imperatives. Some sets of colonial laws are discussed in Clarke, *Parliamentary Privilege*, 279–80. Others of note are *Acts of Assembly Passed in the Island of Barbados, from 1648, to 1718* (London, 1721), especially 1–51 [1648–1666]; and Sir John H. Lefroy, *Memorials of the Discovery and Early Settlement of the Bermudas or Somers Islands, 1515–1685* (2 vols., London, 1877–9): the laws passed by the 1620 assembly in Bermuda will be found in Vol. I, 165–79. It is curious and striking that early colonial legislation is generally rather quiet about the nature and functions of assemblies. There were many more laws passed concerning poultry and liquor than touching the frequency of meetings and their procedure. Since we know that a sufficient number of early legislators cared passionately about their institutional forms and stability, we must assume that they feared to put in print anything that might smack of deviation from English norms, or be offensive to executive forces.

We very much need biographical studies of the leaders of early assemblies. The first men chosen as speakers were usually the most experienced in parliamentary affairs, and they invariably steered the courses of their legislative bodies in significant ways. John Pory of Virginia, Samuel Farmer of Barbados, John Coggeshall, the first "Moderator" of Rhode Island, Samuel Waad of Montserrat, Samuel

Long of Jamaica, George Catchmaid of Albemarle, Thomas Olive of West New Jersey, Thomas Winn of Pennsylvania, Matthias Nicolls and William Pinhorne of New York, all deserve close attention. William S. Powell, "John Pory, His Life, Letters and Work" (unpubl. M.A. thesis [University of North Carolina, 1947]), is especially useful.

The eighteenth-century assemblies were focal points of continuous controversy. The best introduction is Jack P. Greene's "The Role of the Lower Houses of Assembly in Eighteenth Century Politics," *Journal of Southern History* XXVII (1961), 451–74, which should be read alongside H. G. Richardson's "The Commons and Medieval Politics," *Transactions of the Royal Historical Society*, 4th series, XXVIII (1946), 21–45, a thoughtful survey of several centuries. There is some question whether representative government in the Bahamas dates from 1671 or 1729. In *A History of the Bahamas House of Assembly* (Nassau, 1921), Harcourt G. Malcolm argues for the earlier date (see esp. 4–8, 36–46). He admits to a lack of firm evidence, however, and modern students prefer the eighteenth-century point of origin. If proper assemblies did exist after 1670, they were spasmodic and discontinuous, so that a new beginning had to be made in 1729 in any case.

A fascinating and illuminating exchange of views on the nature of assemblies may be found in [Anon.], *A Letter from a Gentleman in Philadelphia to His Friend in Bucks* (Philadelphia, Pa., 1728) [Evans No. 3048] and [Anon.], *The Proceedings of Some Members of the Assembly, at Philadelphia, April 1728, Vindicated from the Unfair Reasoning and Unjust Insinuations of a Certain Remarker* (Philadelphia, Pa., 1728) [Evans No. 3096], which insisted that the House of Commons and the Pennsylvania assembly were essentially dissimilar bodies. The assembly's aggressive assertion of a firm link between taxation and representation, called "A REMONSTRANCE to the Governor from the Assembly," appeared in *The Pennsylvania Gazette*, April 20, 1758, page 1. There is an interesting exchange in New York between J. W., *The Mode of Elections Considered . . .* (broadside, December 29, 1769) [Evans No. 11517] and a critic writing in Parker's *New York Gazette* (May 2, 1770), as to whether New York's manner of electing representatives was superior to that used in Connecticut and Pennsylvania. Jack P. Greene has edited " 'Not to Be Governed or Taxed But by . . . Our Representatives.' Four Essays in Opposition to the Stamp Act by Landon Carter," *Virginia Magazine of History and Biography*, LXXVI (1968), 259–300. For the debate over the nature of representation during the revolutionary era, see Gordon S. Wood, *The Creation of the American Republic, 1776–1787* (Chapel Hill, 1969), 162–96.

The classic statement in modern political thought is John Stuart Mill's "Representative Government," of which the most accessible edition is in R. M. Hutchins, ed., *Great Books of the Western World* (Chicago, 1952), XLIII, 327–442. Michael Oakeshott discusses individualism and the institutions of parliamentary government in "The Masses in Representative Democracy," in *Freedom and Serfdom. An Anthology of Western Thought,* edited by Albert Hunold (Dordrecht, 1961), 151–70. *The Concept of Representation* by Hannah F. Pitkin (Berkeley, 1967) is both a conceptual analysis and a study in the history of political thought. It is unusually lucid and perceptive, and includes an important appendix on the etymology of "representation." Robert G. Dixon, Jr. treats some modern aspects of the problem in *Democratic Representation: Reapportionment in Law and Politics* (New York, 1969).

✑ Index ✑

A NOTE ON THE TYPE

The text of this book is set in Caledonia, a type face designed by W(illiam) A(ddison) Dwiggins for the Mergenthaler Linotype Company in 1939. Dwiggins chose to call his new type face Caledonia, the Roman name for Scotland, because it was inspired by the Scotch types cast about 1833 by Alexander Wilson & Son, Glasgow type founders. However, there is a calligraphic quality about Caledonia that is totally lacking in the Wilson types. Dwiggins referred to an even earlier type face for this "liveliness of action"— one cut around 1790 by William Martin for the printer William Bulmer. Caledonia has more weight than the Martin letters, and the bottom finishing strokes (serifs) of the letters are cut straight across, without brackets, to make sharp angles with the upright stems, thus giving a "modern face" appearance.

W. A. Dwiggins (1880–1956) began an association with the Mergenthaler Linotype Company in 1929 and over the next twenty-seven years designed a number of book types, the most interesting of which are the Metro series, Electra, Caledonia, Eldorado, and Falcon.

This book was composed, printed and bound by The Colonial Press Incorporated, Clinton, Massachusetts. The typography and binding design are by Virginia Tan.

Prolegomenon medieval — p 66

① colonial situation compared to origins of English parliament; legislators as "attorneys" of the people in their district pp. 5-6

    (1a) "medieval concept of attorneyship" p. 8 { also pp. 44,

② early colonial example of the need for the "gov't" or state to legitimate action to the population at large — "Watertown protest" p. 21

③ as early as the 1630s, the relationship between "local" gov't and "central authority" (state of Mass) a problem p. 24

④ Penn/ NJ --- larger rep. bodies n participation pp. 39-40

⑤ legislature in Penn — attempt to restrict to "yea" or "nay" role p. 43 (by William Penn)

⑥ alludes to an "indigenous ideology" in America p. 51

⑦ potential tension between "privacy" and public participation p. 56

    (7a) those wanting religious freedom wanted privacy, not inclined to engage in public life

    (7b) a secure split between state/religion would seem to make public activity more desirable

⑧ representation + consent p. 60